52nd Annual Meeting of the Association for Computational Linguistics (ACL 2014)

System Demonstrations

Baltimore, Maryland, USA
23 – 24 June 2014

ISBN: 978-1-63439-193-1

Printed from e-media with permission by:

Curran Associates, Inc.
57 Morehouse Lane
Red Hook, NY 12571

Some format issues inherent in the e-media version may also appear in this print version.

Printed by Curran Associates, Inc. (2014)

For permission requests, please contact the Association for Computational Linguistics at the address below.

Association for Computational Linguistics
209 N. Eighth Street
Stroudsburg, Pennsylvania 18360

Phone: 1-570-476-8006
Fax: 1-570-476-0860

acl@aclweb.org

Additional copies of this publication are available from:

Curran Associates, Inc.
57 Morehouse Lane
Red Hook, NY 12571 USA
Phone: 845-758-0400
Fax: 845-758-2634
Email: curran@proceedings.com
Web: www.proceedings.com

Preface

Welcome to the proceedings of the system demonstration session. This volume contains the papers of the system demonstrations presented at the 52nd Annual Meeting of the Association for Computational Linguistics, on June 23-24, 2014 in Baltimore, Maryland, USA.

The system demonstrations program offers the presentation of early research prototypes as well as interesting mature systems. The system demonstration chairs and the members of the program committee received 39 submissions, of which 21 were selected for inclusion in the program (acceptance rate of 53.8%) after review by three members of the program committee.

We would like to thank the members of the program committee for their timely help in reviewing the submissions.

Co-Chairs:

Kalina Bontcheva, University of Sheffield
Zhu Jingbo, Northeastern University

Program Committee:

Beatrice Alex, University of Edinburgh
Omar Alonso, Microsoft
Thierry Declerck, DFKI
Leon Derczynski, University of Sheffield
Mark Dras, Macquarie University
Josef van Genabith, Dublin City University
Dirk Hovy, University of Copenhagen
Degen Huang, Dalian Univeristy of Technology
Xuanjing Huang, Institute for Media Computing
Brigitte Kren, OFAI
Oi Yee Kwong, City University of Hong Kong
Maggie Li, The Hong Kong Polytechnic University
Mu Li, Microsoft Research Asia
Wenjie Li, The Hong Kong Polytechnic University
Maria Liakata, University of Warwick
Yuji Matsumoto, Nara Institute of Science and Technology
Nicolas Nicolov, Amazon
Patrick Paroubek, LIMSI
Stelios Piperidis, Athena RC/ILSP
Barbara Plank, University of Copenhagen
Kiril Simov, Bulgarian Academy of Science
Koenraad De Smedt, University of Bergen
Lucia Specia, University of Sheffield
John Tait, johntait.net Ltd.
Keh-Yih Su, BDC
Le Sun, ISCAS
Marc Vilain, MITRE
Leo Wanner, ICREA and Pompeu Fabra University
Derek F. Wong, University of Macau
Wei Xu, New York University
Liang-Chih Yu, Yuan Ze University
Jiajun Zhang, Chinese Academy of Sciences
Yue Zhang, Singapore University of Technology and Design
Tiejun Zhao, Harbin Institute of Technology
Guodong Zhou, Soochow University

Table of Contents

Conference Program

23 June 2014

18:50–21:30 Session A

Cross-Lingual Information to the Rescue in Keyword Extraction
Chung-Chi Huang, Maxine Eskenazi, Jaime Carbonell, Lun-Wei Ku and Ping-Che Yang

Visualization, Search, and Error Analysis for Coreference Annotations
Markus Gärtner, Anders Björkelund, Gregor Thiele, Wolfgang Seeker and Jonas Kuhn

Open-Source Tools for Morphology, Lemmatization, POS Tagging and Named Entity Recognition
Jana Straková, Milan Straka and Jan Hajič

Community Evaluation and Exchange of Word Vectors at wordvectors.org
Manaal Faruqui and Chris Dyer

WINGS:Writing with Intelligent Guidance and Suggestions
Xianjun Dai, Yuanchao Liu, Xiaolong Wang and Bingquan Liu

DKPro Keyphrases: Flexible and Reusable Keyphrase Extraction Experiments
Nicolai Erbs, Pedro Bispo Santos, Iryna Gurevych and Torsten Zesch

Real-Time Detection, Tracking, and Monitoring of Automatically Discovered Events in Social Media
Miles Osborne, Sean Moran, Richard McCreadie, Alexander Von Lunen, Martin Sykora, Elizabeth Cano, Neil Ireson, Craig Macdonald, Iadh Ounis, Yulan He, Tom Jackson, Fabio Ciravegna and Ann O'Brien

The Excitement Open Platform for Textual Inferences
Bernardo Magnini, Roberto Zanoli, Ido Dagan, Kathrin Eichler, Guenter Neumann, Tae-Gil Noh, Sebastian Padó, Asher Stern and Omer Levy

WELT: Using Graphics Generation in Linguistic Fieldwork
Morgan Ulinski, Anusha Balakrishnan, Bob Coyne, Julia Hirschberg and Owen Rambow

The Stanford CoreNLP Natural Language Processing Toolkit
Christopher Manning, Mihai Surdeanu, John Bauer, Jenny Finkel, Steven Bethard and David McClosky

24 June 2014

16:50–19:20 Session B

DKPro TC: A Java-based Framework for Supervised Learning Experiments on Textual Data
Johannes Daxenberger, Oliver Ferschke, Iryna Gurevych and Torsten Zesch

WoSIT: A Word Sense Induction Toolkit for Search Result Clustering and Diversification
Daniele Vannella, Tiziano Flati and Roberto Navigli

A Rule-Augmented Statistical Phrase-based Translation System
Cong Duy Vu Hoang, AiTi Aw and Nhung T. H. Nguyen

KyotoEBMT: An Example-Based Dependency-to-Dependency Translation Framework
John Richardson, Fabien Cromières, Toshiaki Nakazawa and Sadao Kurohashi

kLogNLP: Graph Kernel–based Relational Learning of Natural Language
Mathias Verbeke, Paolo Frasconi, Kurt De Grave, Fabrizio Costa and Luc De Raedt

Automatic Annotation Suggestions and Custom Annotation Layers in WebAnno
Seid Muhie Yimam, Chris Biemann, Richard Eckart de Castilho and Iryna Gurevych

Web Information Mining and Decision Support Platform for the Modern Service Industry
Binyang Li, Lanjun Zhou, Zhongyu Wei, Kam-fai Wong, Ruifeng Xu and Yunqing Xia

FAdR: A System for Recognizing False Online Advertisements
Yi-jie Tang and Hsin-Hsi Chen

lex4all: A language-independent tool for building and evaluating pronunciation lexicons for small-vocabulary speech recognition
Anjana Vakil, Max Paulus, Alexis Palmer and Michaela Regneri

Enhanced Search with Wildcards and Morphological Inflections in the Google Books Ngram Viewer
Jason Mann, David Zhang, Lu Yang, Dipanjan Das and Slav Petrov

Simplified Dependency Annotations with GFL-Web
Michael T. Mordowanec, Nathan Schneider, Chris Dyer and Noah A. Smith

24 June 2014 (continued)

Cross-Lingual Information to the Rescue in Keyword Extraction

[1]Chung-Chi Huang [2]Maxine Eskenazi [3]Jaime Carbonell [4]Lun-Wei Ku [5]Ping-Che Yang
[1,2,3]Language Technologies Institute, CMU, United States
[4]Institute of Information Science, Academia Sinica, Taiwan
[5]Institute for Information Industry, Taipei, Taiwan
{[1]u901571,[4]lunwei.jennifer.ku}@gmail.com
{[2]max+,[3]jgc}@cs.cmu.edu [5]maciaclark@iii.org.tw

Abstract

We introduce a method that extracts keywords in a language with the help of the other. In our approach, we bridge and fuse conventionally irrelevant word statistics in languages. The method involves estimating preferences for keywords w.r.t. domain topics and generating cross-lingual bridges for word statistics integration. At run-time, we transform parallel articles into word graphs, build cross-lingual edges, and exploit PageRank with word keyness information for keyword extraction. We present the system, *BiKEA*, that applies the method to keyword analysis. Experiments show that keyword extraction benefits from PageRank, globally learned keyword preferences, and cross-lingual word statistics interaction which respects language diversity.

1 Introduction

Recently, an increasing number of Web services target extracting keywords in articles for content understanding, event tracking, or opinion mining. Existing keyword extraction algorithm (KEA) typically looks at articles monolingually and calculate word significance in certain language. However, the calculation in another language may tell the story differently since languages differ in grammar, phrase structure, and word usage, thus word statistics on keyword analysis.

Consider the English article in Figure 1. Based on the English content alone, monolingual KEA may not derive the best keyword set. A better set might be obtained by referring to the article and its counterpart in another language (e.g., Chinese). Different word statistics in articles of different languages may help, due to language divergence such as phrasal structure (i.e., word order) and word usage and repetition (resulting from word translation or word sense) and so on. For example, bilingual phrases "social reintegration" and "重返社會" in Figure 1 have inverse word orders ("social" translates into "社會" and "reintegration" into "重返"), both "prosthesis" and "artificial limbs" translate into "義肢", and "physical" can be associated with "物理" and "身體" in "physical therapist" and "physical rehabilitation" respectively. Intuitively, using cross-lingual statistics (implicitly leveraging language divergence) can help look at articles from different perspectives and extract keywords more accurately.

We present a system, *BiKEA*, that learns to identify keywords in a language with the help of the other. The cross-language information is expected to reinforce language similarities and value language dissimilarities, and better understand articles in terms of keywords. An example keyword analysis of an English article is shown in Figure 1. *BiKEA* has aligned the parallel articles at word level and determined the scores of topical keyword preferences for words. *BiKEA* learns these topic-related scores during training by analyzing a collection of articles. We will describe the *BiKEA* training process in more detail in Section 3.

At run-time, *BiKEA* transforms an article in a language (e.g., English) into PageRank word graph where vertices are words in the article and edges between vertices indicate the words' co-occurrences. To hear another side of the story, *BiKEA* also constructs graph from its counterpart in another language (e.g., Chinese). These two independent graphs are then bridged over nodes

Proceedings of 52nd Annual Meeting of the Association for Computational Linguistics: System Demonstrations, pages 1–6,
Baltimore, Maryland USA, June 23-24, 2014.

The English Article:
I've been in Afghanistan for 21 years. I work for the Red Cross and I'm a physical therapist. My job is to make arms and legs -- well it's not completely true. We do more than that. We provide the patients, the Afghan disabled, first with the physical rehabilitation then with the social reintegration. It's a very logical plan, but it was not always like this. For many years, we were just providing them with artificial limbs. It took quite many years for the program to become what it is now. …

Its Chinese Counterpart:
我在阿富汗已經 21 年。 我為紅十字會工作， 我是一名物理治療師。 我的工作是製作胳膊和腿 --恩，這不完全是事實。 我們做的還不止這些。 我們提供給患者， 阿富汗的殘疾人， 首先是身體康復, 然後重返社會。 這是一個非常合理的計劃， 但它並不是總是這樣。 多年來，我們只是給他們提供義肢。 花了很多年的程序 才讓這計劃成為現在的模樣。…

Word Alignment Information:
physical (物理), therapist (治療師), social (社會), reintegration (重返), physical (身體), rehabilitation (康復), prosthesis (義肢), …

Scores of Topical Keyword Preferences for Words:
(English) prosthesis: 0.32; artificial leg: 0.21; physical therapist: 0.15; rehabilitation: 0.08; …
(Chinese) 義肢: 0.41; 物理治療師: 0.15; 康復:0.10; 阿富汗: 0.08, …

English Keywords from Bilingual Perspectives:
prosthesis, artificial, leg, rehabilitation, orthopedic, …

Figure 1. An example *BiKEA* keyword analysis for an article.

that are bilingually equivalent or aligned. The bridging is to take language divergence into account and to allow for language-wise interaction over word statistics. *BiKEA*, then in bilingual context, iterates with learned word keyness scores to find keywords. In our prototype, *BiKEA* returns keyword candidates of the article for keyword evaluation (see Figure 1); alternatively, the keywords returned by *BiKEA* can be used as candidates for social tagging the article or used as input to an article recommendation system.

2 Related Work

Keyword extraction has been an area of active research and applied to NLP tasks such as document categorization (Manning and Schutze, 2000), indexing (Li et al., 2004), and text mining on social networking services ((Li et al., 2010); (Zhao et al., 2011); (Wu et al., 2010)).

The body of KEA focuses on learning word statistics in document collection. Approaches such as tfidf and entropy, using local document and/or across-document information, pose strong baselines. On the other hand, Mihalcea and Tarau (2004) apply PageRank, connecting words locally, to extract essential words. In our work, we leverage globally learned keyword preferences in PageRank to identify keywords.

Recent work has been done on incorporating semantics into PageRank. For example, Liu et al. (2010) construct PageRank synonym graph to accommodate words with similar meaning. And Huang and Ku (2013) weigh PageRank edges based on nodes' degrees of reference. In contrast, we bridge PageRank graphs of parallel articles to facilitate statistics re-distribution or interaction between the involved languages.

In studies more closely related to our work, Liu et al. (2010) and Zhao et al. (2011) present PageRank algorithms leveraging article topic information for keyword identification. The main differences from our current work are that the article topics we exploit are specified by humans not by automated systems, and that our PageRank graphs are built and connected bilingually.

In contrast to the previous research in keyword extraction, we present a system that automatically learns topical keyword preferences and constructs and inter-connects PageRank graphs in bilingual context, expected to yield better and more accurate keyword lists for articles. To the best of our knowledge, we are the first to exploit cross-lingual information and take advantage of language divergence in keyword extraction.

3 The BiKEA System

Submitting natural language articles to keyword extraction systems may not work very well. Keyword extractors typically look at articles from monolingual points of view. Unfortunately, word statistics derived based on a language may be biased due to the language's grammar, phrase structure, word usage and repetition and so on. To identify keyword lists from natural language articles, a promising approach is to automatically bridge the original monolingual framework with bilingual parallel information expected to respect language similarities and diversities at the same time.

3.1 Problem Statement

We focus on the first step of the article recommendation process: identifying a set of words likely to be essential to a given article. These keyword candidates are then returned as the output of the system. The returned keyword list can be examined by human users directly, or passed on to article recommendation systems for article retrieval (in terms of the extracted keywords). Thus, it is crucial that keywords be present in the candidate list and that the list not be too large to overwhelm users or the subsequent (typically computationally expensive) article recommendation systems. Therefore, our goal is to return reasonable-sized set of keyword candidates that, at the same time, must contain essential terms in the article. We now formally state the problem that we are addressing.

Problem Statement: We are given a bilingual parallel article collection of various topics from social media (e.g., TED), an article ART^e in language *e*, and its counterpart ART^c in language *c*. Our goal is to determine a set of words that are likely to contain important words of ART^e. For this, we bridge language-specific statistics of ART^e and ART^c via bilingual information (e.g., word alignments) and consider word keyness w.r.t. ART^e's topic such that cross-lingual diversities are valued in extracting keywords in *e*.

In the rest of this section, we describe our solution to this problem. First, we define strategies for estimating keyword preferences for words under different article topics (Section 3.2). These strategies rely on a set of article-topic pairs collected from the Web (Section 4.1), and are monolingual, language-dependent estimations. Finally, we show how *BiKEA* generates keyword lists for articles leveraging PageRank algorithm with word keyness and cross-lingual information (Section 3.3).

3.2 Topical Keyword Preferences

We attempt to estimate keyword preferences with respect to a wide range of article topics. Basically, the estimation is to calculate word significance in a domain topic. Our learning process is shown in Figure 2.

(1) Generate article-word pairs in training data
(2) Generate topic-word pairs in training data
(3) Estimate keyword preferences for words w.r.t. article topic based on various strategies
(4) Output word-and-keyword-preference-score pairs for various strategies

Figure 2. Outline of the process used to train *BiKEA*.

In the first two stages of the learning process, we generate two sets of article and word information. The input to these stages is a set of articles and their domain topics. The output is a set of pairs of article ID and word in the article, e.g., (ART^e=1, w^e="prosthesis") in language *e* or (ART^c=1, w^c="義肢") in language *c*, and a set of pairs of article topic and word in the article, e.g., (tp^e="disability", w^e="prosthesis") in *e* and (tp^e="disability", w^c="義肢") in *c*. Note that the topic information is shared between the involved languages, and that we confine the calculation of such word statistics in their specific language to respect language diversities and the language-specific word statistics will later interact in PageRank at run-time (See Section 3.3).

The third stage estimates keyword preferences for words across articles and domain topics using aforementioned (*ART*,*w*) and (*tp*,*w*) sets. In our paper, two popular estimation strategies in Information Retrieval are explored. They are as follows.

tfidf. $tfidf(w)=freq(ART,w)/appr(ART',w)$ where term frequency in an article is divided by its appearance in the article collection to distinguish important words from common words.

ent. $\text{entropy}(w)= -\sum_{tp'} Pr(tp'|w)\times\log(Pr(tp'|w))$ where a word's uncertainty in topics is used to estimate its associations with domain topics.

These strategies take global information (i.e., article collection) into account, and will be used as keyword preference models, bilingually intertwined, in PageRank at run-time which locally connects words (i.e., within articles).

3.3 Run-Time Keyword Extraction

Once language-specific keyword preference scores for words are automatically learned, they are stored for run-time reference. *BiKEA* then uses the procedure in Figure 3 to fuse the originally language-independent word statistics to determine keyword list for a given article. In this procedure a machine translation technique (i.e., IBM word aligner) is exploited to glue statistics in the involved languages and make bilingually motivated random-walk algorithm (i.e., PageRank) possible.

```
procedure PredictKW(ART^e,ART^c,KeyPrefs,WA,α,N)
//Construct language-specific word graph for PageRank
(1)  EW^e=constructPRwordGraph(ART^e)
(2)  EW^c=constructPRwordGraph(ART^c)
//Construct inter-language bridges
(3)  EW=α× EW^e+(1-α)× EW^c
       for each word alignment (w_i^c, w_j^e) in WA
         if IsContWord(w_i^c) and IsContWord(w_j^e)
(4a)       EW[i,j]+=1× BiWeight^cont
         else
(4b)       EW[i,j]+=1× BiWeight^noncont
(5)  normalize each row of EW to sum to 1
//Iterate for PageRank
(6)  set KP_1×v to
          [KeyPrefs(w_1), KeyPrefs(w_2), …,KeyPrefs(w_v)]
(7)  initialize KN_1×v to [1/v,1/ v, …,1/v]
     repeat
(8a) KN'=λ× KN× EW+(1-λ)× KP
(8b) normalize KN' to sum to 1
(8c) update KN with KN' after the check of KN and KN'
     until maxIter or avgDifference(KN,KN') ≤ smallDiff
(9)  rankedKeywords=Sort words in decreasing order of KN
     return the N rankedKeywords in e with highest
```

Figure 3. Extracting keywords at run-time.

Once language-specific keyword preference scores for words are automatically learned, they are stored for run-time reference. *BiKEA* then uses the procedure in Figure 3 to fuse the originally language-independent word statistics to determine keyword list for a given article. In this procedure a machine translation technique (i.e., IBM word aligner) is exploited to glue statistics in the involved languages and make bilingually motivated random-walk algorithm (i.e., PageRank) possible.

In Steps (1) and (2) we construct PageRank word graphs for the article ART^e in language *e* and its counterpart ART^c in language *c*. They are built individually to respect language properties (such as subject-verb-object or subject-object-verb structure). Figure 4 shows the algorithm. In this algorithm, **EW** stores normalized edge weights for word w_i and w_j (Step (2)). And **EW** is a *v* by *v* matrix where *v* is the vocabulary size of ART^e and ART^c. Note that the graph is directed (from words to words that follow) and edge weights are words' co-occurrences within window size *WS*. Additionally we incorporate edge weight multiplier $m>1$ to propagate more PageRank scores to content words, with the intuition that content words are more likely to be keywords (Step (2)).

```
procedure constructPRwordGraph(ART)
(1)  EW_v×v=0_v×v
       for each sentence st in ART
         for each word w_i in st
           for each word w_j in st where i<j and j-i≤ WS
             if not IsContWord(w_i) and IsContWord(w_j)
(2a)           EW[i,j]+=1× m
             elif not IsContWord(w_i) and not IsContWord(w_j)
(2b)           EW[i,j]+=1× (1/m)
             elif IsContWord(w_i) and not IsContWord(w_j)
(2c)           EW[i,j]+=1× (1/m)
             elif IsContWord(w_i) and IsContWord(w_j)
(2d)           EW[i,j]+=1× m
       return EW
```

Figure 4. Constructing PageRank word graph.

Step (3) in Figure 3 linearly combines word graphs $\mathbf{EW}^e$ and $\mathbf{EW}^c$ using α. We use α to balance language properties or statistics, and *BiKEA* backs off to monolingual KEA if α is one.

In Step (4) of Figure 3 for each word alignment (w_i^c, w_j^e), we construct a link between the word nodes with the weight *BiWeight*. The inter-language link is to reinforce language similarities and respect language divergence while the weight aims to elevate the cross-language statistics interaction. Word alignments are derived using IBM models 1-5 (Och and Ney, 2003). The inter-language link is directed from w_i^c to w_j^e, basically from language *c* to *e* based on the directional word-aligning entry (w_i^c, w_j^e). The bridging is expected to help keyword extraction in language *e* with the statistics in language *c*. Although alternative approach can be used for bridging, our approach is intuitive, and most importantly in compliance with the directional spirit of PageRank.

Step (6) sets **KP** of keyword preference model using topical preference scores learned from Section 3.2, while Step (7) initializes **KN** of PageRank scores or, in our case, word keyness scores. Then we distribute keyness scores until the number of iteration or the average score differences of two consecutive iterations reach their respective limits. In each iteration, a word's keyness score is the linear combination of its keyword preference score and the sum of the propagation of its inbound words' previous PageRank scores. For the word w_j^e in ART^e, any edge (w_i^e,w_j^e) in ART^e, and any edge (w_k^c,w_j^e) in *WA*, its new PageRank score is computed as below.

$$\mathbf{KN}'[1,j] = \lambda \times \left(\begin{array}{c} \alpha \times \sum_{i \in v} \mathbf{KN}[1,i] \times \mathbf{EW}^{e}[i,j] + \\ (1-\alpha) \times \sum_{k \in v} \mathbf{KN}[1,k] \times \mathbf{EW}[k,j] \end{array} \right) + (1-\lambda) \times \mathbf{KP}[1,j]$$

Once the iterative process stops, we rank words according to their final keyness scores and return top N ranked words in language e as keyword candidates of the given article ART^e. An example keyword analysis for an English article on our working prototype is shown in Figure 1. Note that language similarities and dissimilarities lead to different word statistics in articles of difference languages, and combining such word statistics helps to generate more promising keyword lists.

4 Experiments

BiKEA was designed to identify words of importance in an article that are likely to cover the keywords of the article. As such, *BiKEA* will be trained and evaluated over articles. Furthermore, since the goal of *BiKEA* is to determine a good (representative) set of keywords with the help of cross-lingual information, we evaluate *BiKEA* on bilingual parallel articles. In this section, we first present the data sets for training *BiKEA* (Section 4.1). Then, Section 4.2 reports the experimental results under different system settings.

4.1 Data Sets

We collected approximately 1,500 English transcripts (3.8M word tokens and 63K word types) along with their Chinese counterparts (3.4M and 73K) from TED (www.ted.com) for our experiments. The GENIA tagger (Tsuruoka and Tsujii, 2005) was used to lemmatize and part-of-speech tag the English transcripts while the CKIP segmenter (Ma and Chen, 2003) segment the Chinese.

30 parallel articles were randomly chosen and manually annotated for keywords on the English side to examine the effectiveness of *BiKEA* in English keyword extraction with the help of Chinese.

4.2 Experimental Results

Table 1 summarizes the performance of the baseline *tfidf* and our best systems on the test set. The evaluation metrics are nDCG (Jarvelin and Kekalainen, 2002), precision, and mean reciprocal rank.

(a) @N=5	nDCG	P	MRR
tfidf	.509	.213	.469
PR+tfidf	.676	.400	.621
BiKEA+tfidf	.703	.406	.655

(b) @N=7	nDCG	P	MRR
tfidf	.517	.180	.475
PR+tfidf	.688	.323	.626
BiKEA+tfidf	.720	.338	.660

(c) @N=10	nDCG	P	MRR
tfidf	.527	.133	.479
PR+tfidf	.686	.273	.626
BiKEA+tfidf	.717	.304	.663

Table 1. System performance at (a) N=5 (b) N=7 (c) N=10.

As we can see, monolingual PageRank (i.e., *PR*) and bilingual PageRank (*BiKEA*), using global information tfidf, outperform *tfidf*. They relatively boost nDCG by 32% and P by 87%. The MRR scores also indicate their superiority: their top-two candidates are often keywords vs. the 2nd place candidates from *tfidf*. Encouragingly, *BiKEA+tfidf* achieves better performance than the strong monolingual *PR+tfidf* across N's. Specifically, it further improves nDCG relatively by 4.6% and MRR relatively by 5.4%.

Overall, the topical keyword preferences, and the inter-language bridging and the bilingual score propagation in PageRank are simple yet effective. And respecting language statistics and properties helps keyword extraction.

5 Summary

We have introduced a method for extracting keywords in bilingual context. The method involves estimating keyword preferences, word-aligning parallel articles, and bridging language-specific word statistics using PageRank. Evaluation has shown that the method can identify more keywords and rank them higher in the candidate list than monolingual KEAs. As for future work, we would like to explore the possibility of incorporating the articles' reader feedback into keyword extraction. We would also like to examine the proposed methodology in a multi-lingual setting.

Acknowledgement

This study is conducted under the "Online and Offline integrated Smart Commerce Platform (1/4)" of the Institute for Information Industry which is subsidized by the Ministry of Economy Affairs of the Republic of China.

References

Scott A. Golder and Bernardo A. Huberman. 2006. Usage patterns of collaborative tagging systems. *Information Science*, 32(2): 198-208.

Harry Halpin, Valentin Robu, and Hana Shepherd. 2007. The complex dynamics of collaborative tagging. In *Proceedings of the WWW*, pages 211-220.

Chung-chi Huang and Lun-wei Ku. 2013. Interest analysis using semantic PageRank and social interaction content. In *Proceedings of the ICDM Workshop on Sentiment Elicitation from Natural Text for Information Retrieval and Extraction*, pages 929-936.

Kalervo Jarvelin and Jaana Kekalainen. 2002. Cumulated gain-based evaluation of IR technologies. *ACM Transactions on Information Systems*, 20(4): 422-446.

Philipp Koehn, Franz Josef Och, and Daniel Marcu. 2003. Statistical phrase-based translation. In *Proceedings of the North American Chapter of the Association for Computational Linguistics*, pages 48-54.

Quanzhi Li, Yi-Fang Wu, Razvan Bot, and Xin Chen. 2004. Incorporating document keyphrases in search results. In *Proceedings of the Americas Conference on Information Systems*.

Zhenhui Li, Ging Zhou, Yun-Fang Juan, and Jiawei Han. 2010. Keyword extraction for social snippets. In *Proceedings of the WWW*, pages 1143-1144.

Marina Litvak and Mark Last. 2008. Graph-based keyword extraction for single-document summarization. In *Proceedings of the ACL Workshop on Multi-Source Multilingual Information Extraction and Summarization*, pages 17-24.

Zhengyang Liu, Jianyi Liu, Wenbin Yao, Cong Wang. 2010. Keyword extraction using PageRank on synonym networks. In *Proceedings of the ICEEE*, pages 1-4.

Zhiyuan Liu, Wenyi Huang, Yabin Zheng, and Maosong Sun. 2010. Automatic keyphrase extraction via topic decomposition. In *Proceedings of the EMNLP*, pages 366-376.

Wei-Yun Ma and Keh-Jiann Chen. 2003. Introduction to CKIP Chinese word segmentation system for the first international Chinese word segmentation bakeoff. In *Proceedings of the ACL Workshop on Chinese Language Processing*.

Chris D. Manning and Hinrich Schutze. 2000. *Foundations of statistical natural language processing*. MIT Press.

Rada Mihalcea and Paul Tarau. 2004. TextRank: Bringing orders into texts. In *Proceedings of the EMNLP*, pages 404-411.

Franz Josef Och and Hermann Ney. 2003. A systematic comparison of various statistical alignment models. *Computational Linguistics*, 29(1): 19-51.

Yoshimasa Tsuruoka and Jun'ichi Tsujii. 2005. Bidirectional inference with the easiest-first strategy for tagging sequence data. In *Proceedings of the EMNLP*, pages 467-474.

Peter D. Turney. 2000. Learning algorithms for keyphrase extraction. *Information Retrieval*, 2(4): 303-336.

Wei Wu, Bin Zhang, and Mari Ostendorf. 2010. Automatic generation of personalized annotation tags for Twitter users. In *Proceedings of the NAACL*, pages 689-692.

Wayne Xin Zhao, Jing Jiang, Jing He, Yang Song, Palakorn Achananuparp, Ee-Peng Lim, and Xiaoming Li. 2011. Topical keyword extraction from Twitter. In *Proceedings of the ACL*, pages 379-388.

Visualization, Search, and Error Analysis for Coreference Annotations

Markus Gärtner Anders Björkelund Gregor Thiele Wolfgang Seeker Jonas Kuhn
Institute for Natural Language Processing
University of Stuttgart
{thielegr,seeker,gaertnms,anders,kuhn}@ims.uni-stuttgart.de

Abstract

We present the ICARUS Coreference Explorer, an interactive tool to browse and search coreference-annotated data. It can display coreference annotations as a tree, as an entity grid, or in a standard text-based display mode, and lets the user switch freely between the different modes. The tool can compare two different annotations on the same document, allowing system developers to evaluate errors in automatic system predictions. It features a flexible search engine, which enables the user to graphically construct search queries over sets of documents annotated with coreference.

1 Introduction

Coreference resolution is the task of automatically grouping references to the same real-world entity in a document into a set. It is an active topic in current NLP research and has received considerable attention in recent years, including the 2011 and 2012 CoNLL shared tasks (Pradhan et al., 2011; Pradhan et al., 2012).

Coreference relations are commonly represented by sets of mentions, where all mentions in one set (or coreference **cluster**) are considered coreferent. This type of representation does not support any internal structure within the clusters. However, many automatic coreference resolvers establish links between pairs of mentions which are subsequently transformed to a cluster by taking the transitive closure over all links, i.e., placing all mentions that are directly or transitively classified as coreferent in one cluster. This is particularly the case for several state-of-the-art resolvers (Fernandes et al., 2012; Durrett and Klein, 2013; Björkelund and Kuhn, 2014). These pairwise decisions, which give rise to a clustering, can be exploited for detailed error analysis and more fine-grained search queries on data automatically annotated for coreference.

We present the ICARUS Coreference Explorer (ICE), an interactive tool to browse and search coreference-annotated data. In addition to standard text-based display modes, ICE features two other display modes: an **entity-grid** (Barzilay and Lapata, 2008) and a **tree** view, which makes use of the internal pairwise links within the clusters. ICE builds on ICARUS (Gärtner et al., 2013), a platform for search and exploration of dependency treebanks.[1]

ICE is geared towards two (typically) distinct users: The *NLP developer* who designs coreference resolution systems can inspect the predictions of his system using the three different display modes. Moreover, ICE can compare the predictions of a system to a gold standard annotation, enabling the developer to inspect system errors interactively. The second potential user is the *corpus linguist*, who might be interested in browsing or searching a document, or a (large) set of documents for certain coreference relations. The built-in search engine of ICARUS now also allows search queries over sets of documents in order to meet the needs of this type of user.

2 Data Representation

ICE reads the formats used in the 2011 and 2012 CoNLL shared tasks as well as the SemEval 2010 format (Recasens et al., 2010).[2] Since these formats cannot accommodate pairwise links, an auxiliary file with standoff annotation can be provided, which we call *allocation*. An allocation is a list of pairwise links between mentions. Multiple

[1] ICE is written in Java and is therefore platform independent. It is open source (under GNU GPL) and we provide both sources and binaries for download on http://www.ims.uni-stuttgart.de/data/icarus.html

[2] These two formats are very similar tabular formats, but differ slightly in the column representations.

Proceedings of 52nd Annual Meeting of the Association for Computational Linguistics: System Demonstrations, pages 7–12, Baltimore, Maryland USA, June 23-24, 2014.

allocations can be associated with a single document and the user can select one of these for display or search queries. An allocation can also include *properties* on mentions and links. The set of possible properties is not constrained, and the user can freely specify properties as a list of key-value pairs. Properties on mentions may include, e.g., grammatical gender or number, or information status labels. Additionally, a special property that indicates the head word of a mention can be provided in an allocation. The head property enables the user to access head words of mentions for display or search queries.

The motivation for keeping the allocation file separate from the CoNLL or SemEval files is two-fold: First, it allows ICE to work without having to provide an allocation file, thereby making it easy to use with the established formats for coreference. The user is still able to introduce additional structure by the use of the allocation file. Second, multiple allocation files allow the user to switch between different allocations while exploring a set of documents. Moreover, as we will see in Section 3.3, ICE can also compare two different allocations in order to highlight the differences.

In addition to user-specified allocations, ICE will always by default provide an internal structure for the clusters, in which the correct antecedent of every mention is the closest coreferent mention with respect to the linear order of the document (this is equivalent to the training instance creation heuristic proposed by Soon et al. (2001)). Therefore, the user is not required to define an allocation on their own.

3 Display Modes

In this section we describe the entity grid and tree display modes by means of screenshots. ICE additionally includes a standard text-based view, similar to other coreference visualization tools. The example document is taken from the CoNLL 2012 development set (Pradhan et al., 2012) and we use two allocations: (1) the predictions output by Björkelund and Kuhn (2014) system (*predicted*) and (2) a gold allocation that was obtained by running the same system in a restricted setting, where only links between coreferent mentions are allowed (*gold*). The complete document can be seen in the lower half of Figure 1.

3.1 Entity grid

Barzilay and Lapata (2008) introduce the *entity grid*, a tabular view of entities in a document. Specifically, rows of the grid correspond to sentences, and columns to entities. The cells of the table are used to indicate that an entity is mentioned in the corresponding sentence. Entity grids provide a compact view on the distribution of mentions in a document and allow the user to see how the description of an entity changes from mention to mention.

Figure 1 shows ICE's entity-grid view for the example document using the predicted allocation. When clicking on a cell in the entity grid the immediate textual context of the cell is shown in the lower pane. In Figure 1, the cell with the blue background has been clicked, which corresponds to the two mentions *firms from Taiwan* and *they*. These mentions are thus highlighted in the lower pane. The user can also right-click on a cell and jump straight to the tree view, centered around the same mentions.

3.2 Label Patterns

The information that is displayed in the cells of the entity grid (and also on the nodes in the tree view, see Section 3.3) can be fully customized by the user. The customization is achieved by defining *label patterns*. A label pattern is a string that specifies the format according to which a mention will be displayed. The pattern can extract information on a mention according to three axes: (1) at the token- level for the full mention, extracting, e.g., the sequence of surface forms or the part-of-speech tags of a mention; (2) at the mention- level, extracting an arbitrary property of a mention as defined in an allocation; (3) token-level information from the head word of a mention.

Label patterns can be defined interactively while displaying a document and the three axes are referenced by dedicated operators. For instance, the label pattern `$form$` extracts the full surface form of a mention, whereas `#form#` only extracts the surface form of the head word of a mention. All properties defined by the user in the allocation (see Section 2) are accessible via label patterns.

For example, the allocations we use for Figure 1 include a number of properties on the mentions, most of which are internally computed by the coreference system: The TYPE of a mention, which can take any of the values

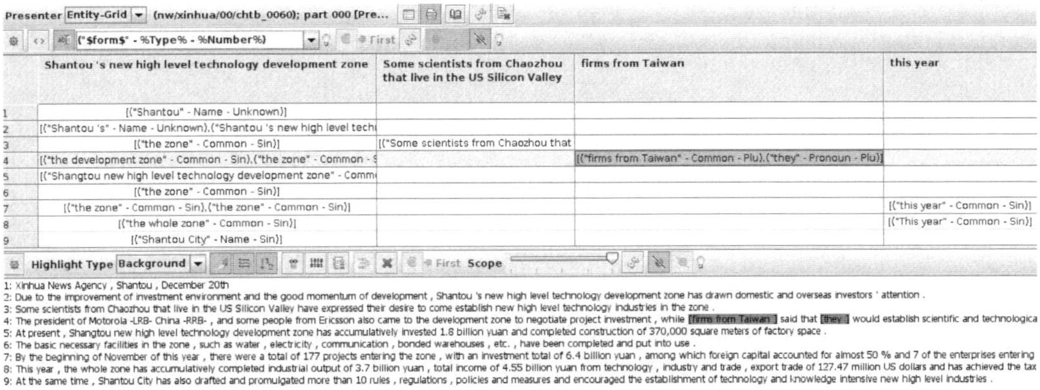

Figure 1: Entity grid over the predicted clustering in the example document.

{Name, Common, Pronoun} and is inferred from the part- of-speech tags in the CoNLL file; The grammatical NUMBER of a mention, which is assigned based on the number and gender data compiled by Bergsma and Lin (2006) and can take the values {Sin, Plu, Unknown}. The label pattern for displaying the number property associated with a mention would be %Number%.

The label pattern used in Figure 1 is defined as ("$form$" - %Type% - %Number%). This pattern accesses the full surface form of the mentions ($form$), as well as the TYPE (%Type%) and grammatical NUMBER (%Number%) properties defined in the allocation file.

Custom properties and label patterns can be used for example to display the entity grid in the form proposed by Barzilay and Lapata (2008): In the allocation, we assign a coarse-grained grammatical function property (denoted GF) to every mention, where each mention is tagged as either *subject*, *object*, or *other* (denoted S, O, X, respectively).[3] The label pattern %GF% then displays the grammatical function of each mention in the entity grid, as shown in Figure 2.

3.3 Tree view

Pairwise links output by an automatic coreference system can be treated as arcs in a directed graph. Linking the first mention of each cluster to an artificial root node creates a tree structure that encodes the entire clustering in a document. This representation has been used in coreference resolvers (Fernandes et al., 2012; Björkelund and Kuhn, 2014), but ICE uses it to display links between mentions introduced by an automatic (pairwise) resolver.

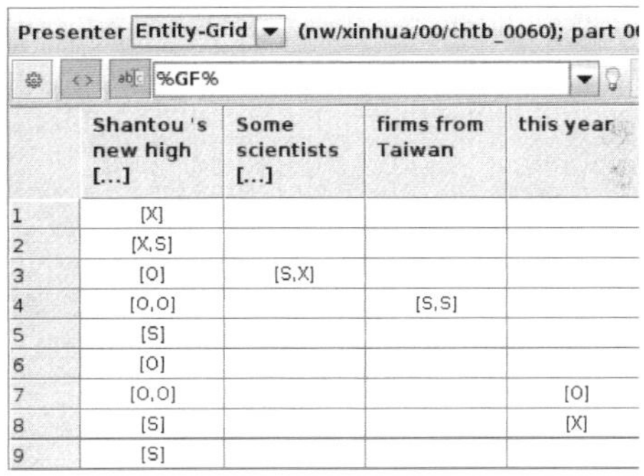

Figure 2: Example entity grid, using the labels by Barzilay and Lapata (2008).

Figure 3 shows three examples of the tree view of the same document as before: The gold allocation (3a), the predicted allocation (3b), as well as the differential view, where the two allocations are compared (3c). Each mention corresponds to a node in the trees and all mentions are directly or transitively dominated by the artificial root node. Every subtree under the root constitutes its own cluster and a *solid* arc between two mentions denotes that the two mentions are coreferent according to a coreference allocation. The information displayed in the nodes of the tree can be customized using label patterns.

In the differential view (Figure 3c), solid arcs correspond to the predicted allocation. Dashed nodes and arcs are present in the gold allocation, but not in the prediction. Discrepancies between the predicted and the gold allocations are marked

[3]The grammatical function was assigned by converting the phrase-structure trees in the CoNLL file (which lack grammatical function information) to Stanford dependencies (de Marneffe and Manning, 2008), and then extracting the grammatical function from the head word in each mention.

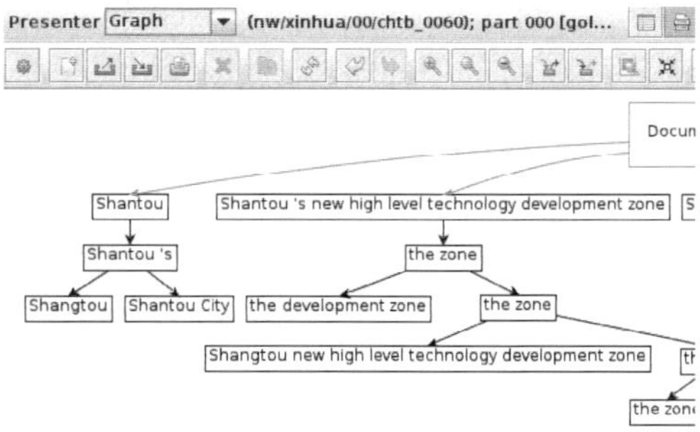

(a) Tree representing the gold allocation.

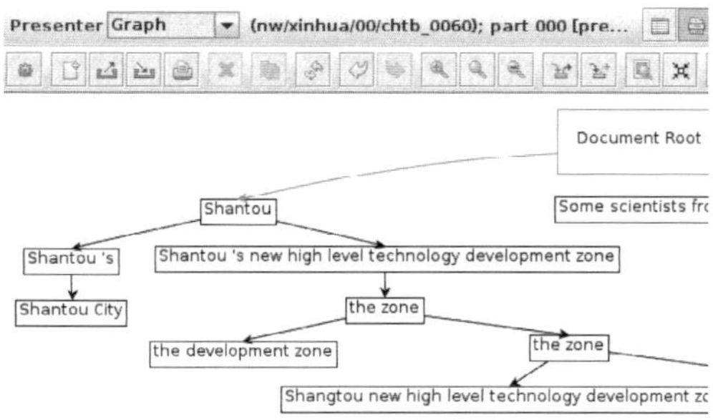

(b) Tree representing the predicted allocation.

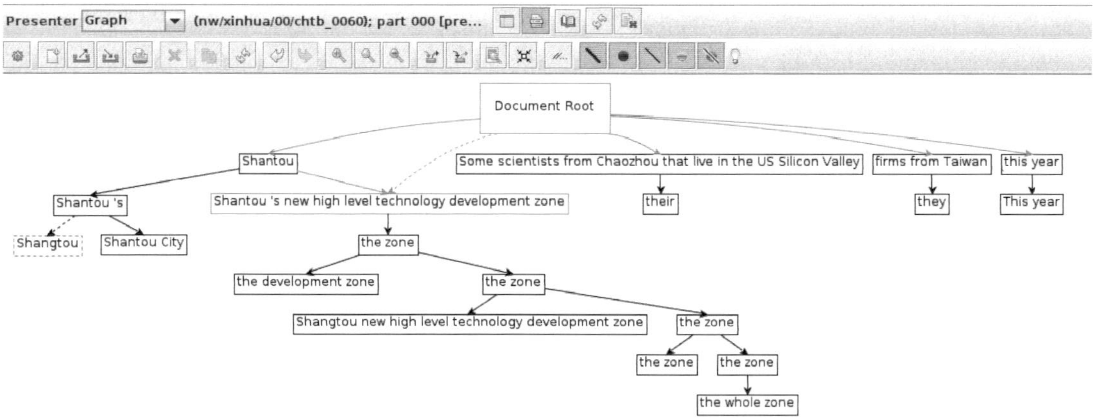

(c) Differential view displaying the difference between the gold and predicted allocations.

Figure 3: Tree view over the example document (gold, predicted, differential).

with different colors denoting different types of errors. The example in Figure 3c contains two errors made by the system:

1. A **false negative mention**, denoted by the dashed red node *Shangtou*. In the gold standard (Figure 3a) this mention is clustered with other mentions such as *Shantou 's*, *Shantou City*, etc. The dashed arc between *Shantou 's* and *Shangtou* is taken from the gold allocation, and indicates what the system prediction should have been like.[4]

2. A **foreign antecedent**, denoted by the solid orange arc between *Shantou 's new high level technology development zone* and *Shantou*. In this case, the coreference system erroneously clustered these two mentions. The correct antecedent is indicated by the dashed arc that originates from the document root. This error is particularly interesting since the system effectively merges the two clusters corresponding to *Shantou* and *Shantou' s new high level technology development zone*. The tree view, however, shows that the error stems from a single link between these two mentions, and that the developer needs to address this.

Since the tree-based view makes pairwise decisions explicit, the differential view shown in Figure 3c is more informative to NLP developers when inspecting errors by automatic system than comparing a gold standard clustering to a predicted one. The problem with analyzing the error on clusterings instead of trees is that the clusters would be merged, i.e., it is not clear where the actual mistake was made.

Additional error types not illustrated by Figure 3c include **false positive** mentions, where the system invents a mention that is not part of the gold allocation. When a false positive mention is assigned as an antecedent of another

[4]This error likely stems from the fact that *Shantou* is spelled two different ways within the same document which causes the resolver's string-matching feature to fail.

mention, the corresponding link is marked as an **invented antecedent**. Links that erroneously start a new cluster when it is coreferent with other mentions to the left is marked as **false new**.

4 Searching

The search engine in ICE makes the annotations in the documents searchable for, e. g., a corpus linguist who is interested in specific coreference phenomena. It allows the user to express queries over mentions related through the tree. Queries can access the different layers of annotation, both from the allocation file and the underlying document, using various constructs such as, e.g., transitivity, regular expressions, and/or disjunctions. The user can construct queries either textually (through a query language) or graphically (by creating nodes and configuring constraints in dialogues). For a further discussion of the search engine we refer to the original ICARUS paper (Gärtner et al., 2013).

Figure 4 shows a query that matches cataphoric pronouns, i.e., pronouns that precede their antecedents. The figure shows the query expressed as a subgraph (on the left) and the corresponding results (right) obtained on the development set of the English CoNLL 2012 data using the manual annotation represented in the gold allocation.

The query matches two mentions that are directly or transitively connected through the graph. The first mention (red node) matches mentions of the type `Pronoun` that have to be attached to the document root node. In the tree formalism we adopt, this implies that it must be the first mention of its cluster. The second mention (green node) matches any mention that is not of the type `Pronoun`.

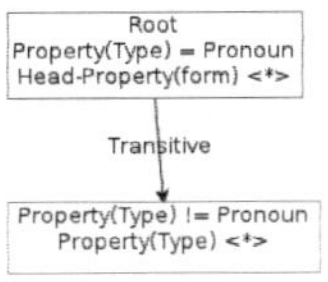

(a)

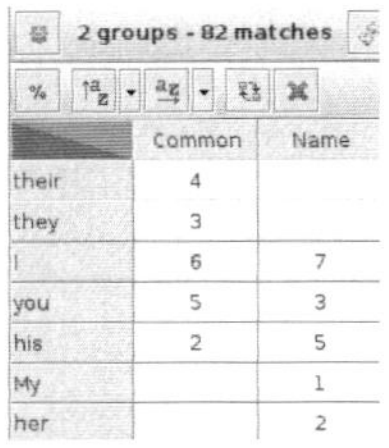

(b)

Figure 4: Example search query and corresponding results.

The search results are grouped along two axes: the surface form of the head word of the first (red) node, and the type property of the second mention (green node), indicated by the special *grouping operator* <∗> inside the boxes. The corresponding results are shown in the right half of Figure 4, where the first group (surface form) runs vertically, and the second group (mention type) runs horizontally. The number of hits for each configuration is shown in the corresponding cell. For example, the case that the first mention of a chain is the pronoun *I* and the closest following coreferent mention that is not a pronoun is of type `Common`, occurs 6 times. By clicking on a cell, the user can jump straight to a list of the matches, and browse them using any of the three display modes.

5 Related Work

Two popular annotation and visualization tools for coreference are PAlinkA (Orăsan, 2003) and MMAX2 (Müller and Strube, 2006), which focus on a (customizable) textual visualization with highlighting of clusters. The TrED (Pajas and Štěpánek, 2009) project is a very flexible multi-level annotation tool centered around tree-based annotations that can be used to annotate and visualize coreference. It also features a powerful search engine. Recent annotation tools include the web-based BRAT (Stenetorp et al., 2012) and its extension WebAnno (Yimam et al., 2013). A dedicated query and exploration tool for multi-level annotations is ANNIS (Zeldes et al., 2009).

The aforementioned tools are primarily meant as annotation tools. They have a tendency of locking the user into one type of visualization (tree- or text-based), while often lacking advanced search functionality. In contrast to them, ICE is not meant to be yet another annotation tool, but was designed as a dedicated coreference exploration tool, which enables the user to swiftly switch between different views. Moreover, none of the existing tools provide an entity-grid view.

ICE is also the only tool that can graphically compare predictions of a system to a gold standard with a fine-grained distinction on the types of differences. Kummerfeld and Klein (2013) present an algorithm that transforms a predicted coreference clustering into a gold clustering and records the necessary transformations, thereby quantifying different types of errors. However, their algorithm only works on clusterings (sets of mentions), not pairwise links, and is therefore not able to pinpoint some of the mistakes that ICE can (such as the foreign antecedent described in Section 3).

6 Conclusion

We presented ICE, a flexible coreference visualization and search tool. The tool complements standard text-based display modes with entity-grid and tree visualizations. It is also able to display discrepancies between two different coreference annotations on the same document, allowing NLP developers to debug coreference systems in a graphical way. The built-in search engine allows corpus linguists to construct complex search queries and provide aggregate result views over large sets of documents. Being based on the ICARUS platform's plugin-engine, ICE is extensible and can easily be extended to cover additional data formats.

Acknowledgments

This work was funded by the German Federal Ministry of Education and Research (BMBF) via CLARIN-D, No. 01UG1120F and the German Research Foundation (DFG) via the SFB 732, project D8.

References

Regina Barzilay and Mirella Lapata. 2008. Modeling Local Coherence: An Entity-Based Approach. *Computational Linguistics*, 34(1):1–34.

Shane Bergsma and Dekang Lin. 2006. Bootstrapping path-based pronoun resolution. In *COLING-ACL*, pages 33–40, Sydney, Australia, July.

Anders Björkelund and Jonas Kuhn. 2014. Learning Structured Perceptrons for Coreference Resolution with Latent Antecedents and Non-local Features. In *ACL*, Baltimore, MD, USA, June.

Marie-Catherine de Marneffe and Christopher D. Manning. 2008. The stanford typed dependencies representation. In *COLING Workshop on Cross-framework and Cross-domain Parser Evaluation*.

Greg Durrett and Dan Klein. 2013. Easy Victories and Uphill Battles in Coreference Resolution. In *EMNLP*, pages 1971–1982, Seattle, Washington, USA, October.

Eraldo Fernandes, Cícero dos Santos, and Ruy Milidiú. 2012. Latent Structure Perceptron with Feature Induction for Unrestricted Coreference Resolution. In *EMNLP-CoNLL: Shared Task*, pages 41–48, Jeju Island, Korea, July.

Markus Gärtner, Gregor Thiele, Wolfgang Seeker, Anders Björkelund, and Jonas Kuhn. 2013. ICARUS – An Extensible Graphical Search Tool for Dependency Treebanks. In *ACL: System Demonstrations*, pages 55–60, Sofia, Bulgaria, August.

Jonathan K. Kummerfeld and Dan Klein. 2013. Error-Driven Analysis of Challenges in Coreference Resolution. In *EMNLP*, pages 265–277, Seattle, Washington, USA, October.

Christoph Müller and Michael Strube. 2006. Multi-level annotation of linguistic data with MMAX2. In *Corpus Technology and Language Pedagogy: New Resources, New Tools, New Methods*, pages 197–214. Peter Lang.

Constantin Orăsan. 2003. PALinkA: A highly customisable tool for discourse annotation. In Akira Kurematsu, Alexander Rudnicky, and Syun Tutiya, editors, *Proceedings of the Fourth SIGdial Workshop on Discourse and Dialogue*, pages 39–43.

Petr Pajas and Jan Štěpánek. 2009. System for Querying Syntactically Annotated Corpora. In *ACL-IJCNLP: Software Demonstrations*, pages 33–36, Suntec, Singapore.

Sameer Pradhan, Lance Ramshaw, Mitchell Marcus, Martha Palmer, Ralph Weischedel, and Nianwen Xue. 2011. CoNLL-2011 Shared Task: Modeling Unrestricted Coreference in OntoNotes. In *CoNLL: Shared Task*, pages 1–27, Portland, Oregon, USA, June.

Sameer Pradhan, Alessandro Moschitti, Nianwen Xue, Olga Uryupina, and Yuchen Zhang. 2012. CoNLL-2012 Shared Task: Modeling Multilingual Unrestricted Coreference in OntoNotes. In *EMNLP-CoNLL: Shared Task*, pages 1–40, Jeju Island, Korea, July.

Marta Recasens, Lluís Màrquez, Emili Sapena, M. Antònia Martí, Mariona Taulé, Véronique Hoste, Massimo Poesio, and Yannick Versley. 2010. Semeval-2010 task 1: Coreference resolution in multiple languages. In *Proceedings of the 5th International Workshop on Semantic Evaluation*, pages 1–8, Uppsala, Sweden, July.

Wee Meng Soon, Hwee Tou Ng, and Daniel Chung Yong Lim. 2001. A machine learning approach to coreference resolution of noun phrases. *Computational Linguistics*, 27(4):521–544.

Pontus Stenetorp, Sampo Pyysalo, Goran Topić, Tomoko Ohta, Sophia Ananiadou, and Jun'ichi Tsujii. 2012. brat: a Web-based Tool for NLP-Assisted Text Annotation. In *EACL: Demonstrations*, pages 102–107, April.

Seid Muhie Yimam, Iryna Gurevych, Richard Eckart de Castilho, and Chris Biemann. 2013. WebAnno: A Flexible, Web-based and Visually Supported System for Distributed Annotations. In *ACL: System Demonstrations*, pages 1–6, August.

Amir Zeldes, Julia Ritz, Anke Lüdeling, and Christian Chiarcos. 2009. ANNIS: a search tool for multi-layer annotated corpora. In *Proceedings of Corpus Linguistics*.

Open-Source Tools for Morphology, Lemmatization, POS Tagging and Named Entity Recognition

Jana Straková and **Milan Straka** and **Jan Hajič**
Charles University in Prague
Faculty of Mathematics and Physics
Institute of Formal and Applied Linguistics
{strakova,straka,hajic}@ufal.mff.cuni.cz

Abstract

We present two recently released open-source taggers: NameTag is a free software for named entity recognition (NER) which achieves state-of-the-art performance on Czech; MorphoDiTa (Morphological Dictionary and Tagger) performs morphological analysis (with lemmatization), morphological generation, tagging and tokenization with state-of-the-art results for Czech and a throughput around 10-200K words per second. The taggers can be trained for any language for which annotated data exist, but they are specifically designed to be efficient for inflective languages, Both tools are free software under LGPL license and are distributed along with trained linguistic models which are free for non-commercial use under the CC BY-NC-SA license. The releases include standalone tools, C++ libraries with Java, Python and Perl bindings and web services.

1 Introduction

Morphological analysis, part-of-speech tagging and named entity recognition are one of the most important components of computational linguistic applications. They usually represent initial steps of language processing. It is no wonder then that they have received a great deal of attention in the computational linguistics community and in some respect, these tasks can even be considered very close to being "solved".

However, despite the fact that there is a considerable number of POS taggers available for English and other languages with a large number of active users, we lacked a POS tagger and NE recognizer which would

- be well suited and trainable for languages with very rich morphology and thus a large tagset of possibly several thousand plausible combinations of morphologically related attribute values,
- provide excellent, preferably state-of-the-art results for Czech,
- be distributed along with trained linguistic models for Czech,
- allow the user to train custom models for any language,
- be extremely efficient in terms of RAM and disc usage to be used commercially,
- offer a full end-to-end solution for users with little computational linguistics background,
- be distributed as a library without additional dependencies,
- offer API in many programming languages,
- be open-source, free software.

Following these requirements, we have developed a morphological dictionary and tagger software, which is described and evaluated in Section 3; and a named entity recognizer, which is described and evaluated in Section 4. The software performance and resource usage are described in Section 5 and the release and licensing condition information is given in Section 6. We conclude the paper in Section 7.

2 Related Work

2.1 POS Tagging

In English, the task of POS tagging has been in the center of computational linguists' attention for decades (Kucera and Francis, 1967), with renewed interest after significant improvements achieved by (Collins, 2002). The recent state-of-the-art for English POS supervised tagging without external data for training is by (Shen et al., 2007) and there are many available taggers, such as well-known Brill tagger (Brill, 1992), TnT tagger (Brants, 2000) and many others.

Proceedings of 52nd Annual Meeting of the Association for Computational Linguistics: System Demonstrations, pages 13–18,
Baltimore, Maryland USA, June 23-24, 2014. ©2014 Association for Computational Linguistics

In Czech, the POS tagging research has been carried out mostly by Czech speaking linguistic community and the current state-of-the-art was reported by (Spoustová et al., 2009) in Morče research project[1]. Based on this project, two taggers were released: Morče tagger (released as part of COMPOST[2] containing morphological analyzer, tagger and trained models, available to registered users only) and Featurama[3] (source code only, no trained models publicly available).

2.2 Named Entity Recognition

For English, many NE datasets and shared tasks exist, e.g. CoNLL-2003 (Tjong Kim Sang and De Meulder, 2003), MUC7 (Chinchor, 1998). These shared tasks and the associated freely available NE annotated corpora allowed wide and successful research in NE recognition in English. For example, the systems which published high scores on the CoNLL-2003 task include (Suzuki and Isozaki, 2008), (Ando and Zhang, 2005) and to our knowledge, the best currently known results on this dataset were published by (Ratinov and Roth, 2009). One should also mention a well-known and widely used Stanford parser (Finkel et al., 2005).

In Czech, the referential corpus for NE recognition is called the Czech Named Entity Corpus[4] (Ševčíková et al., 2007) and we describe its' properties further in Section 4.2. The development of the Czech NE recognition research is easy to follow: started by a pilot project by (Ševčíková et al., 2007), the results were improved by (Kravalová and Žabokrtský, 2009), (Konkol and Konopík, 2011) and (Konkol and Konopík, 2013). The current state-of-the-art results for CNEC are reported by (Straková et al., 2013). So far, there was no freely available Czech NE recognizer.

3 MorphoDiTa: Morphological Dictionary and Tagger

3.1 Morphological Dictionary Methodology

The morphological dictionary is specially designed for inflective languages with large number of suffixes (endings) and we propose an effective method for handling rich morphology.

In inflective languages,[5] words take endings (suffixes) to mark linguistic cases, grammatical number, gender etc. Therefore, many forms may be related to one lemma. For example, the lemma "zelený" ("green" in Czech) can appear as "zelený", "zelenější", "zelenému" etc. – there are several tens of forms for this type of adjective. Corpus-wise, there are 168K unique forms and 72K lemmas in a corpus of 2M words (Prague Dependency Treebank 2.5 (Bejček et al., 2012)) in Czech. It is therefore crucial to handle the endings effectively and to reduce the processing costs where regularities are found.

Given a resource with forms, lemmas and tags,[6] MorphoDiTa estimates regular patterns based on common form endings and automatically clusters them into morphological "templates" without linguistic knowledge about the language. We now describe the method for template set creation.

During template set creation, MorphoDiTa takes lemmas one by one. For each lemma, it collects all corresponding forms and builds a trie (De La Briandais, 1959; Knuth, 1997). Trie is a tree structure in which one character corresponds to a node and all descendants of a node share the same prefix. The procedure then finds a suitable common ancestor in the trie (common prefix or stem). The heuristics is "such a node whose subtree has depth at most N and at the same time has the maximal number of ancestors with one child". Intuitively, this means we want to select a long prefix (stem) – hence "maximal number of ancestors" but at the same time, the linguistic endings are not too long (at most N). Having selected a common prefix, all the endings (including their corresponding tags) in its subtree define a template. A rich trie with many subtrees may be split into multiple templates. For example, a simple trie for noun "hrad" ("castle" in Czech) with one template, and also two lemmas sharing two templates are shown in Fig. 1. When processing the next lemma and its corresponding forms, either new template is created, or the templates are reused if the set of endings is the same. Larger N leads to longer endings and larger number of classes, and smaller N leads to short endings and less classes.[7]

[1] http://ufal.mff.cuni.cz/morce/index.php

[2] http://ufal.mff.cuni.cz/compost/

[3] http://sourceforge.net/projects/featurama/

[4] http://ufal.mff.cuni.cz/cnec/

[5] In the following, we describe features of a core group of inflective languages, such as Slavic languages of all types. Sometimes, the word "inflective" is used also for agglutinative languages such as Turkish, Hungarian or Finnish; we believe our tools are suitable for these, too, but we have not tested them on this group yet.

[6] In Czech, the resource used was Morfflex CZ by Jan Hajič: http://ufal.mff.cuni.cz/morfflex.

[7] Our morphological dictionary representation cannot be replaced with a minimized finite state automaton with marked

The number of templates determines the efficiency of dictionary encoding. When too few templates are used, many are needed to represent a lemma. When too many are used, the representation of the templates themselves is large.

The morphological dictionary is then saved in binary form and the software offers a higher level access: given a form, morphological analysis lists all possible lemma-tag pairs; given a lemma-tag pair, MorphoDiTa generates the respective form. The analysis function is then used in tagging, which we describe in the next section.

The heuristics described above does not require linguistic knowledge about the language and handles linguistic regularities very well. The major advantage is a significant data compression leading to efficient resource usage: in our setting, the original morphology dictionary, the Czech Morfflex, contains 120M form-tag pairs derived from 1M unique lemmas, using 3 922 different tags, of total size 6.7GB.[8] Using the proposed heuristics with $N = 8$, there are 7 080 templates created, such that the whole dictionary is encoded using 3M template instances. The resulting binary form of the dictionary uses 2MB, which is 3 000 times smaller than the original dictionary.

In order to look up a word form in the dictionary, we split it into a prefix and an ending for all ending lengths from 1 to N. We then find templates associated with both the prefix and the ending. For each such template, we return the lemma corresponding to the prefix and the tag corresponding to the ending. The result is a set of lemma-tag pairs found during this procedure. This algorithm can be implemented efficiently – our implementation performs 500k word form lookups per second in the Czech morphological dictionary.

3.2 POS Tagger Methodology

The POS tagger is an offspring of Morče and Featurama research projects based on (Spoustová et al., 2009). For each form in the text, the morphological dictionary suggests all possible lemma-tag candidates and these lemma-tag pairs are disambiguated by the tagger. The tagger is implemented as supervised, rich feature averaged perceptron (Collins, 2002) and the classification features are adopted from (Spoustová et al., 2009).

lemmas, because the process of minimization cannot capture templates containing word forms (or their prefixes) of multiple lemmas.

[8]Which compresses to 454MB using `gzip -9`.

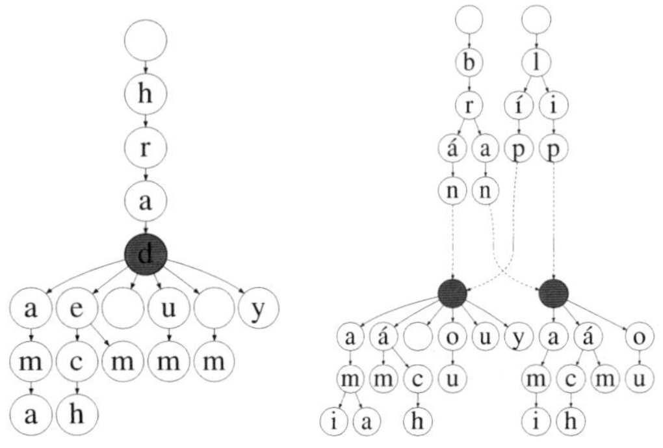

Figure 1: A simple trie for noun "hrad" (castle in Czech), and two lemmas sharing templates.

Czech language was trained on the training part of the Prague Dependency Treebank 2.5 (Bejček et al., 2012). The English language was trained on the standard training portion (Sections 0-18) of the Wall Street Journal part of the Penn Treebank (Marcus et al., 1993). In both cases, the system was tuned on the development set (Sections 19-21 in PTB/WSJ in English) and tested on the testing section (Sections 22-24 in PTB/WSJ in English).

3.3 POS Tagger Evaluation

An evaluation of POS taggers, which do not use external data, is shown in Table 1 for Czech and in Table 2 for English. MorphoDiTa reaches state-of-the-art results for Czech and nearly state-of-the-art results for English. The results are very similar for the three Czech systems, Morče, Featurama and MorphoDiTa, because in all three cases, they are implementations of (Spoustová et al., 2009). However, MorphoDiTa is the first end-to-end application released under a free license.

Due to rich morphosyntactic complexity of the Czech language and the positional tagging scheme proposed by (Hajič, 2004), there are 3 922 plausible tags in Czech (although only 1 571 unique tags actually appear in training data).

However, in many applications, only the first two tagging positions, which correspond to POS and sub-POS,[9] are actually needed for further processing, which greatly reduces the complexity of the task, leaving only 67 possible tags (64 in training data), although some morphological information, such as case, is lost.

[9]Sub-POS is detailed set of POS labels, which includes basic properties such as the type of pronouns, conjunctions, adjectives, also some tense and active/passive/mood information for verbs, etc.

Tagger	Task	Accuracy
Morče	tag	95.67%
Featurama	tag	95.66%
MorphoDiTa	tag	95.75%
MorphoDiTa	lemma	97.80%
MorphoDiTa	lemma+tag	95.03%
MorphoDiTa	tag-first two pos.	99.18%

Table 1: Evaluation of Czech POS taggers.

Tagger	Accuracy
Morče (Spoustová et al., 2009)	97.23%
(Shen et al., 2007)	97.33%
MorphoDiTa	97.27%

Table 2: Evaluation of the English taggers.

An example of a full 15-position tag and the restricted 2-position tag for an adjective "zelený" is "`AAIS1----1A----`" and "`AA`", respectively. The first two positions are in fact quite similar to what the Penn-style tags encode (for English). MorphoDiTa therefore also offers models trained on such a restricted tagging scheme. The tagger evaluation for the 2-position, restricted tags is given in the last row of Table 1.

4 NameTag: Named Entity Recognizer

4.1 NER Methodology

The NE recognizer is an implementation of a research project by (Straková et al., 2013). The recognizer is based on a Maximum Entropy Markov Model. First, maximum entropy model predicts, for each word in a sentence, the full probability distribution of its classes and positions with respect to an entity. Consequently, a global optimization via dynamic programming determines the optimal combination of classes and named entities chunks (lengths). The classification features utilize morphological analysis, two-stage prediction, word clustering and gazetteers and are described in (Straková et al., 2013).

The recognizer is available either as a run-time implementation with trained linguistic models for Czech, or as a package which allows custom models to be trained using any NE-annotated data.

4.2 Czech Named Entity Corpus

For training the recognizer, Czech Named Entity Corpus(Ševčíková et al., 2007) was used. In this corpus, Czech entities are classified into a two-level hierarchy classification: a fine-grained set of 42 classes or a more coarse classification of 7 super-classes. Like other authors, we report the evaluation on both hierarchy levels.

System	F-measure (42 classes)	F-measure (7 classes)
(Ševčíková et al., 2007)	62.00	68.00
(Kravalová et al., 2009)	68.00	71.00
(Konkol and Konopík, 2013)	NA	79.00
(Straková et al., 2013)	79.23	82.82
NameTag CNEC 1.1	77.88	81.01
NameTag CNEC 2.0	77.22	80.30

Table 3: Evaluation of the Czech NE recognizers.

Corpus	Words / sec	RAM	Model size
CNEC 1.1	40K	54MB	3MB
CNEC 2.0	45K	65MB	4MB

Table 4: Evaluation of the NE recognizer tagger throughput, RAM and model size.

Czech Named Entity Corpus annotation allows ambiguous labels, that is, one entity can be labeled with two classes; however, NameTag predicts exactly one label per named entity, just like the previous work does (Straková et al., 2013).

Furthermore, CNEC also allows embedded entities, which is also somewhat problematic. NameTag always predicts only the outer-most entity (the embedding entity), although it is penalized by the evaluation score which includes correct prediction of the nested entities.

4.3 NER Evaluation

For comparison with previous work, we report results for the first version of the Czech Named Entity Corpus (CNEC 1.1). The linguistic models released with NameTag are trained on the most current version of the Czech Named Entity Corpus (CNEC 2.0), which has been recently released. We report our results for both CNEC 1.1 and CNEC 2.0 in Table 3.

5 Software Performance

We designed MorphoDiTa and NameTag as lightweight, efficient software with low resource usage.

Depending on the morphosyntactic complexity of the language and the selected tagging scheme, the MorphoDiTa tagger has a throughput around 10-200K words per second on 2.9GHz Pentium computer with 4GB RAM. Table 4 shows the system word throughput, allocated RAM and model size on such a machine for NameTag and Table 5 shows these parameters for MorphoDiTa.

Task	System	Words / sec	RAM	Model size
Czech tag	Morče (Spoustová et al., 2009)	1K	902MB	178MB
Czech tag	Featurama	2K	747MB	210MB
Czech tag	MorphoDiTa	10K	52MB	16MB
Czech tag–first two pos.	MorphoDiTa	200K	15MB	2MB
English Penn style	Morče (Spoustová et al., 2009)	3K	268MB	42MB
English Penn style	Featurama	10K	195MB	49MB
English Penn style	MorphoDiTa	50K	30MB	6MB

Table 5: Evaluation of the POS tagger throughput, RAM and model size.

	MorphoDiTa	NameTag
Binaries and source code	https://github.com/ufal/morphodita	https://github.com/ufal/nametag
Project website	http://ufal.mff.cuni.cz/morphodita	http://ufal.mff.cuni.cz/nametag
Demo	http://lindat.mff.cuni.cz/services/morphodita/	http://lindat.mff.cuni.cz/services/nametag/
Web services	http://lindat.mff.cuni.cz/services	
Language models	http://lindat.mff.cuni.cz	

Table 6: Web links to MorphoDiTa and NameTag downloads.

6 Release

Both MorphoDiTa and NameTag are free software under LGPL and their respective linguistic models are free for non-commercial use and distributed under CC BY-NC-SA license, although for some models the original data used to create the model may impose additional licensing conditions. Both MorphoDiTa and NameTag can be used as:

- a standalone tool,
- C++ library with Java, Python, Perl bindings,
- a web service, which does not require any installation at the user's machine whatsoever,
- an on-line demo.

MorphoDiTa and NameTag are platform independent and do not require any additional libraries. Web services and demo for the Czech and English languages are also available.

Table 6 lists the web links to all resources. The pre-compiled binaries and source code are available on GitHub, the language models are available from the LINDAT/CLARIN infrastructure and the documentation can be found at the respective project websites.

7 Conclusion

We released two efficient, light-weight POS- and NE taggers (especially efficient for inflective languages), which are available to a wide audience as an open-source, free software with rich API and also as an end-to-end application. The taggers reach state-of-the-art results for Czech and are distributed with the models. We are currently working on more language releases (Slovak, Polish and Arabic). We are also aware that the creation of the dictionary relies on the existence of a resource annotated with forms, lemmas and tags, which may not be readily available. Therefore, our future work includes developing a guesser for analyzing previously unseen but valid word forms in inflective languages, using only data annotated with disambiguated POS tags. We hope the release for Czech will prove useful for broad audience, for example for shared tasks which include Czech language data.

Acknowledgments

This work has been partially supported and has been using language resources developed and/or stored and/or distributed by the LINDAT/CLARIN project of the Ministry of Education of the Czech Republic (project LM2010013). This research was also partially supported by SVV project number 260 104. We are grateful to the reviewers for comments which helped us to improve the paper.

References

Rie Kubota Ando and Tong Zhang. 2005. A high-performance semi-supervised learning method for text chunking. In *Proceedings of the 43rd Annual Meeting on Association for Computational Linguistics*, ACL '05, pages 1–9. Association for Computational Linguistics.

Eduard Bejček, Jarmila Panevová, Jan Popelka, Pavel Straňák, Magda Ševčíková, Jan Štěpánek, and Zdeněk Žabokrtský. 2012. Prague Dependency Treebank 2.5 – a revisited version of PDT 2.0. In

Martin Kay and Christian Boitet, editors, *Proceedings of the 24th International Conference on Computational Linguistics (Coling 2012)*, pages 231–246, Mumbai, India. IIT Bombay, Coling 2012 Organizing Committee.

Thorsten Brants. 2000. TnT: A Statistical Part-of-speech Tagger. In *Proceedings of the Sixth Conference on Applied Natural Language Processing*, ANLC '00, pages 224–231, Stroudsburg, PA, USA. Association for Computational Linguistics.

Eric Brill. 1992. A Simple Rule-based Part of Speech Tagger. In *Proceedings of the Third Conference on Applied Natural Language Processing*, ANLC '92, pages 152–155, Stroudsburg, PA, USA. Association for Computational Linguistics.

Nancy A. Chinchor. 1998. Proceedings of the Seventh Message Understanding Conference (MUC-7) Named Entity Task Definition. In *Proceedings of the Seventh Message Understanding Conference (MUC-7)*, page 21 pages, April.

Michael Collins. 2002. Discriminative Training Methods for Hidden Markov Models: Theory and Experiments with Perceptron Algorithms. In *Proceedings of the 2002 Conference on Empirical Methods in Natural Language Processing*, pages 1–8. Association for Computational Linguistics, July.

Rene De La Briandais. 1959. File Searching Using Variable Length Keys. In *Papers Presented at the the March 3-5, 1959, Western Joint Computer Conference*, IRE-AIEE-ACM '59 (Western), pages 295–298, New York, NY, USA. ACM.

Jenny Rose Finkel, Trond Grenager, and Christopher Manning. 2005. Incorporating non-local information into information extraction systems by Gibbs sampling. In *Proceedings of the 43rd Annual Meeting on Association for Computational Linguistics*, ACL '05, pages 363–370. Association for Computational Linguistics.

J. Hajič. 2004. *Disambiguation of Rich Inflection: Computational Morphology of Czech*. Karolinum Press.

Donald Knuth, 1997. *The Art of Computer Programming, Volume 3: Sorting and Searching, Third Edition*, chapter Section 6.3: Digital Searching, pages 492–512. Addison-Wesley.

Michal Konkol and Miloslav Konopík. 2011. Maximum Entropy Named Entity Recognition for Czech Language. In *Text, Speech and Dialogue*, volume 6836 of *Lecture Notes in Computer Science*, pages 203–210. Springer Berlin Heidelberg.

Michal Konkol and Miloslav Konopík. 2013. CRF-Based Czech Named Entity Recognizer and Consolidation of Czech NER Research. In Ivan Habernal and Vclav Matouek, editors, *Text, Speech, and Dialogue*, volume 8082 of *Lecture Notes in Computer Science*, pages 153–160. Springer Berlin Heidelberg.

Jana Kravalová and Zdeněk Žabokrtský. 2009. Czech named entity corpus and SVM-based recognizer. In *Proceedings of the 2009 Named Entities Workshop: Shared Task on Transliteration*, NEWS '09, pages 194–201. Association for Computational Linguistics.

H. Kucera and W. N. Francis. 1967. *Computational analysis of present-day American English*. Brown University Press, Providence, RI.

Mitchell P. Marcus, Beatrice Santorini, and Mary Ann Marcinkiewicz. 1993. Building a Large Annotated Corpus of English: The Penn Treebank. *COMPUTATIONAL LINGUISTICS*, 19(2):313–330.

Lev Ratinov and Dan Roth. 2009. Design challenges and misconceptions in named entity recognition. In *CoNLL '09: Proceedings of the Thirteenth Conference on Computational Natural Language Learning*, pages 147–155. Association for Computational Linguistics.

Libin Shen, Giorgio Satta, and Aravind Joshi. 2007. Guided Learning for Bidirectional Sequence Classification. In *Proceedings of the 45th Annual Meeting of the Association of Computational Linguistics*, pages 760–767, Prague, Czech Republic, June. Association for Computational Linguistics.

Drahomíra "johanka" Spoustová, Jan Hajič, Jan Raab, and Miroslav Spousta. 2009. Semi-Supervised Training for the Averaged Perceptron POS Tagger. In *Proceedings of the 12th Conference of the European Chapter of the ACL (EACL 2009)*, pages 763–771, Athens, Greece, March. Association for Computational Linguistics.

Jana Straková, Milan Straka, and Jan Hajič. 2013. A New State-of-The-Art Czech Named Entity Recognizer. In Ivan Habernal and Václav Matoušek, editors, *Text, Speech and Dialogue: 16th International Conference, TSD 2013. Proceedings*, volume 8082 of *Lecture Notes in Computer Science*, pages 68–75, Berlin / Heidelberg. Západočeská univerzita v Plzni, Springer Verlag.

Jun Suzuki and Hideki Isozaki. 2008. Semi-Supervised Sequential Labeling and Segmentation using Giga-word Scale Unlabeled Data. *Computational Linguistics*, (June):665–673.

Erik F. Tjong Kim Sang and Fien De Meulder. 2003. Introduction to the CoNLL-2003 Shared Task: Language-Independent Named Entity Recognition. In *Proceedings of CoNLL-2003*, pages 142–147. Edmonton, Canada.

Magda Ševčíková, Zdeněk Žabokrtský, and Oldřich Krůza. 2007. Named entities in Czech: annotating data and developing NE tagger. In *Proceedings of the 10th international conference on Text, speech and dialogue*, TSD'07, pages 188–195. Springer-Verlag.

Community Evaluation and Exchange of Word Vectors at wordvectors.org

Manaal Faruqui and **Chris Dyer**
Carnegie Mellon University
Pittsburgh, PA, 15213, USA
{mfaruqui, cdyer}@cs.cmu.edu

Abstract

Vector space word representations are useful for many natural language processing applications. The diversity of techniques for computing vector representations and the large number of evaluation benchmarks makes reliable comparison a tedious task both for researchers developing new vector space models and for those wishing to use them. We present a website and suite of offline tools that that facilitate evaluation of word vectors on standard lexical semantics benchmarks and permit exchange and archival by users who wish to find good vectors for their applications. The system is accessible at: www.wordvectors.org.

1 Introduction

Data-driven learning of vector-space word embeddings that capture lexico-semantic properties is a technique of central importance in natural language processing. Using co-occurrence statistics from a large corpus of text (Deerwester et al., 1990; Turney and Pantel, 2010), it is possible to construct high-quality semantic vectors — as judged by both correlations with human judgements of semantic relatedness (Turney, 2006; Agirre et al., 2009) and as features for downstream applications (Turian et al., 2010). A number of approaches that use the internal representations from models of word sequences (Collobert and Weston, 2008) or continuous bags-of-context wordsets (Mikolov et al., 2013) to arrive at vector representations have also been shown to likewise capture co-occurrence tendencies and meanings.

With an overwhelming number of techniques to obtain word vector representations the task of comparison and choosing the vectors best suitable for a particular task becomes difficult. This is further aggravated by the large number of existing lexical semantics evaluation benchmarks being constructed by the research community. For example, to the best of our knowledge, for evaluating word similarity between a given pair of words, there are currently at least 10 existing benchmarks[1] that are being used by researchers to prove the effectiveness of their word vectors.

In this paper we describe an online application that provides the following utilities:

- Access to a suite of word similarity evaluation benchmarks
- Evaluation of user computed word vectors
- Visualizing word vectors in $\mathbb{R}^2$
- Evaluation and comparison of the available open-source vectors on the suite
- Submission of user vectors for exhaustive offline evaluation and leader board ranking
- Publicly available repository of word vectors with performance details

Availability of such an evaluation system will help in enabling better consistency and uniformity in evaluation of word vector representations as well as provide an easy to use interface for end-users in a similar spirit to Socher et al. (2013a), a website for text classification.[2] Apart from the online demo version, we also provide a software that can be run in an offline mode on the command line. Both the online and offline tools will be kept updated with continuous addition of new relevant tasks and vectors.

[1] www.wordvectors.org/suite.php
[2] www.etcml.com

Proceedings of 52nd Annual Meeting of the Association for Computational Linguistics: System Demonstrations, pages 19–24,
Baltimore, Maryland USA, June 23-24, 2014.

2 Word Similarity Benchmarks

We evaluate our word representations on 10 different benchmarks that have been widely used to measure word similarity. The first one is the **WS-353**[3] dataset (Finkelstein et al., 2001) containing 353 pairs of English words that have been assigned similarity ratings by humans. This data was further divided into two fragments by Agirre et al. (2009) who claimed that *similarity* (**WS-SIM**) and *relatedness* (**WS-REL**)[4] are two different kinds of relations and should be dealt with separately. The fourth and fifth benchmarks are the **RG-65** (Rubenstein and Goodenough, 1965) and the **MC-30** (Miller and Charles, 1991) datasets that contain 65 and 30 pairs of nouns respectively and have been given similarity rankings by humans. These differ from **WS-353** in that it contains only nouns whereas the former contains all kinds of words.

The sixth benchmark is the **MTurk-287**[5] (Radinsky et al., 2011) dataset that constitutes 287 pairs of words and is different from the previous benchmarks in that it has been constructed by crowdsourcing the human similarity ratings using Amazon Mechanical Turk (AMT). Similar in spirit is the **MTruk-771**[6] (Halawi et al., 2012) dataset that contains 771 word pairs whose similarity was crowdsourced from AMT. Another, AMT created dataset is the **MEN**[7] benchmark (Bruni et al., 2012) that consists of 3000 word pairs, randomly selected from words that occur at least 700 times in the freely available ukWaC and Wackypedia[8] corpora combined.

The next two benchmarks were created to put emphasis on different kinds of word types. To specifically emphasize on verbs, Yang and Powers (2006) created a new benchmark **YP-130** of 130 verb pairs with human similarity judgements. Since, most of the earlier discussed datasets contain word pairs that are relatively more frequent in a corpus, Luong et al. (2013) create a new benchmark (**Rare-Word**)[9] that contains rare-words by sampling words from different frequency bins to a total of 2034 word pairs.

We calculate similarity between a given pair of words by the *cosine* similarity between their corresponding vector representation. We then report Spearman's rank correlation coefficient (Myers and Well, 1995) between the rankings produced by our model against the human rankings.

Multilingual Benchmarks. As is the case with most NLP problems, the lexical semantics evaluation benchmarks for languages other than English have been limited. Currently, we provide a link to some of these evaluation benchmarks from our website and in future will expand the website to encompass vector evaluation for other languages.

3 Visualization

The existing benchmarks provide ways of vector evaluation in a quantitative setting. To get an idea of what kind of information the vectors encode it is important to see how these vectors represent words in n-dimensional space, where n is the length of the vector. Visualization of high-dimensional data is an important problem in many different domains, and deals with data of widely varying dimensionality. Over the last few decades, a variety of techniques for the visualization of such high-dimensional data have been proposed (de Oliveira and Levkowitz, 2003).

Since visualization in n dimensions is hard when $n >= 3$, we use the t-SNE (van der Maaten and Hinton, 2008) tool[10] to project our vectors into $\mathbb{R}^2$. t-SNE converts high dimensional data set into a matrix of pairwise similarities between individual elements and then provides a way to visualize these distances in a way which is capable of capturing much of the local structure of the high-dimensional data very well, while also revealing global structure such as the presence of clusters at several scales.

In the demo system, we give the user an option to input words that they need to visualize which are fed to the t-SNE tool and the produced images are shown to the user on the webpage. These images can then be downloaded and used. We have

[3] http://www.cs.technion.ac.il/~gabr/resources/data/wordsim353/

[4] http://alfonseca.org/eng/research/wordsim353.html

[5] http://tx.technion.ac.il/~kirar/Datasets.html

[6] http://www2.mta.ac.il/~gideon/mturk771.html

[7] http://clic.cimec.unitn.it/~elia.bruni/MEN.html

[8] http://wacky.sslmit.unibo.it/doku.php?id=corpora

[9] http://www-nlp.stanford.edu/~lmthang/morphoNLM/

[10] http://homepage.tudelft.nl/19j49/t-SNE_files/tsne_python.zip

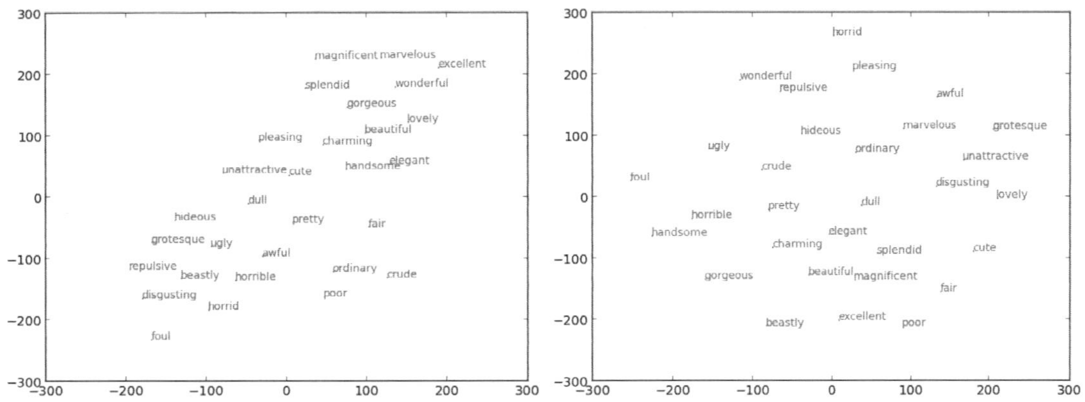

Figure 1: Antonyms (red) and synonyms (green) of *beautiful* represented by Faruqui and Dyer (2014) (left) and Huang et al. (2012) (right).

included two datasets by default which exhibit different properties of the language:

- Antonyms and synonyms of *beautiful*
- Common male-female nouns and pronouns

In the first plot, ideally the antonyms (*ugly, hideous, ...*) and synonyms (*pretty, gorgeous, ...*) of beautiful should form two separate clusters in the plot. Figure 1 shows the plots of the antonyms and synonyms of the word *beautiful* for two available embeddings. The second default word plot is the gender data set, every word in which has a male and a female counterpart (ex. *grandmother* and *grandfather*), this data set exhibits both local and global properties. Locally, the male and female counterparts should occur in pairs together and globally there should be two separate clusters of male and female.

4 Word Vector Representations

4.1 Pre-trained Vectors

We haves collected several standard pre-trained word vector representations freely available for research purposes and provide a utility for the user to test them on the suite of benchmarks, as well as try out the visualization functionality. The user can also choose the option to choose two different types of word vectors and compare their performance on the benchmarks. We will keep adding word vectors on the website as and when they are released. The following word vectors have been included in our collection:

Metaoptimize. These word embeddings [11] have been trained in (Turian et al., 2010) using a neural network language model and were shown to be useful for named entity recognition (NER) and phrase chunking.

SENNA. It is a software[12] which outputs a host of predictions: part-of-speech (POS) tags, chunking, NER etc (Collobert et al., 2011). The software uses neural word embeddings trained over Wikipedia data for over 2 months.

RNNLM. The recurrent neural network language modeling toolkit[13] comes with some pre-trained embeddings on broadcast news data (Mikolov et al., 2011).

Global Context. Huang et al. (2012) present a model to incorporate document level information into embeddings to generate semantically more informed word vector representations. These embeddings[14] capture both local and global context of the words.

Skip-Gram. This model is a neural network language model except for that it does not have a hidden layer and instead of predicting the target word, it predicts the context given the target word (Mikolov et al., 2013). These embeddings are much faster to train[15] than the other neural embeddings.

[11] http://metaoptimize.com/projects/wordreprs/

[12] http://ronan.collobert.com/senna/

[13] http://rnnlm.org/

[14] http://nlp.stanford.edu/~socherr/ACL2012_wordVectorsTextFile.zip

[15] https://code.google.com/p/word2vec/

Select?	Name	Dimensions	Vocabulary	Reference
	Metaoptimize	50	268810	Turian et al, 2010
	Senna	50	130000	Collobert et al, 2011
	RNN	80	82390	Mikolov et al, 2011
	RNN	640	82390	Mikolov et al, 2011
	Global Context	50	100232	Socher et al, 2012
	Skip-Gram	640	180834	Mikolov et al 2013
	Multilingual	512	180834	Faruqui and Dyer, 2014

Figure 2: Vector selection interface (right) of the demo system.

Multilingual. Faruqui and Dyer (2014) propose a method based on canonical correlation analysis to produce more informed monolingual vectors using multilingual knowledge. Their method is shown to perform well for both neural embeddings and LSA (Deerwester et al., 1990) based vectors.[16]

4.2 User-created Vectors

Our demo system provides the user an option to upload their word vectors to perform evaluation and visualization. However, since the size of the word vector file will be huge due to a lot of infrequent words that are not useful for evaluation, we give an option to filter the word vectors file to only include the words required for evaluation. The script and the vocabulary file can be found on the website online.

5 Offline Evaluation & Public Access

We provide an online portal where researchers can upload their vectors which are then be evaluated on a variety of NLP tasks and then placed on the leader board.[17] The motivation behind creating such a portal is to make it easier for a user to select the kind of vector representation that is most suitable for their task. In this scenario, instead of asking the uploader to filter their word vectors for a small vocabulary, they will be requested to upload their vectors for the entire vocabulary.

[16] http://cs.cmu.edu/~mfaruqui/soft.html

[17] We provide an initial list of some such tasks to which we will later add more tasks as they are developed.

5.1 Offline Evaluation

Syntactic & semantic relations. Mikolov et al. (2013) present a new semantic and syntactic relation dataset composed of analogous word pairs of size 8869 and 10675 pairs resp.. It contains pairs of tuples of word relations that follow a common relation. For example, in *England : London :: France : Paris*, the two given pairs of words follow the country-capital relation. We use the vector offset method (Mikolov et al., 2013) to compute the missing word in these relations. This is non-trivial $|V|$-way classification task where V is the size of the vocabulary.

Sentence Completion. The Microsoft Research sentence completion dataset contains 1040 sentences from each of which one word has been removed. The task is to correctly predict the missing word from a given list of 5 other words per sentence. We average the word vectors of a given sentence $q_{sent} = \sum_{i=1,i\neq j}^{N} q_{w_i}/N$, where w_j is the missing word and compute the cosine similarity of q_{sent} vector with each of the options. The word with the highest similarity is chosen as the missing word placeholder.

Sentiment Analysis Socher et al. (2013b) have created a treebank which contains sentences annotated with fine-grained sentiment labels on both the phrase and sentence level. They show that compositional vector space models can be used to predict sentiment at these levels with high accuracy. The coarse-grained treebank, containing only positive and negative classes has been split into training, development and test datasets con-

Serial	Dataset	Num Pairs	Not found	Rho
1	EN-MC-30.txt	30	0	0.8198
2	EN-MTurk-287.txt	287	1	0.5365
3	EN-RG-65.txt	65	0	0.7554
4	EN-RW-STANFORD.txt	2034	598	0.4232
5	EN-WS-353-ALL.txt	353	0	0.6809
6	EN-WS-353-REL.txt	252	0	0.6462
7	EN-WS-353-SIM.txt	203	0	0.7440
8	EN-MEN-TR-3k.txt	3000	1	0.7585

Figure 3: Screenshot of the command line version showing word similarity evaluation.

taining 6920, 872 and 1821 sentences respectively. We train a logistic regression classifier with $L2$ regularization on the average of the word vectors of a given sentence to predict the coarse-grained sentiment tag at the sentence level.

TOEFL Synonyms. These are a set of 80 questions compiled by Landauer and Dutnais (1997), where a given word needs to be matched to its closest synonym from 4 given options. A number of systems have reported their results on this dataset.[18] We use cosine similarity to identify the closest synonym.

5.2 Offline Software

Along with the web demo system we are making available a software which can be downloaded and be used for evaluation of vector representations offline on all the benchmarks listed above. Since, we cannot distribute the evaluation benchmarks along with the software because of licensing issues, we would give links to the resources which should be downloaded prior to using the software. This software can be run on a command line interface. Figure 3 shows a screenshot of word similarity evaluation using the software.

5.3 Public Access

Usually corpora that the vectors are trained upon are not available freely because of licensing issues but it is easier to release the vectors that have been trained on them. In the system that we have developed, we give the user an option to either make the vectors freely available for everyone to use under a GNU General Public License[19] or a Creative Commons License.[20] If the user chooses not to make the word vectors available, we would evaluate the vectors and give it a position in the leader board with proper citation to the publications/softwares.

[18] http://aclweb.org/aclwiki/index.php?title=TOEFL_Synonym_Questions_(State_of_the_art)

[19] https://www.gnu.org/copyleft/gpl.html

[20] https://creativecommons.org/licenses/by-nc-sa/4.0/legalcode

6 Conclusion

In this paper we have presented a demo system that supports rapid and consistent evaluation of word vector representations on a variety of tasks, visualization with an easy-to-use web interface and exchange and comparison of different word vector representations. The system also provides access to a suite of evaluation benchmarks both for English and other languages. The functionalities of the system are aimed at: (1) Being a portal for systematic evaluation of lexical semantics tasks that heavily rely on word vector representation, (2) Making it easier for an end-user to choose the most suitable vector representation schema.

Acknowledgements

We thank members of Noah's Ark and c-lab for their helpful comments about the demo system. Thanks to Devashish Thakur for his help in setting up the website. This work was supported by the NSF through grant IIS-1352440.

References

Eneko Agirre, Enrique Alfonseca, Keith Hall, Jana Kravalova, Marius Paşca, and Aitor Soroa. 2009. A study on similarity and relatedness using distributional and wordnet-based approaches. In *Proceedings of NAACL*, NAACL '09, pages 19–27, Stroudsburg, PA, USA.

Elia Bruni, Gemma Boleda, Marco Baroni, and Nam Khanh Tran. 2012. Distributional semantics in technicolor. In *Proceedings of the 50th Annual Meeting of the Association for Computational Linguistics (Volume 1: Long Papers)*, pages 136–145, Jeju Island, Korea, July. Association for Computational Linguistics.

Ronan Collobert and Jason Weston. 2008. A unified architecture for natural language processing: deep neural networks with multitask learning. In *Proceedings of the 25th international conference on Machine learning*, ICML '08, pages 160–167, New York, NY, USA. ACM.

Ronan Collobert, Jason Weston, Léon Bottou, Michael Karlen, Koray Kavukcuoglu, and Pavel Kuksa. 2011. Natural language processing (almost) from scratch. *J. Mach. Learn. Res.*, 12:2493–2537, November.

Maria Cristina Ferreira de Oliveira and Haim Levkowitz. 2003. From visual data exploration to visual data mining: A survey. *IEEE Trans. Vis. Comput. Graph.*, 9(3):378–394.

S. C. Deerwester, S. T. Dumais, T. K. Landauer, G. W. Furnas, and R. A. Harshman. 1990. Indexing by latent semantic analysis. *Journal of the American Society for Information Science*.

Manaal Faruqui and Chris Dyer. 2014. Improving vector space word representations using multilingual correlation. In *Proceedings of the 14th Conference of the European Chapter of the Association for Computational Linguistics*, Gothenburg, Sweden, April. Association for Computational Linguistics.

Lev Finkelstein, Evgeniy Gabrilovich, Yossi Matias, Ehud Rivlin, Zach Solan, Gadi Wolfman, and Eytan Ruppin. 2001. Placing search in context: the concept revisited. In *WWW '01: Proceedings of the 10th international conference on World Wide Web*, pages 406–414, New York, NY, USA. ACM Press.

Guy Halawi, Gideon Dror, Evgeniy Gabrilovich, and Yehuda Koren. 2012. Large-scale learning of word relatedness with constraints. In *KDD*, pages 1406–1414.

Eric H Huang, Richard Socher, Christopher D Manning, and Andrew Y Ng. 2012. Improving word representations via global context and multiple word prototypes. In *Proceedings of the 50th ACL: Long Papers-Volume 1*, pages 873–882.

Thomas K Landauer and Susan T. Dutnais. 1997. A solution to platos problem: The latent semantic analysis theory of acquisition, induction, and representation of knowledge. *Psychological review*, pages 211–240.

Minh-Thang Luong, Richard Socher, and Christopher D. Manning. 2013. Better word representations with recursive neural networks for morphology. In *CoNLL*, Sofia, Bulgaria.

Tomas Mikolov, Stefan Kombrink, Anoop Deoras, Lukar Burget, and J Cernocký. 2011. Rnnlm–recurrent neural network language modeling toolkit. *Proc. of the 2011 ASRU Workshop*, pages 196–201.

Tomas Mikolov, Kai Chen, Greg Corrado, and Jeffrey Dean. 2013. Efficient estimation of word representations in vector space. *arXiv preprint arXiv:1301.3781*.

George A. Miller and Walter G. Charles. 1991. Contextual correlates of semantic similarity. *Language and Cognitive Processes*, 6(1):1–28.

Jerome L. Myers and Arnold D. Well. 1995. *Research Design & Statistical Analysis*. Routledge, 1 edition, June.

Kira Radinsky, Eugene Agichtein, Evgeniy Gabrilovich, and Shaul Markovitch. 2011. A word at a time: computing word relatedness using temporal semantic analysis. In *Proceedings of the 20th international conference on World wide web*, WWW '11, pages 337–346, New York, NY, USA. ACM.

Herbert Rubenstein and John B. Goodenough. 1965. Contextual correlates of synonymy. *Commun. ACM*, 8(10):627–633, October.

Richard Socher, Romain Paulus, Bryan McCann, Kai Sheng Tai, and Andrew Y. Hu, JiaJi Ng. 2013a. etcml.com - easy text classification with machine learning. In *Advances in Neural Information Processing Systems (NIPS 2013)*.

Richard Socher, Alex Perelygin, Jean Wu, Jason Chuang, Christopher D. Manning, Andrew Y. Ng, and Christopher Potts. 2013b. Recursive deep models for semantic compositionality over a sentiment treebank. In *Proceedings of the 2013 Conference on Empirical Methods in Natural Language Processing*, pages 1631–1642, Stroudsburg, PA, October. Association for Computational Linguistics.

Joseph Turian, Lev Ratinov, and Yoshua Bengio. 2010. Word representations: a simple and general method for semi-supervised learning. In *Proceedings of the 48th ACL*, ACL '10, pages 384–394, Stroudsburg, PA, USA.

Peter D. Turney and Patrick Pantel. 2010. From frequency to meaning : Vector space models of semantics. *Journal of Artificial Intelligence Research*, pages 141–188.

Peter D. Turney. 2006. Similarity of semantic relations. *Comput. Linguist.*, 32(3):379–416, September.

Laurens van der Maaten and Geoffrey Hinton. 2008. Visualizing Data using t-SNE. *Journal of Machine Learning Research*, 9:2579–2605, November.

Dongqiang Yang and David M. W. Powers. 2006. Verb similarity on the taxonomy of wordnet. In *In the 3rd International WordNet Conference (GWC-06), Jeju Island, Korea*.

WINGS: Writing with Intelligent Guidance and Suggestions

Xianjun Dai, Yuanchao Liu*, Xiaolong Wang, Bingquan Liu
School of Computer Science and Technology
Harbin Institute of Technology, China
{xjdai, lyc, wangxl, liubq}@insun.hit.edu.cn

Abstract

Without inspirations, writing may be a frustrating task for most people. In this study, we designed and implemented *WINGS*, a Chinese input method extended on IBus-Pinyin with intelligent writing assistance. In addition to supporting common Chinese input, *WINGS* mainly attempts to spark users' inspirations by recommending both word level and sentence level writing suggestions. The main strategies used by *WINGS*, including providing syntactically and semantically related words based on word vector representation and recommending contextually related sentences based on LDA, are discussed and described. Experimental results suggest that *WINGS* can facilitate Chinese writing in an effective and creative manner.

1 Introduction

Writing articles may be a challenging task, as we usually have trouble in finding the suitable words or suffer from lack of ideas. Thus it may be very helpful if some writing reference information, e.g., words or sentences, can be recommended while we are composing an article.

On the one hand, for non-english users, e.g., Chinese, the Chinese input method is our first tool for interacting with a computer. Nowadays, the most popular Chinese input methods are Pinyin-based ones, such as Sougou Pinyin[1] and Google Pinyin[2]. These systems only present accurate results of Pinyin-to-Character conversion. Considering these systems' lack of suggestions for related words, they hardly provide writers with substantial help in writing. On the other hand, try to meet the need of writing assistance, more and more systems facilitating Chinese writing have been available to the public, such as WenXin Super Writing Assistant[3] and BigWriter[4], and among others. However, due to their shortcomings of building examples library manually and lack of corpus mining techniques, most of the time the suggestions made by these systems are not creative or contextual.

Thus, in this paper, we present Writing with INtelligent Guidance and Suggestions (*WINGS*)[5], a Chinese input method extended with intelligent writing assistance. Through *WINGS*, users can receive intelligent, real-time writing suggestions, including both word level and sentence level. Different from existing Chinese writing assistants, *WINGS* mainly attempts to spark users' writing inspirations from two aspects: providing diverse related words to expand users' minds and recommending contextual sentences according to their writing intentions. Based on corpus mining with Natural Language Processing techniques, e.g., word vector representation and LDA model, *WINGS* aims to facilitate Chinese writing in an effective and creative manner.

For example, when using *WINGS* to type "xuxurusheng", a sequence of Chinese Pinyin characters for "栩栩如生" (vivid/vividly), the Pinyin-to-Character Module will generate "栩栩如生" and some other candidate Chinese words.

Then the Words Recommending Module generates word recommendations for "栩栩如生". The recommended words are obtained through calculating word similarities based on word vector representations as well as rule-based strategy (POS patterns).

In the Sentences Recommending Module, we first use "栩栩如生" to retrieve example sentences from sentences library. Then the topic similarities between the local context and the candidate sentences are evaluated for contextual

* Corresponding author

[1] http://pinyin.sogou.com

[2] http://www.google.com/intl/zh-CN/ime/pinyin

[3] http://www.xiesky.com

[4] http://www.zidongxiezuo.com/bigwriter_intro.php

[5] The DEB package for Ubuntu 64 and recorded video of our system demonstration can be accessed at this URL: http://yunpan.cn/Qp4gM3HW446Rx (password:63b3)

Proceedings of 52nd Annual Meeting of the Association for Computational Linguistics: System Demonstrations, pages 25–30,
Baltimore, Maryland USA, June 23-24, 2014.

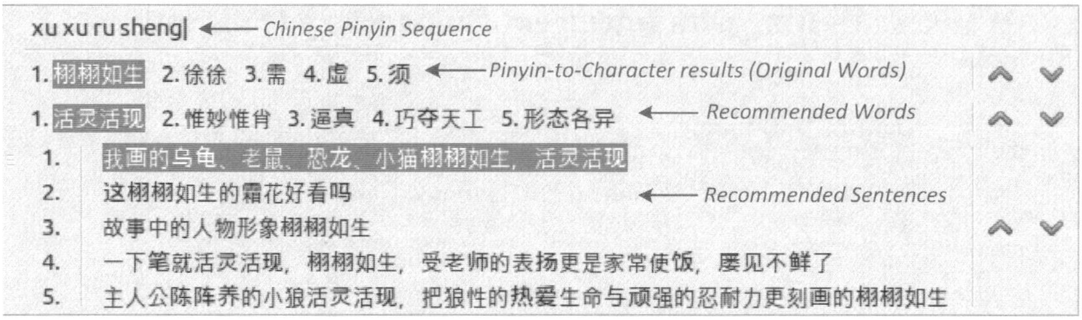

Figure 1. Screenshot of *WINGS*.

sentence recommendations.

At last in consideration of users' feedback, we introduce a User Feedback Module to our system. The recorded feedback data will in turn influence the scores of words and sentences in Recommending Modules above.

Figure 1 shows a screenshot of *WINGS*.

2 Related Work

2.1 Input Method

Chinese input method is one of the most important tools for Chinese PC users. Nowadays, Pinyin-based input method is the most popular one. The main strategy that Pinyin-based input method uses is automatically converting Pinyin to Chinese characters (Chen and Lee, 2000).

In recent years, more and more intelligent strategies have been adopted by different input methods, such as Triivi[6], an English input method that attempts to increase writing speed by suggesting words and phrases, and PRIME (Komatsu et al., 2005), an English/Japanese input system that utilizes visited documents to predict the user's next word to be input.

In our system the basic process was Pinyin → Characters (words) → Writing Suggestions (including words and sentences). We mainly focused on writing suggestions from Characters (words) in this paper. As the Pinyin-to-Character was the underlining work, we developed our system directly on the open source framework of the IBus (an intelligent input Bus for Linux and Unix OS) and IBus-Pinyin[7] input method.

2.2 Writing Assistant

As previously mentioned, several systems are available in supporting Chinese writing, such as WenXin Super Writing Assistant and Big Writer. These systems are examples of a retrieval-based writing assistant, which is primarily based on a large examples library and provides users with a search function.

In contrast, other writing assistants employ special NLP strategies. Liu et al. (2011, 2012) proposed two computer writing assistants: one for writing love letters and the other for blog writing. In these two systems, some special techniques were used, including text generation, synonym substitution, and concept expansion. PENS (Liu et al., 2000) and FLOW (Chen et al., 2012) are two writing assistants designed for students of English as a Foreign Language (EFL) practicing writing, which are mainly based on Statistical Machine Translation (SMT) strategies.

Compared with the above mentioned systems, *WINGS* is closer to retrieval-based writing assistants in terms of function. However, *WINGS* can provide more intelligent suggestions because of the introduction of NLP techniques, e.g., word vector representation and topic model.

2.3 Word Representations in Vector Space

Recently, Mikolov et al. (2013) proposed novel model architectures to compute continuous vector representations of words obtained from very large data sets. The quality of these representations was assessed through a word similarity task, and according to their report, the word vectors provided state-of-the-art performance for measuring syntactic and semantic word similarities in their test set. Their research produced the open source tool word2vec[8].

In our system, we used word2vec to train the word vectors from a corpus we processed beforehand. For the Words Recommending Module, these vectors were used to determine the similarity among different words.

[6] http://baike.baidu.com/view/4849876.htm
[7] https://code.google.com/p/ibus
[8] https://code.google.com/p/word2vec

2.4 Latent Dirichlet Allocation

The topic model Latent Dirichlet Allocation (LDA) is a generative probabilistic model of a corpus. In this model, documents are represented as random mixtures of latent topics, where each topic is characterized by the distribution of words (Blei et al., 2003). Each document can thus be represented as a distribution of topics.

Gibbs Sampling is a popular and efficient strategy used for LDA parameter estimation and inference. This technique is used in implementing several open sourcing LDA tools, such as GibbsLDA++[9] (Phan and Nguyen, 2007), which was used in this paper.

In order to generate contextual sentence suggestions, we ensured that the sentences recommended to the user were topic related to the local context (5-10 words previously input) based on the LDA model.

3 Overview of WINGS

Figure 2 illustrates the overall architecture of *WINGS*.

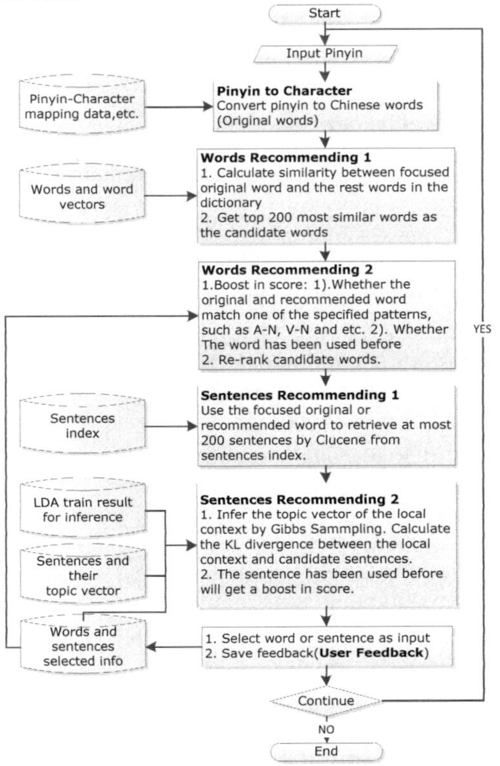

Figure 2. Overall architecture of *WINGS*.

3.1 System Architecture

Our system is composed of four different modules: **Pinyin-to-Character Module**, **Words Recommending Module**, **Sentences Recommending Module**, and **User Feedback Module**. The following sub-sections discuss these modules in detail.

3.2 Pinyin-to-Character Module

Our system is based on the open sourcing input framework IBus and extended on the IBus-Pinyin input method. Thus, the Pinyin-to-Character module is adopted from the original IBus-Pinyin system. This module converts the input Chinese Pinyin sequence into a list of candidate Chinese words, which we refer to as **original words**.

3.3 Words Recommending Module

- **Words vector representations**

In this preparatory step for word recommendation, words vector representations are obtained using the word2vec tool. This will be described in detail in Section 4.

- **Obtain the most related words**

Our system will obtain the focused **original word** and calculate the cosine similarities between this word and the rest of the words in the dictionary. Thus, we can obtain the top 200 most similar words according to their cosine values. These words are referred to as **recommended words**. According to Mikolov et al. (2013), these words are syntactically and semantically similar to the original word.

- **Re-rank the recommended words**

In order to further improve word recommending, we introduce several special POS patterns (Table 1). If the POS of the original word and the recommended word satisfy one of the POS patterns we specified, the score (based on the cosine similarity) of the recommended word will be boosted. In addition, the score of the word selected by the user before will also be boosted. Therefore, these words will be ranked higher in the recommended words list.

POS of original word	**POS of recommended word**
N (noun)	A (adjective)
A (adjective)	N (noun)
N (noun)	V (verb)
Any POS	Same with the original word
Any POS	L (idiom)

Table 1. Special POS patterns.

3.4 Sentences Recommending Module

- **Sentences topic distribution**

In this preparatory step for sentence

[9] http://gibbslda.sourceforge.net

recommendation, sentences topic distribution vectors and other parameters are trained using the GibbsLDA++. This step will be discussed in Section 4.

- **Retrieve relative sentences via CLucene**

The focused original or recommended word will be used to search the most related sentences in the sentences index via CLucene[10]. At most 200 sentences will be taken as candidates, which will be called **recommended sentences**.

- **Re-rank the recommended sentences**

To ensure that the recommended sentences are topic related to our local input context (5-10 words previously input), we use Gibbs Sampling to infer the topic vector of the local context, and calculate the KL divergence between the local context and each recommended sentence. Finally, the recommended sentences will be re-ranked based on their KL divergences value with respect to the local context and the boost score derived from the feedback information.

3.5 User Feedback Module

This module saves the users' feedback information, particularly the number of times when users select the recommended words and sentences. This information will be used as a boost factor for the **Words** and **Sentences Recommending Modules**. Our reasons for introducing this module are two-fold: the users' feedback reflects their preference, and at the same time, this information can somewhat indicate the quality of the words and sentences.

4 Data Pre-processing

In this section, the procedure of our data pre-processing is discussed in detail. Firstly, our raw corpus was crawled from DiYiFanWen[11], a Chinese writing website that includes all types of writing materials. After extracting useful composition examples from each raw html file, we merged all articles into a single file named **large corpus**. Finally, a total of 324,302 articles were merged into the large corpus (with a total size of 320 MB).

For words recommending, each of the articles in our large corpus was segmented into words by ICTCLAS [12] with POS tags. Subsequently, word2vec tool was used on the words sequence (with useless symbols filtered). Finally, the words, their respective vector representations and main POS tags were combined, and we built these data into one binary file.

For sentences recommending, the large corpus was segmented into sentences based on special punctuations. Sentences that were either too long or too short were discarded. Finally, 2,567,948 sentences were left, which we called **original sentences**. An index was created on these sentences using CLucene. Moreover, we segmented these original sentences and filtered the punctuations and stop words. Accordingly, these new sentences were named **segmented sentences**. We then ran GibbsLDA++ on the segmented sentences, and the Gibbs sampling result and topic vector of each sentence were thus obtained. Finally, we built the original sentence and their topic vectors into a binary file. The Gibbs sampling data used for inference was likewise saved into a binary file.

Table 2 lists all information on the resources of *WINGS*.

Items	Information
Articles corpus size	320 MB
Articles total count	324,302
Words total count	101,188
Sentences total count	2,567,948

Table 2. Resources information.

5 Experimental Results

This section discusses the experimental results of *WINGS*.

5.1 Words Recommending

The top 20 recommended words for the sample word "老师" (teacher) are listed in Table 3. Compared with traditional methods (using Cilin, Hownet, and so forth.), using the word vectors to determine related words will identify more diverse and meaningful related words and this quality of *WINGS* is shown in Table 4. With the diversity of recommended words, writers' minds can be expanded easily.

1-10: 同学(student), 上课(conduct class), 语文课(Chinese class), 语重心长(with sincere words and earnest wishes), 和蔼可亲(affability), 教导(guide), 讲课(lecture), 讲台(dais), 不厌其烦(patient), 全班(the whole class)
11-20: 下课(finish class), 一番话(remarks), 数学课(math class), 开小差(be absent-minded), 戒尺(ferule), 班主任(class adviser), 忐忑不安(restless), 记得(remember), 青出于蓝而胜于蓝(excel one's master), 听讲(listen to)

Table 3. Top 20 recommended words for "老师" (teacher).

[10] http://sourceforge.net/projects/clucene
[11] http://www.diyifanwen.com
[12] http://ictclas.nlpir.org

Words about	Words
Person	同学，班主任，全班
Quality	语重心长，和蔼可亲，不厌其烦
Course	语文课，数学课
Teaching	教导，讲课，上课，下课
Teaching facility	讲台，戒尺
Student behaviour	听讲，开小差，忐忑不安
Special idiom	青出于蓝而胜于蓝
Others	记得，一番话

Table 4. Diversity of recommended words for "老师" (teacher).

5.2 Sentences Recommending

By introducing the topic model LDA, the sentences recommended by *WINGS* are related to the topic of the local context. Table 5 presents the top 5 recommended sentences for the word "栩栩如生" (vivid/vividly) in two different local contexts: one refers to characters in books; the other refers to statues and sculptures. Most sentences in the first group are related to the first context, and most from the second group are related to the second context.

In order to assess the performance of *WINGS* in sentence recommendation, the following evaluation was implemented. A total of 10 Chinese words were randomly selected, and each word was given two or three different local contexts as above (contexts varied for different words). Finally, we obtained a total of 24 groups of data, each of which included an original word, a local context, and the top 10 sentences recommended by *WINGS*. To avoid the influence of personal preferences, 12 students were invited to judge whether each sentence in the 24 different groups was related to their respective local context. We believed that a sentence was related to its context only when at least 70% of the evaluators agreed. The Precision@10 measure in Information Retrieval was used, and the total average was 0.76, as shown in Table 6.

Additionally, when we checked the sentences which were judged not related to their respective local context, we found that these sentences were generally too short after stop words removal, and as a result the topic distributions inferred from Gibbs Sampling were not that reliable.

Context 1 is about characters in books: 故事(story), 人物(character), 形象(image), 作品(works)
1 这本书刻画了许多栩栩如生的人物 (The characters of this book are depicted vividly) 2 这本书人物描写栩栩如生，故事叙述有声有色 (The characters of this book are depicted vividly and the story is impressive narrative) 3 故事中的人物形象栩栩如生 (The characters of this story are depicted vividly) 4 他的作品情节惊险曲折人物栩栩如生结局出人意料 (His works are full of plot twists, vivid characters, and surprising endings) 5 书中的人物都被葛竞姐姐描写得栩栩如生 (The characters in the book are depicted vividly by Jing Zhuge)
Context 2 is about statues and sculptures: 塑像(statue), 雕塑(sculpture), 石刻(stone inscription), 寺庙(temple)
1 墙上绘满了威武的龙，栩栩如生 (The walls are painted with mighty and vivid dragons) 2 两侧的十八罗汉神态各异，栩栩如生 (On both sides there are standing 18 vivid Arhats with different manners) 3 大雄宝殿气势恢弘，殿内人物栩栩如生 (the Great Buddha Hall is grand and the statues there are vivid) 4 每尊都栩栩如生，活灵活现 (Each statue is vivid and lifelike) 5 檐角上各有七个栩栩如生的飞禽走兽像，它们各有其寓意 (On each of the eave angles there are 7 vivid statues of animals and birds with special meanings)

Table 5. Top 5 recommended sentences for "栩栩如生" (vivid/vividly) in two different local contexts.

Local Context	word 1	word 2	word 3	word 4	word 5	word 6	word 7	word 8	word 9	word 10
1	0.9	0.3	0.9	0.6	0.7	0.8	0.6	0.8	1.0	0.9
2	0.4	0.7	1.0	0.9	0.9	0.7	1.0	0.5	0.9	0.5
3	0.9	N/A	N/A	N/A	N/A	0.9	0.8	N/A	N/A	0.7
Average Precision@10 value of the 24 groups data								**0.76**		

Table 6. Precision@10 value of each word under their respective context and the total average.

5.3 Real Time Performance

In order to ensure the real time process for each recommendation, we used CLucene to index and retrieve sentences and memory cache strategy to reduce the time cost of fetching sentences' information. Table 7 shows the average and max responding time of each recommendation of randomly selected 200 different words (Our test environment is 64-bit Ubuntu 12.04 LTS OS on PC with 4GB memory and 3.10GHz Dual-Core CPU).

Item	Responding time
Average	154 ms
Max	181 ms

Table 7. The average and max responding time of 200 different words' recommending process

6 Conclusion and Future Work

In this paper, we presented *WINGS*, a Chinese input method extended with writing assistance that provides intelligent, real-time suggestions for writers. Overall, our system provides syntactically and semantically related words, as well as recommends contextually related sentences to users. As for the large corpus, on which the recommended words and sentences are based, and the corpus mining based on NLP techniques (e.g., word vector representation and topic model LDA), experimental results show that our system is both helpful and meaningful. In addition, given that the writers' feedback is recorded, *WINGS* will become increasingly effective for users while in use. Thus, we believe that *WINGS* will considerably benefit writers.

In future work, we will conduct more user experiments to understand the benefits of our system to their writing. For example, we can integrate *WINGS* into a crowdsourcing system and analyze the improvement in our users' writing. Moreover, our system may still be improved further. For example, we are interested in adding a function similar to Google Suggest, which is based on the query log of the search engine, in order to provide more valuable suggestions for users.

References

David M. Blei, Andrew Y. Ng and Michael I. Jordan. 2003. Latent dirichlet allocation. *the Journal of machine Learning research,* 3, pages 993-1022.

Mei-Hua Chen, Shih-Ting Huang, Hung-Ting Hsieh, Ting-Hui Kao and Jason S. Chang. 2012. FLOW: a first-language-oriented writing assistant system. In *Proceedings of the ACL 2012 System Demonstrations,* pages 157-162.

Zheng Chen and Kai-Fu Lee. 2000. A new statistical approach to Chinese Pinyin input. In *Proceedings of the 38th annual meeting on association for computational linguistics,* pages 241-247.

Hiroyuki Komatsu, Satoru Takabayash and Toshiyuki Masui. 2005. Corpus-based predictive text input. In *Proceedings of the 2005 international conference on active media technology,* pages 75–80.

Chien-Liang Liu, Chia-Hoang Lee, Ssu-Han Yu and Chih-Wei Chen. 2011. Computer assisted writing system. *Expert Systems with Applications, 38(1),* pages 804-811.

Chien-Liang Liu, Chia-Hoang Lee and Bo-Yuan Ding. 2012. Intelligent computer assisted blog writing system. Expert Systems with Applications, 39(4), pages 4496-4504.

Ting Liu, Ming Zhou, Jianfeng Gao, Endong Xun and Changning Huang. 2000. PENS: A machine-aided English writing system for Chinese users. In *Proceedings of the 38th Annual Meeting on Association for Computational Linguistics,* pages 529-536.

Tomas Mikolov, Kai Chen, Greg Corrado and Jeffrey Dean. 2013. Efficient estimation of word representations in vector space. arXiv:1301.3781.

Xuan-Hieu Phan and Cam-Tu Nguyen. 2007. GibbsLDA++: A C/C++ implementation of latent Dirichlet allocation (LDA).

DKPro Keyphrases: Flexible and Reusable Keyphrase Extraction Experiments

Nicolai Erbs[†], Pedro Bispo Santos[†], Iryna Gurevych[†‡] and Torsten Zesch[§‡]

† UKP Lab, Technische Universität Darmstadt
‡ Information Center for Education, DIPF, Frankfurt
§ Language Technology Lab, University of Duisburg-Essen
http://www.ukp.tu-darmstadt.de

Abstract

DKPro Keyphrases is a keyphrase extraction framework based on UIMA. It offers a wide range of state-of-the-art keyphrase experiments approaches. At the same time, it is a workbench for developing new extraction approaches and evaluating their impact. DKPro Keyphrases is publicly available under an open-source license.[1]

1 Introduction

Keyphrases are single words or phrases that provide a summary of a text (Tucker and Whittaker, 2009) and thus might improve searching (Song et al., 2006) in a large collection of texts. As manual extraction of keyphrases is a tedious task, a wide variety of keyphrase extraction approaches has been proposed. Only few of them are freely available which makes it hard for researchers to replicate previous results or use keyphrase extraction in some other application, such as information retrieval (Manning et al., 2008), or question answering (Kwok et al., 2001).

In this paper, we describe our keyphrase extraction framework called DKPro Keyphrases. It integrates a wide range of state-of-the-art approaches for keyphrase extraction that can be directly used with limited knowledge of programming. However, for developers of new keyphrase extraction approaches, DKPro Keyphrases also offers a programming framework for developing new extraction algorithms and for evaluation of resulting effects. DKPro Keyphrases is based on the Unstructured Information Management Architecture (Ferrucci and Lally, 2004), which provides a rich source of libraries with preprocessing components.

[1]http://code.google.com/p/dkpro-keyphrases/

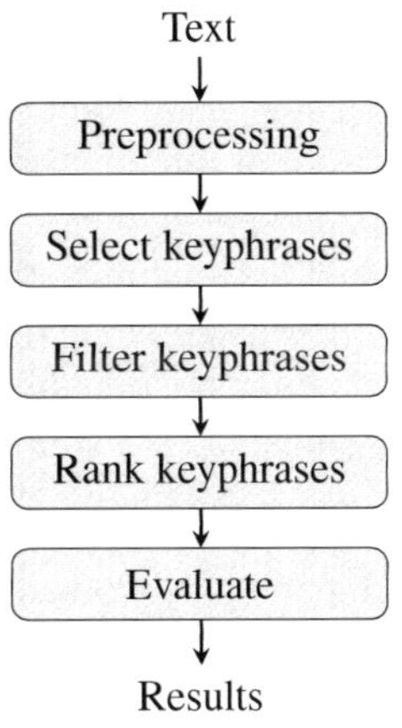

Figure 1: Architecture overview of DKPro Keyphrases

2 Architecture

The architecture of DKPro Keyphrases models the five fundamental steps of keyphrase extraction: (i) Reading of input data and enriching it with standard linguistic preprocessing, (ii) selecting phrases as keyphrase candidates based on the preprocessed text, (iii) filtering selected keyphrases, (iv) ranking remaining keyphrases, and (v) evaluating ranked keyphrases against a gold standard. This process is visualized in Figure 1. In this section, we will describe details of each step, including components already included in DKPro Keyphrases.

2.1 Preprocessing

DKPro Keyphrases relies on UIMA-based preprocessing components developed in the natural language processing framework DKPro Core (Gurevych et al., 2007; Eckart de Castilho and Gurevych, 2009). Thus, a wide range of linguistic preprocessing components are readily available such as word segmentation, lemmatization, part-of-speech tagging, named entity recognition, syn-

Proceedings of 52nd Annual Meeting of the Association for Computational Linguistics: System Demonstrations, pages 31–36,
Baltimore, Maryland USA, June 23-24, 2014.

tactic parsing, or co-reference resolution.

2.2 Selecting Keyphrases

In this step, DKPro Keyphrases selects all phrases as keyphrases that match user-specified criteria. A criterium is typically a linguistic type, e.g. tokens, or more sophisticated types such as noun phrases. The resulting list of keyphrases should cover all gold keyphrases and at the same time be as selective as possible. We use the following sentence with the two gold keyphrases "dog" and "old cat" as a step through example:

> A [dog] chases an [old cat] in my garden.

Taking all uni- and bi-grams as keyphrases will easily match both gold keyphrases, but it will also result in many other less useful keyphrases like "in my".

In the given example, the keyphrase list consists of nine tokens (lemmas, resp.) but covers only one gold keyphrase (i.e. "dog"). Noun chunks and named entities are alternative keyphrases, limiting the set of keyphrases further. Experiments where noun chunks are selected as keyphrases perform best for this example. Named entities are too restrictive, but applicable for identifying relevant entities in a text. This is useful for tasks that are targeted towards entities, e.g. for finding experts (Dörner et al., 2007) in a collection of domain-dependent texts. The selection of a linguistic type is not limited as preprocessing components might introduce further types.

2.3 Filtering

Filtering can be used together with over-generating selection approaches like taking all n-grams to decrease the number of keyphrases before ranking. One possible approach is based on POS patterns. For example, using the POS patterns, `Adjective-Noun`, `Adjective`, and `Noun` limits the set of possible keyphrases to "dog", "old cat", "cat", and "garden" in the previous example. This step can also been performed as part of the selection step, however, keeping it separated enables researchers to apply filters to keyphrases of any linguistic type. DKPro Keyphrases provides the possibility to use controlled-vocabulary keyphrase extraction by filtering out all keyphrases which are not included in a keyphrase list.

Developers of keyphrase extraction approaches can create their own filter simply by extending from a base class and adding filter-specific code. Additionally, DKPro Keyphrases does not impose workflow-specific requirements, such as a fixed number of filters. This leaves room for keyphrase extraction experiments testing new or extended filters.

2.4 Ranking

In this step, a ranker assigns a score to each remaining keyphrase candidate. DKPro Keyphrases contains rankers based on the candidate position, frequency, tf-idf, TextRank (Mihalcea and Tarau, 2004), and LexRank (Erkan and Radev, 2004).

DKPro Keyphrases also contains a special extension of tf-idf, called tf-idf$_{web}$, for which Google web1t (Brants and Franz, 2006) is used for obtaining approximate *df* counts. In case of keyphrase extraction for a single document or for domain-independent keyphrase extraction, web1t provides reliable n-gram statistics without any domain-dependence.

2.5 Evaluation

DKPro Keyphrases ships with all the metrics that have been traditionally used for evaluating keyphrase extraction. Kim et al. (2010) use precision and recall for a different number of keyphrases (5, 10 and 15 keyphrases). These metrics are widely used for evaluation in information retrieval. Precision @5 is the ratio of true positives in the set of extracted keyphrases when 5 keyphrases are extracted. Recall @5 is the ratio of true positives in the set of gold keyphrases when 5 keyphrases are extracted. Moreover, DKPro Keyphrases evaluates with MAP and R-precision. MAP is the mean average precision of extracted keyphrases from the highest scored keyphrase to the total number of extracted keyphrases. For each position in the rank, the precision at that position will be computed. Summing up the precision at each recall point and then taking its average will return the average precision for the text being evaluated. The mean average precision will be the mean from the sum of each text's average precision from the dataset. R-precision is the ratio of true positives in the set of extracted keyphrases, when the set is limited to the same size as the set of gold keyphrases (Zesch and Gurevych, 2009).

3 Experimental framework

In this section, we show how researchers can perform experiments covering many different configurations for preprocessing, selection, and ranking. To facilitate the construction of experiments, the framework contains a module to make its architecture compatible to the DKPro Lab framework (Eckart de Castilho and Gurevych, 2011), thus allowing to sweep through the *parameter space* of configurations. The parameter space is the combination of all possible parameters, e.g. one parameter with two possible values for preprocessing and a second parameter with two values for rankers lead to four possible combinations. We refer to *parameter sweeping experiments* when running the experiment with all possible combinations.

DKPro Keyphrases divides the experimental setup in three *tasks*. Tasks are processing steps defined in the Lab framework, which – in case of keyphrase extraction – are based on the steps described in Section 2. In the first task, the input text is fed into a pipeline and preprocessed. In the second task, the keyphrases are selected and filtered. In the third and final task they are ranked and evaluated. The output of the first two tasks are serialized objects which can be processed further by the following task. The output of the third task is a report containing all configurations and results in terms of all evaluation metrics.

The division into three tasks speeds up processing of the entire experiment. Each task has multiple configuration parameters which influence the forthcoming tasks. Instead of running the preprocessing tasks for every single possible combination, the intermediate objects are stored once and then used for every possible configuration in the keyphrase selection step.

To illustrate the advantages of experimental settings in DKPro Keyphrases, we run the previously used example sentence through the entire parameter space. Hence, tokens, lemmas, n-grams, noun chunks, and named entities will be combined with all filters and all rankers (not yet considering all possible parameters). This results in more than 10,000 configurations. Although the number of configurations is high, the computation time is low[2] as not the entire pipeline needs to run that often. This scales well for longer texts.

The experimental framework runs all possible combinations automatically and collects individual results in a report, such as a spreadsheet or text file. This allows for comparing results of different rankers, mitigating the influence of different preprocessing and filtering components. This way, the optimal experimental configuration can be found empirically. It is a great improvement for researchers because a variety of system configurations can be compared without the effort of reimplementing the entire pipeline.

Code example 1 shows the main method of an example experiment, selecting all tokens as possible keyphrases and ranking them with their tf-idf values. Lines 1 to 34 show values for dimensions which span the parameter space. A dimension consists of an identifier, followed by one or more values. Lines 36 to 40 show the creation of tasks, and in lines 42 to 48 the tasks and a report are added to one *batch task*, which is then executed. Researchers can run multiple configurations by setting multiple values to a dimension. Line 25 shows an example of a dimension with two values (using the logarithm or unchanged text frequency), in this case two configurations[3] for the ranker based on tf-idf scores.

Code example 1: Example experiment

```
1  ParameterSpace params = new
       ParameterSpace(
2   Dimension.create("language", "en"),
3   Dimension.create("frequencies",
       "web1t"),
4   Dimension.create("tfidfFeaturePath",
       Token.class"),
5
6   Dimension.create("dataset",
       datasetPath),
7   Dimension.create("goldSuffix", ".key"),
8
9  //Selection
10  Dimension.create("segmenter",
       OpenNlpSegmenter.class),
11  Dimension.create("keyphraseFeaturePath",
       Token.class),
12
13 //PosSequence filter
14  Dimension.create("runPosSequenceFilter",
       true),
15  Dimension.create("posSequence",
       standard),
16
17 //Stopword filter
18  Dimension.create("runStopwordFilter",
       true),
19  Dimension.create("stopwordlists",
       "stopwords.txt"),
20
21 // Ranking
```

[2] Less than five minutes on a desktop computer with a 3.4 GHz 8-core processor.

[3] DKPro Keyphrases provides ways to configure experiments using Groovy and JSON.

```
    Dimension.create("rankerClass",
        TfidfRanking.class),

//TfIdf
    Dimension.create("weightingModeTf",
        NORMAL, LOG),
    Dimension.create("weightingModeIdf",
        LOG),
    Dimension.create("tfidfAggregate",
        MAX),

//Evaluator
    Dimension.create("evalMatchingType",
        MatchingType.Exact),
    Dimension.create("evalN", 50),
    Dimension.create("evalLowercase",
        true),
    Dimension.create("evalType",
        EvaluatorType.Lemma),
);

Task preprocessingTask = new
    PreprocessingTask();
Task filteringTask = new
    KeyphraseFilteringTask();
candidateSelectionTask.addImport(
    preprocessingTask,
    PreprocessingTask.OUTPUT,
    KeyphraseFilteringTask.INPUT);
Task keyphraseRankingTask = new
    KeyphraseRankingTask();
keyphraseRankingTask.addImport(
    filteringTask,
    KeyphraseFilteringTask.OUTPUT,
    KeyphraseRankingTask.INPUT);

BatchTask batch = new BatchTask();
batch.setParameterSpace(params);
batch.addTask(preprocessingTask);
batch.addTask(candidateSelectionTask);
batch.addTask(keyphraseRankingTask);
batch.addReport(
    KeyphraseExtractionReport.class);
Lab.getInstance().run(batch);
```

A use case for the experimental framework is the evaluation of new preprocessing components. For example, keyphrase extraction should be evaluated with Twitter data: One collects a dataset with tweets and their corresponding keyphrases (possibly, the hash tags). The standard preprocessing will most likely fail as non-canonical language will be hard to process (e.g. *hash tags* or emoticons).

The preprocessing components can be set as a parameter and compared directly without changing the remaining parameters for filters and rankers. This allows researchers to perform reliable extrinsic evaluation of their components in a keyphrase extraction setting.

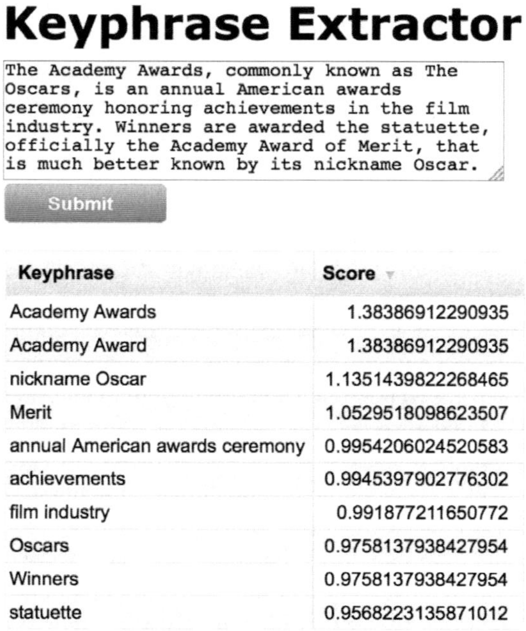

Figure 2: Screenshot of web demo in DKPro Keyphrases

4 Visualization and wrappers

To foster analysis of keyphrase extraction experiments, we created a web-based visualization framework with Spring[4]. It allows for running off-the-shelf experiments and manually inspecting results without the need to install any additional software. Figure 2 shows a visualization of one preconfigured experiment. The web demo is available online.[5] Currently, a table overview of extracted keyphrases is implemented, but developers can change it to highlighting all keyphrases. The latter is recommend for a binary classification of keyphrases. This is the case, if a system only returns keyphrases with a score above a certain threshold. The table in Figure 2 shows keyphrases with the assigned scores, which can be sorted to get a ranking of keyphrases. However, the visualization framework does not provide any evaluation capabilities.

To help new users of DKPro Keyphrases, it includes a module with two demo experiments using preconfigured parameter sets. This is especially useful for applying keyphrase extraction in other tasks, e.g. text summarization (Goldstein et

[4]http://projects.spring.io/spring-ws/

[5]https://dkpro.ukp.informatik.tu-darmstadt.de/DKProWebDemo/livedemo/3

al., 2000). Both demo experiments are frequently used keyphrase extraction systems. The first one is based on TextRank (Mihalcea and Tarau, 2004) and the second one is based on the supervised system KEA (Witten et al., 1999). Both configurations do not require any additional installation of software packages.

This module offers setters to configure parameters, e.g. the size of co-occurrence windows in case of the TextRank extractor.

5 Related work

Most work on keyphrase extraction is not accompanied with free and open software. The tools listed in this section allow users to combine different configurations with respect to preprocessing, keyphrase selection, filtering, and ranking. In the following, we give an overview of software tools for keyphrase extraction.

KEA (Witten et al., 1999) provides a Java API, which offers automatic keyphrase extraction from texts. They provide a supervised approach for keyphrase extraction. For each keyphrase, KEA computes frequency, position, and semantic relatedness as features. Thus, for using KEA, the user needs to provide annotated training data. KEA generates keyphrases from n-grams with length from 1 to 3 tokens. A controlled vocabulary can be used to filter keyphrases. The configuration for keyphrase selection and filtering is limited compared to DKPro Keyphrases, which offers capabilities for changing the entire preprocessing or adding filters.

Maui (Medelyan et al., 2009) enhances KEA by allowing the computation of semantic relatedness of keyphrases. It uses Wikipedia as a thesaurus and computes the keyphraseness of each keyphrase, which is the number of times a candidate was used as keyphrase in the training data (Medelyan et al., 2009).

Although Maui provides training data along with their software, this training data is highly domain-specific. A shortcoming of KEA and Maui is the lack of any evaluation capabilities or the possibility to run parameter sweeping experiments. DKPro Keyphrases provides evaluation tools for automatic testing of many parameter settings.

Besides KEA and Mau, which are Java systems, there are several modules in Python, e.g. topia.termextract[6], which offer capabilities for tokenization, part-of-speech tagging and keyphrase extraction. Keyphrase extraction from topia.termextract is based on noun phrases and ranks them according to their frequencies.

BibClassify[7] is a python module which automatically extracts keywords from a text based on the occurrence of terms in a thesaurus. The ranker is frequency-based like topia.termextract. BibClassify and topia.termextract do not provide evaluation capabilities or parameter sweeping experiments.

Besides these software tools, there exist web services for keyphrase extraction. AlchemyAPI[8] offers a web service for keyword extraction. It may return keyphrases encoded in various markup languages. TerMine[9] offers a SOAP service for extracting keyphrases from documents and a web demo. The input must be a String and the extracted terms will be returned as a String. Although web services can be integrated easily due to their protocol stacks, they are not extensible and replicability cannot be guaranteed over time.

6 Conclusions and future work

We presented DKPro Keyphrases, a framework for flexible and reusable keyphrase extraction experiments. This helps researchers to effectively develop new keyphrase extraction components without the need to re-implement state-of-the-art approaches.

The UIMA-based architecture of DKPro Keyphrases allows users to easily evaluate keyphrase extraction configurations. Researchers can integrate keyphrase extraction with different existing linguistic preprocessing components offered by the open-source community and evaluate them in terms of all commonly used evaluation metrics.

As future work, we plan to wrap further third-party libraries with keyphrase extraction approaches in DKPro Keyphrases and to add a supervised system using the unsupervised components as features. We expect that a supervised system using a large variety of features would improve the state of the art in keyphrase extraction.

---

[6] https://pypi.python.org/pypi/topia.termextract/

[7] http://invenio-demo.cern.ch/help/admin/bibclassify-admin-guide

[8] http://www.alchemyapi.com/api/keyword-extraction/

[9] http://www.nactem.ac.uk/software/termine/

Acknowledgments

This work has been supported by the Volkswagen Foundation as part of the Lichtenberg-Professorship Program under grant No. I/82806, by the Klaus Tschira Foundation under project No. 00.133.2008, and by the German Federal Ministry of Education and Research (BMBF) within the context of the Software Campus project *open window* under grant No. 01IS12054. The authors assume responsibility for the content. We thank Richard Eckart de Castilho and all contributors for their valuable collaboration and the we thank the anonymous reviewers for their helpful comments.

References

Thorsten Brants and Alex Franz. 2006. Web 1T 5-Gram Corpus Version 1.1. Technical report, Google Research.

Christian Dörner, Volkmar Pipek, and Markus Won. 2007. Supporting Expertise Awareness: Finding Out What Others Know. In *Proceedings of the 2007 Symposium on Computer Human Interaction for the Management of Information Technology*.

Richard Eckart de Castilho and Iryna Gurevych. 2009. DKPro-UGD: A Flexible Data-Cleansing Approach to Processing User-Generated Discourse. In *Online-proceedings of the First French-speaking meeting around the framework Apache UIMA*.

Richard Eckart de Castilho and Iryna Gurevych. 2011. A Lightweight Framework for Reproducible Parameter Sweeping in Information Retrieval. In *Proceedings of the 2011 Workshop on Data Infrastructures for Supporting Information Retrieval Evaluation*, pages 7–10.

Günes Erkan and Dragomir Radev. 2004. LexRank: Graph-based Lexical Centrality as Salience in Text Summarization. *Journal of Artificial Intelligence Research*, 22:457–479.

David Ferrucci and Adam Lally. 2004. UIMA: An Architectural Approach to Unstructured Information Processing in the Corporate Research Environment. *Natural Language Engineering*, 10(3-4):327–348.

Jade Goldstein, Vibhu Mittal, Jaime Carbonell, and Mark Kantrowitz. 2000. Multi-Document Summarization By Sentence Extraction. In *Proceedings of the NAACL-ANLP 2000 Workshop: Automatic Summarization*, pages 40–48.

Iryna Gurevych, Max Mühlhäuser, Christof Müller, Jürgen Steimle, Markus Weimer, and Torsten Zesch. 2007. Darmstadt Knowledge Processing Repository Based on UIMA. In *Proceedings of the First Workshop on Unstructured Information Management Architecture at Biannual Conference of the Society for Computational Linguistics and Language Technology*.

Su Nam Kim, Olena Medelyan, Min-Yen Kan, and Timothy Baldwin. 2010. Semeval-2010 Task 5: Automatic Keyphrase Extraction from Scientific Articles. In *Proceedings of the 5th International Workshop on Semantic Evaluation*, pages 21–26.

Cody Kwok, Oren Etzioni, and Daniel S. Weld. 2001. Scaling Question Answering to the Web. *ACM Transactions on Information Systems*, 19(3):242–262.

Christopher D Manning, Prabhakar Raghavan, and Hinrich Schütze. 2008. *An Introduction to Information Retrieval*. Cambridge University Press Cambridge.

Olena Medelyan, Eibe Frank, and Ian H Witten. 2009. Human-competitive Tagging using Automatic Keyphrase Extraction. In *Proceedings of the 2009 Conference on Empirical Methods in Natural Language Processing*, pages 1318–1327.

Rada Mihalcea and Paul Tarau. 2004. TextRank: Bringing Order into Texts. In *Proceedings of the Conference on Empirical Methods in Natural Language Processing*, pages 404–411.

Min Song, Il Yeol Song, Robert B. Allen, and Zoran Obradovic. 2006. Keyphrase Extraction-based Query Expansion in Digital Libraries. In *Proceedings of the 6th ACM/IEEE-CS Joint Conference on Digital Libraries*, pages 202–209.

Simon Tucker and Steve Whittaker. 2009. Have A Say Over What You See: Evaluating Interactive Compression Techniques. In *Proceedings of the 2009 International Conference on Intelligent User Interfaces*, pages 37–46.

Ian H. Witten, Gordon W. Paynter, Eibe Frank, Carl Andrew Gutwin, and Craig G . Nevill-Manning. 1999. KEA: Practical Automatic Keyphrase Extraction. In *Proceedings of the 4th ACM Conference on Digital Libraries*, pages 254–255.

Torsten Zesch and Iryna Gurevych. 2009. Approximate Matching for Evaluating Keyphrase Extraction. In *Proceedings of the 7th International Conference on Recent Advances in Natural Language Processing*, pages 484–489.

Real-Time Detection, Tracking, and Monitoring of Automatically Discovered Events in Social Media

Miles Osborne* Edinburgh
Sean Moran Edinburgh
Richard McCreadie Glasgow
Alexander Von Lunen Loughborough
Martin Sykora Loughborough
Elizabeth Cano Aston
Neil Ireson Sheffield
Craig Macdonald Glasgow
Iadh Ounis Glasgow
Yulan He Aston
Tom Jackson Loughborough
Fabio Ciravegna Sheffield
Ann O'Brien Loughborough

Abstract

We introduce **ReDites**, a system for real-time event detection, tracking, monitoring and visualisation. It is designed to assist Information Analysts in understanding and exploring complex events as they unfold in the world. Events are automatically detected from the Twitter stream. Then those that are categorised as being security-relevant are tracked, geolocated, summarised and visualised for the end-user. Furthermore, the system tracks changes in emotions over events, signalling possible flashpoints or abatement. We demonstrate the capabilities of **ReDites** using an extended use case from the September 2013 Westgate shooting incident. Through an evaluation of system latencies, we also show that enriched events are made available for users to explore within seconds of that event occurring.

1 Introduction and Challenges

Social Media (and especially Twitter) has become an extremely important source of real-time information about a massive number of topics, ranging from the mundane (what I had for breakfast) to the profound (the assassination of Osama Bin Laden). Detecting events of interest, interpreting and monitoring them has clear economic, security and humanitarian importance.

The use of social media message streams for event detection poses a number of opportunities and challenges as these streams are: very high in volume, often contain duplicated, incomplete, imprecise and incorrect information, are written in informal style (i.e. short, unedited and conversational), generally concern the short-term zeitgeist; and finally relate to unbounded domains. These characteristics mean that while massive and timely information sources are available, domain-relevant information may be mentioned very infrequently. The scientific challenge is therefore the detection of the signal within that noise. This challenge is exacerbated by the typical requirement that documents must be processed in (near) real-time, such that events can be promptly acted upon.

The **ReDites** system meets these requirements and performs event detection, tracking, summarisation, categorisation and visualisation. To the best of our understanding, it is the first published, large-scale, (near) real-time Topic Detection and Tracking system that is tailored to the needs of information analysts in the security sector. Novel aspects of **ReDites** include the first large-scale treatment of spuriously discovered events and tailoring the event stream to the security domain.

*Corresponding author: miles@inf.ed.ac.uk

Proceedings of 52nd Annual Meeting of the Association for Computational Linguistics: System Demonstrations, pages 37–42, Baltimore, Maryland USA, June 23-24, 2014. ©2014 Association for Computational Linguistics

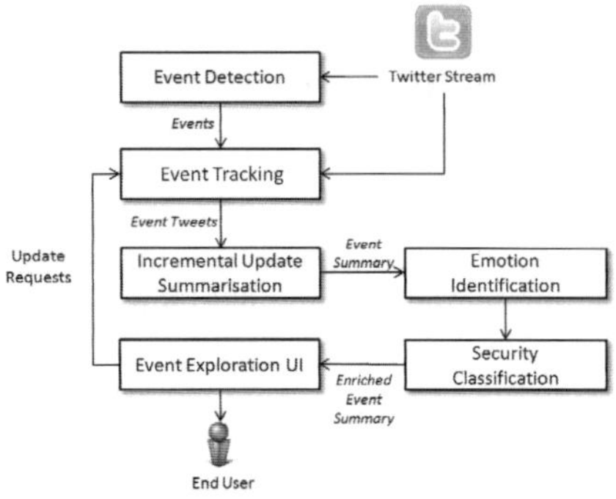

Figure 1: System Diagram

2 Related Work

A variety of event exploration systems have previously been proposed within the literature. For instance, *Trend Miner*[1] enables the plotting of term times series, drawn from Social Media (Preoţiuc-Pietro and Cohn, 2013). It has a summarisation component and is also multilingual. In contrast, our system is focussed instead upon documents (Tweets) and is more strongly driven by real-time considerations. The *Social Sensor* (Aiello et al., 2013) system facilitates the tracking of predefined events using social streams.

In contrast, we track all automatically discovered events we find in the stream. The *Twitcident* (Abel et al., 2012) project deals with user-driven searching through Social Media with respect to crisis management. However, unlike **ReDites**, these crises are not automatically discovered. The *LRA Crisis Tracker*[2] has a similar purpose as **ReDites**. However, while LRA uses crowdsourcing, our **ReDites** system is fully automatic.

3 System Overview and Architecture

Figure 1 gives a high-level system description. The system itself is loosely coupled, with services from different development teams coordinating via a Thrift interface. An important aspect of this decoupled design is that it enables geographically dispersed teams to coordinate with each other. Event processing is comprised of the following main 4 steps:

1) New events are detected. An event is described by the first Tweet that we find discussing it and is defined as something that is captured within a single Tweet (Petrovic et al., 2010).

2) When an event is first discovered it may initially have little information associated with it. Furthermore, events evolve over time. Hence, the second step involves tracking the event – finding new posts relating to it as they appear and maintaining a concise updated summary of them.

3) Not all events are of interest to our intended audience, so we organise them. In particular, we determine whether an event is security-related (or otherwise), geolocate it, and detect how prominent emotions relating to that event evolve.

4) Finally, we visualise the produced stream of summarised, categorised and geolocated events for the analyst(s), enabling them to better make sense of the mass of raw information present within the original Twitter stream.

Section 6 further describes these four steps.

4 Data and Statistics

For the deployment of **ReDites**, we use the Twitter 1% streaming sample. This provides approximately four million Tweets per day, at a rate of about 50 Tweets a second. Table 1 gives some illustrative statistics on a sample of data from September 2013 to give a feel for the rate of data and generated events we produce. Table 2 gives timing information, corresponding with the major components of our system: time to process and time to transfer to the next component, which is usually a service on another machine on the internet. The latency of each step is measured in seconds over a 1000 event sample. 'Transfer' latencies is the time between one step completing and the output arriving at the next step to be processed (Thrift transfer time). Variance is the average deviation from the mean latency over the event sample.

When processing the live stream, we ingest data at an average rate of 50 Tweets per second and detect an event (having geolocated and filtered out non-English or spam Tweets) with a per-Tweet latency of 0.6 ± 0.55 seconds. Figure 2 gives latencies for the various major components of the system. All processing uses commodity machines.

5 The Westgate Shopping Mall Attack

As an illustrative example of a complex recent event, we considered a terrorist attack on the 21st of September, 2013.[3] This event is used to demonstrate how our system can be used to understand it.

[1] http://www.trendminer-project.eu/

[2] http://www.lracrisistracker.com/

[3] https://en.wikipedia.org/wiki/Westgate_shopping_mall_shooting

Measure	Event Detection	Tracking and Summ			Emotion Ident		Security Class	
	Detection	Transfer	Ranking	Summ	Transfer	Ident	Transfer	Class
Latency (sec.)	0.6226	0.7929	2.2892	0.0409	0.0519	0.2881	0.1032	0.1765
Variance (sec.)	0.5518	0.2987	1.3079	0.0114	0.0264	0.1593	0.0195	0.0610

Table 2: Event exploration timing and timing variance (seconds)

Data	Rate
Tweets	35 Million
Detected events	533k
Categorised (security-related) events	5795

Table 1: Data statistics, 1st September - 30th September 2013

In summary, a shopping Mall in Kenya was attacked from the 21st of September until the 24th of September. This event was covered by traditional newswire, by victims caught up in it as well as by terrorist sympathisers, often in real-time. As we later show, even though we only operate over 1% of the Twitter Stream, we are still able to find many (sub) events connected with this attack. There were 6657 mentions of Westgate in September 2013 in our 1% of sample Tweets.

6 Major Components

6.1 Event Detection

Building upon an established Topic Detection and Tracking (TDT) methodology, which assumes that each new event corresponds with seeing some novel document. the event detection component uses a hashing approach that finds novel events[4] in constant time (Petrovic et al., 2010). To make it scale and process thousands of documents each second, it can optionally be distributed over a cluster of machines (via Storm[5]) (McCreadie et al., 2013). The system favours recall over precision and has been shown to have high recall, but a low precision (Petrovic et al., 2013). Given that we are presenting discovered events to a user and we do not want to overload them with false positives, we need to take steps to increase precision (ie present fewer false positives).

We use a *content categoriser* to determine whether a discovered event is worth reporting. Using more than 100k automatically discovered events from the Summer of 2011, we created a training set and manually labelled each Tweet: was it content bearing (what you might want to read about in traditional newswire) or irrelevant / not useful. With this labelled data, we used a Passive-Aggressive algorithm to build a content classifier. Features were simply unigrams in Tweets. This dramatically improves precision, to 70%, with a drop in recall to 25% (when tested on 73k unseen events, manually labelled by two annotators). We can change the precision-recall boundary as needed by adjusting the associated decision boundary. We do not consider non-English language Tweets in this work and they are filtered out (Lui and Baldwin, 2012).

Geolocation is important, as we are particularly interested in events that occur at a specific location. We therefore additionally geolocate any Tweets that were not originally geolocated. To geotag those Tweets that do not have any geo-location information we use the Tweet text and additional Tweet metadata (language, city/state/country name, user description etc), to learn a L_1 penalised least squares regressor (LASSO) to predict the latitude and longitude. The model is learnt on nearly 20 million geolocated Tweets collected from 2010-2014. Experiments on a held-out test dataset show we can localise Tweets to within a mean distance of 433 km of their true location. This performance is based on the prediction of *individual* tweet location and not, as in most previous work, on the location of a user who is represented by a set of tweets. Furthermore we are not restricted to a single, well-defined area (such as London) and we also evaluate over a very large set of unfiltered tweets.

Turning to the Westgate example, the first mention of it in our data was at 10:02 UTC. There were 57 mentions of Westgate in discovered events, of which 42 mentioned Kenya and 44 mentioned Nairobi. The first mention itself in Twitter was at 09:38 UTC. We declared it an event (having seen enough evidence and post-processing it) less than one second later:

> Westgate under siege. Armed thugs. Gunshots reported. Called the managers, phones are off/busy. Are cops on the way?

We also captured numerous informative sub-

[4] An event is defined as something happening at a given time and place. Operationally, this means something that can be described within a Tweet.

[5] http://storm.incubator.apache.org/

events covering different aspects and sides of the central Westgate siege event, four of these are illustrated below:

Post Time	Tweet
10:05am	RT @ItsMainaKageni: My friend Ruhila Adatia passed away together with her unborn child. Please keep her family and new husband in your thou
10:13am	RT howden_africa: Kenya police firing tear gas and warning shots at Kenyan onlookers. Crowd getting angry #westgate
10:10am	RT @BreakingNews: Live video: Local news coverage of explosions, gunfire as smoke billows from Nairobi, Kenya, mall - @KTNKenya
10:10am	"Purportedly official Twitter account for al-Shabaab Tweeting on the Kenyan massacre HSM_Press (http://t.co/XnCz9BulGj)

6.2 Tracking and Summarisation

The second component of the event exploration system is *Tracking and Summarisation (TaS)*. The aim of this component is to use the underlying Tweet stream to produce an overview for each event produced by the event detection stage, updating this overview as the event evolves. Tracking events is important when dealing with live, ongoing disasters, since new information can rapidly emerge over time.

TaS takes as input a Tweet representing an event and emits a list of Tweets summarising that event in more detail. TaS is comprised of two distinct sub-components, namely: real-time tracking; and event summarisation. The real-time tracking component maintains a sliding window of Tweets from the underlying Tweet stream. As an event arrives, the most informative terms contained[6] form a search query that is used to retrieve new Tweets about the event. For example, taking the Tweet about the Westgate terrorist attack used in the previous section as input on September 21st 2013 at 10:15am, the real-time tracking subcomponent retrieved the following related Tweets from the Twitter Spritzer (1%) steam[7] (only 5/100 are shown):

ID	Post Time	Tweet	Score
1	10:05am	Westgate under siege. Armed thugs. Gunshots reported. Called the managers, phones are off/busy. Are cops on the way?	123.7
2	10:13am	DO NOT go to Westgate Mall. Gunshots and mayhem, keep away until further notice.	22.9
3	10:13am	RT DO NOT go to Westgate Mall. Gunshots and mayhem, keep away until further notice.	22.9
4	10:10am	Good people please avoid Westgate Mall. @PoliceKE @IGkimaiyo please act ASAP, reports of armed attack at #WestgateMall	22.2
5	10:07am	RT @steve_enzo: @kirimiachieng these thugs won't let us be	11.5

[6]Nouns, adjectives, verbs and cardinal numbers

[7]https://dev.twitter.com/docs/streaming-apis/streams/public

The second TaS sub-component is event summarisation. This sub-component takes as input the Tweet ranking produced above and performs extractive summarisation (Nenkova and McKeown, 2012) upon it, i.e. it selects a subset of the ranked Tweets to form a summary of the event. The goals of event summarisation are two-fold. First, to remove any Tweets from the above ranking that are not relevant to the event (e.g. Tweet 5 in the example above). Indeed when an event is first detected, there may be few relevant Tweets yet posted. The second goal is to remove redundancy from within the selected Tweets, such as Tweets 2 and 3 in the above example, thereby focussing the produced summary on novelty. To tackle the first of these goals, we leverage the score distribution of Tweets within the ranking to identify those Tweets that are likely background noise. When an event is first detected, few relevant Tweets will be retrieved, hence the mean score over the Tweets is indicative of non-relevant Tweets. Tweets within the ranking whose scores diverge from the mean score in the positive direction are likely to be on-topic. We therefore, make an include/exclude decision for each Tweet t in the ranking R:

$$include(t,R) = \begin{cases} 1 \; if & score(t) - SD(R) > 0 \\ \quad and & |SD(R) - score(t)| > \\ & \theta \cdot \frac{1}{|R|}\sum_{t' \in R}|SD(R) - score(t')| \\ 0 & \text{otherwise} \end{cases} \quad (1)$$

where $SD(R)$ is the standard deviation of scores in R, $score(t)$ is the retrieval score for Tweet t and θ is a threshold parameter that describes the magnitude of the divergence from the mean score that a Tweet must have before it is included within the summary. Then, to tackle the issue of redundancy, we select Tweets in a greedy time-ordered manner (earliest first). A similarity (cosine) threshold between the current Tweet and each Tweet previously selected is used to remove those that are textually similar, resulting in the following extractive summary:

ID	Post Time	Tweet	Score
1	10:05am	Westgate under siege. Armed thugs. Gunshots reported. Called the managers, phones are off/busy. Are cops on the way?	123.7
2	10:13am	DO NOT go to Westgate Mall. Gunshots and mayhem, keep away until further notice.	22.9
4	10:10am	Good people please avoid Westgate Mall. @PoliceKE @IGkimaiyo please act ASAP, reports of armed attack at #WestgateMall	22.2

Finally, the TaS component can be used to track

events over time. In this case, instead of taking a new event as input from the event detection component, a previously summarised event can be used as a surrogate. For instance, a user might identify an event that they want to track. The real-time search sub-component retrieves new Tweets about the event posted since that event was last summarised. The event summarisation sub-component then removes non-relevant and redundant Tweets with respect to those contained within the previous summary, producing a new updated summary.

6.3 Organising Discovered Events

The events we discover are not targeted at information analysts. For example, they contain sports updates, business acquisitions as well as those that are genuinely relevant and can bear various opinions and degrees of emotional expression. We therefore take steps to filter and organise them for our intended audience: we predict whether they have a specific security-focus and finally predict an emotional label for events (which can be useful when judging changing viewpoints on events and highlighting extreme emotions that could possibly motivate further incidents).

6.3.1 Security-Related Event Detection

We are particularly interested in security-related events such as violent events, natural disasters, or emergency situations. Given a lack of in-domain labelled data, we resort to a weakly supervised Bayesian modelling approach based on the previously proposed Violence Detection Model (VDM) (Cano et al., 2013) for identifying security events.

In order to differentiate between security and non-security related events, we extract words relating to security events from existing knowledge sources such as DBpedia and incorporate them as priors into the VDM model learning. It should be noted that such a word lexicon only provides initial prior knowledge into the model. The model will automatically discover new words describing security-related events.

We trained the VDM model on a randomly sampled 10,581 Tweets from the TREC Microblog 2011 corpus (McCreadie et al., 2012) and tested the model on 1,759 manually labelled Tweets which consist of roughly the same number of security-related and non-security related Tweets. Our results show that the VDM model achieved 85.8% in F-measure for the identification of security-related Tweets, which is not far from the F-measure of 90% obtained using the supervised Naive Bayes classifier despite using no labelled data in the model.

Here, we derived word priors from a total of 32,174 documents from DBpedia and extracted 1,612 security-related words and 1,345 non-security-related words based on the measurement of relative word entropy. We then trained the VDM model by setting the topic number to 50 and using 7,613 event Tweets extracted from the Tweets collected during July-August 2011 and September 2013 in addition to 10,581 Tweets from the TREC Microblog 2011 corpus. In the aforementioned Westgate example, we classify 24% of Tweets as security-related out of a total of 7,772 summary Tweets extracted by the TaS component. Some of the security-related Tweets are listed below[8]:

ID	Post Time	Tweet
1	9:46am	Like Bin Laden kind of explosion? "@The_realBIGmeat: There is an explosion at westgate!"
2	10:08am	RT @SmritiVidyarthi: DO NOT go to Westgate Mall. Gunshots and mayhem, keep away till further notice.
3	10:10am	RT @juliegichuru: Good people please avoid Westgate. @PoliceKE @IGkimaiyo please act ASAP, reports of armed attack at #WestgateMall.
4	10:13am	there has bn shooting @ Westgate which is suspected to b of gangs.......there is tension rt nw....

6.3.2 Emotion

Security-related events can be fraught, with emotionally charged posts possibly evolving over time, reflecting ongoing changes in underlying events. Eight basic emotions, as identified in the psychology literature (see (Sykora et al., 2013a) for a detailed review of this literature) are covered, specifically; anger, confusion, disgust, fear, happiness, sadness, shame and surprise. Extreme values –as well as their evolution– can be useful to an analyst (Sykora et al., 2013b). We detect enotions in Tweets and support faceted browing. The emotion component assigns labels to Tweets representing these emotions. It is based upon a manually constructed ontology, which captures the relationships between these emotions and terms (Sykora et al., 2013a).

We sampled the summarised Tweets of the Westgate attack, starting from the event detection and following the messages over a course of seven days. In the relevant Tweets, we detected that

[8]Note some Tweets happen on following days.

8.6% had emotive terms in them, which is in line with the aforementioned literature. Some example expressions of emotion include:

Time	Tweet	Emotions
03:34	-) Ya so were those gunshots outside of gables?! I'm terrified ?	Fear
06:27	-) I'm so impressed @ d way. Kenyans r handling d siege.	Surprise
14:32	-) All you xenophobic idiots spewing anti-Muslim bullshit need to -get in one of these donation lines and see how wrong you ?	Fear Disgust

For Westgate, the emotions of sadness, fear and surprise dominated. Very early on the emotions of fear and sadness were expressed, as Twitter users were terrified by the event and saddened by the loss of lives. Sadness and fear were – over time – the emotions that were stated most frequently and constantly, with expressions of surprise, as users were shocked about what was going on, and some happiness relating to when people managed to escape or were rescued from the mall. Generally speaking, factual statements in the Tweets were more prominent than emotive ones. This coincides with the emotive Tweets that represented fear and surprise in the beginning, as it was not clear what had happened and Twitter users were upset and tried to get factual information about the event.

6.4 Visual Analytics

The visualisation component is designed to facilitate the understanding and exploration of detected events. It offers faceted browsing and multiple visualisation tools to allow an information analyst to gain a rapid understanding of ongoing events. An analyst can constrain the detected events using information both from the original Tweets (e.g. hashtags, locations, user details) and from the updated summaries derived by **ReDites**. The analyst can also view events using facet values, locations/keywords in topic maps and time/keywords in multiple timelines. By combining information dimensions, the analyst can determine patterns across dimensions to determine if an event should be acted upon – e.g the analyst can choose to view Tweets, which summarise highly emotive events, concerning middle eastern countries.

7 Discussion

We have presented **ReDites**, the first published system that carries out large-scale event detection, tracking summarisation and visualisation for the security sector. Events are automatically identified and those that are relevant to information analysts are quickly made available for ongoing monitoring. We showed how the system could be used to help understand a complex, large-scale security event. Although our system is initially specialised to the security sector, it is easy to repurpose it to other domains, such as natural disasters or smart cities. Key aspects of our approach include scalability and a rapid response to incoming data.

Acknowledgements

This work was funded by EPSRC grant EP/L010690/1. MO also acknowledges support from grant ERC Advanced Fellowship 249520 GRAMPLUS.

References

F. Abel, C. Hauff, G.-J. Houben, R. Stronkman, and K. T. Semantics + filtering + search = twitcident. exploring information in social web streams. In *Proc. of HT*, 2012.

L. M. Aiello et al. L. Aiello, G. Petkos, C. Martin, D. Corney, S. Papadopoulos, R. Skraba, A. Goker, Y. Kompatsiaris, A. Jaimes Sensing trending topics in Twitter. Transactions on Multimedia Journal, 2012.

A.E. Cano, Y. He, K. Liu, and J. Zhao. A weakly supervised bayesian model for violence detection in social media. In *Proc. of IJCNLP*, 2013.

M. Lui and T. Baldwin. Langid.py: An off-the-shelf language identification tool. In *Proc. of ACL*, 2012.

R. McCreadie, C. Macdonald, I. Ounis, M. Osborne, and S. Petrovic. Scalable distributed event detection for twitter. In *Proc. of Big Data*, 2013.

R. McCreadie, I. Soboroff, J. Lin, C. Macdonald, I. Ounis and D. McCullough. On building a reusable Twitter corpus. In *Proc. of SIGIR*, 2012.

A. Nenkova and K. McKeown. A survey of text summarization techniques. In *Mining Text Data Journal*, 2012.

S. Petrovic, M. Osborne, and V. Lavrenko. Streaming first story detection with application to Twitter. In *Proc. of NAACL*, 2010.

S. Petrovic, M. Osborne, R. McCreadie, C. Macdonald, I. Ounis, and L. Shrimpton. Can Twitter replace newswire for breaking news? In *Proc. of WSM*, 2012.

D. Preoţiuc-Pietro and T. Cohn. A temporal model of text periodicities using gaussian processes. In *Proc. of EMNLP*, 2012.

M. D. Sykora, T. W. Jackson, A. O'Brien, and S. Elayan. Emotive ontology: Extracting fine-grained emotions from terse, informal messages. *Computer Science and Information Systems Journal*, 2013.

M. D. Sykora, T. W. Jackson, A. O'Brien, and S. Elayan. National security and social media monitoring. In *Proc. of EISIC*, 2013.

The Excitement Open Platform for Textual Inferences

Bernardo Magnini*, **Roberto Zanoli***, **Ido Dagan**°, **Kathrin Eichler**†, **Günter Neumann**†, **Tae-Gil Noh**‡, **Sebastian Pado**‡, **Asher Stern**°, **Omer Levy**°

*FBK (magnini|zanoli@fbk.eu) ‡Heidelberg, Stuttgart Univ. (pado|noh@cl.uni-heidelberg.de)

†DFKI (neumann|eichler@dfki.de) °Bar Ilan University (dagan|sterna3|omerlevy@cs.biu.ac.il)

Abstract

This paper presents the Excitement Open Platform (EOP), a generic architecture and a comprehensive implementation for textual inference in multiple languages. The platform includes state-of-art algorithms, a large number of knowledge resources, and facilities for experimenting and testing innovative approaches. The EOP is distributed as an open source software.

1 Introduction

In the last decade textual entailment (Dagan et al., 2009) has been a very active topic in Computational Linguistics, providing a unifying framework for textual inference. Several evaluation exercises have been organized around Recognizing Textual Entailment (RTE) challenges and many methodologies, algorithms and knowledge resources have been proposed to address the task. However, research in textual entailment is still fragmented and there is no unifying algorithmic framework nor software architecture.

In this paper, we present the Excitement Open Platform (EOP), a generic architecture and a comprehensive implementation for multilingual textual inference which we make available to the scientific and technological communities. To a large extent, the idea is to follow the successful experience of the Moses open source platform (Koehn et al., 2007) in Machine Translation, which has made a substantial impact on research in that field. The EOP is the result of a two-year coordinated work under the international project EXCITEMENT.[1] A consortium of four academic partners has defined the EOP architectural specifications, implemented the functional interfaces of the EOP components, imported existing entailment engines into the EOP and finally designed and implemented a rich environment to support open source distribution.

The goal of the platform is to provide functionality for the automatic identification of entailment relations among texts. The EOP is based on a modular architecture with a particular focus on *language-independent* algorithms. It allows developers and users to combine linguistic pipelines, entailment algorithms and linguistic resources within and across languages with as little effort as possible. For example, different entailment decision approaches can share the same resources and the same subcomponents in the platform. A classification-based algorithm can use the distance component of an edit-distance based entailment decision approach, and two different approaches can use the same set of knowledge resources. Moreover, the platform has various multilingual components for languages like English, German and Italian. The result is an ideal software environment for experimenting and testing innovative approaches for textual inferences. The EOP is distributed as an open source software[2] and its use is open both to users interested in using inference in applications and to developers willing to extend the current functionalities.

The paper is structured as follows. Section 2 presents the platform architecture, highlighting how the EOP component-based approach favors interoperability. Section 3 provides a picture of the current population of the EOP in terms of both entailment algorithms and knowledge resources. Section 4 introduces expected use cases of the platform. Finally, Section 5 presents the main features of the open source package.

2 Architecture

The EOP platform takes as input two text portions, the first called the Text (abbreviated with T), the second called the Hypothesis (abbreviated with H).

[1] http://www.excitement-project.eu

[2] http://hltfbk.github.io/Excitement-Open-Platform/

Proceedings of 52nd Annual Meeting of the Association for Computational Linguistics: System Demonstrations, pages 43–48, Baltimore, Maryland USA, June 23-24, 2014.

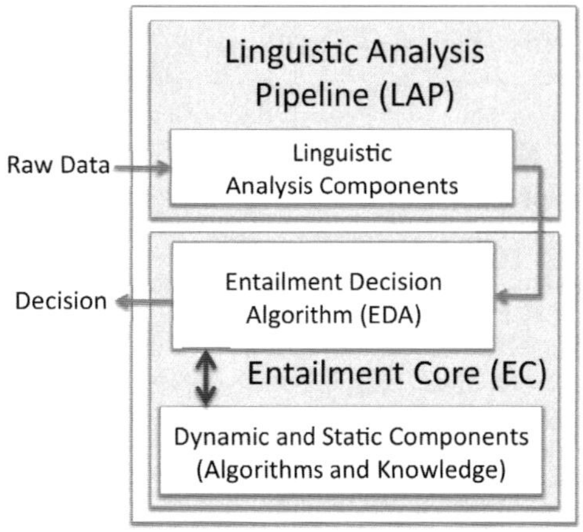

Figure 1: EOP architecture

The output is an entailment judgement, either "Entailment" if T entails H, or "NonEntailment" if the relation does not hold. A confidence score for the decision is also returned in both cases.

The EOP architecture (Padó et al., 2014) is based on the concept of modularization with pluggable and replaceable components to enable extension and customization. The overall structure is shown in Figure 1 and consists of two main parts. The Linguistic Analysis Pipeline (LAP) is a series of linguistic annotation components. The Entailment Core (EC) performs the actual entailment recognition. This separation ensures that (a) the components in the EC only rely on linguistic analysis in well-defined ways and (b) the LAP and EC can be run independently of each other. Configuration files are the principal means of configuring the EOP. In the rest of this section we first provide an introduction to the LAP, then we move to the EC and finally describe the configuration files.

2.1 Linguistic Analysis Pipeline (LAP)

The Linguistic Analysis Pipeline is a collection of annotation components for Natural Language Processing (NLP) based on the Apache UIMA framework.[3] Annotations range from tokenization to part of speech tagging, chunking, Named Entity Recognition and parsing. The adoption of UIMA enables interoperability among components (e.g., substitution of one parser by another one) while ensuring language independence. Input and output of the components are represented in an extended version of the DKPro type system based on UIMA Common Analysis Structure (CAS) (Gurevych et al., 2007; Noh and Padó, 2013).

2.2 Entailment Core (EC)

The Entailment Core performs the actual entailment recognition based on the preprocessed text made by the Linguistic Analysis Pipeline. It consists of one or more Entailment Decision Algorithms (EDAs) and zero or more subordinate components. An EDA takes an entailment decision (i.e., "entailment" or "no entailment") while components provide static and dynamic information for the EDA.

Entailment Decision Algorithms are at the top level in the EC. They compute an entailment decision for a given Text/Hypothesis (T/H) pair, and can use components that provide standardized algorithms or knowledge resources. The EOP ships with several EDAs (cf. Section 3).

Scoring Components accept a Text/Hypothesis pair as an input, and return a vector of scores. Their output can be used directly to build minimal classifier-based EDAs forming complete RTE systems. An extended version of these components are the *Distance Components* that can produce normalized and unnormalized distance/similarity values in addition to the score vector.

Annotation Components can be used to add different annotations to the Text/Hypothesis pairs. An example of such a type of component is one that produces word or phrase alignments between the Text and the Hypothesis.

Lexical Knowledge Components describe semantic relationships between words. In the EOP, this knowledge is represented as directed rules made up of two word–POS pairs, where the LHS (left-hand side) entails the RHS (right-hand side), e.g., $(shooting\_star, Noun) \implies (meteorite, Noun)$. Lexical Knowledge Components provide an interface that allows for (a) listing all RHS for a given LHS; (b) listing all LHS for a given RHS; and (c) checking for an entailment relation for a given LHS–RHS pair. The interface also wraps all major lexical knowledge sources currently used in RTE research, including manually constructed ontologies like WordNet, and encyclopedic resources like Wikipedia.

Syntactic Knowledge Components capture entailment relationships between syntactic and

[3] `http://uima.apache.org/`

lexical-syntactic expressions. We represent such relationships by entailment rules that link (optionally lexicalized) dependency tree fragments that can contain variables as nodes. For example, the rule *fall of X* $\Longrightarrow$ *X falls*, or *X sells Y to Z* $\Longrightarrow$ *Z buys Y from X* express general paraphrasing patterns at the predicate-argument level that cannot be captured by purely lexical rules. Formally, each syntactic rule consists of two dependency tree fragments plus a mapping from the variables of the LHS tree to the variables of the RHS tree.[4]

2.3 Configuration Files

The EC components can be combined into actual *inference engines* through configuration files which contain information to build a complete inference engine. A configuration file completely describes an experiment. For example, it specifies the resources that the selected EDA has to use and the data set to be analysed. The LAP needed for data set preprocessing is another parameter that can be configured too. The platform ships with a set of predefined configuration files accompanied by supporting documentation.

3 Entailment Algorithms and Resources

This section provides a description of the Entailment Algorithms and Knowledge Resources that are distributed with the EOP.

3.1 Entailment Algorithms

The current version of the EOP platform ships with three EDAs corresponding to three different approaches to RTE: an EDA based on transformations between T and H, an EDA based on edit distance algorithms, and a classification based EDA using features extracted from T and H.

Transformation-based EDA applies a sequence of transformations on T with the goal of making it identical to H. If each transformation preserves (fully or partially) the meaning of the original text, then it can be concluded that the modified text (which is actually the Hypothesis) can be inferred from the original one. Consider the following simple example where the text is "The boy was located by the police" and the Hypothesis is "The child was found by the police". Two transformations for "boy" $\rightarrow$ "child" and "located" $\rightarrow$ "found" do the job.

[4]Variables of the LHS may also map to null, when material of the LHS must be present but is deleted in the inference step.

In the EOP we include a transformation based inference system that adopts the knowledge based transformations of Bar-Haim et al. (2007), while incorporating a probabilistic model to estimate transformation confidences. In addition, it includes a search algorithm which finds an optimal sequence of transformations for any given T/H pair (Stern et al., 2012).

Edit distance EDA involves using algorithms casting textual entailment as the problem of mapping the whole content of T into the content of H. Mappings are performed as sequences of editing operations (i.e., insertion, deletion and substitution) on text portions needed to transform T into H, where each edit operation has a cost associated with it. The underlying intuition is that the probability of an entailment relation between T and H is related to the distance between them; see Kouylekov and Magnini (2005) for a comprehensive experimental study.

Classification based EDA uses a Maximum Entropy classifier to combine the outcomes of several scoring functions and to learn a classification model for recognizing entailment. The scoring functions extract a number of features at various linguistic levels (bag-of-words, syntactic dependencies, semantic dependencies, named entities). The approach was thoroughly described in Wang and Neumann (2007).

3.2 Knowledge Resources

As described in Section 2.2, knowledge resources are crucial to recognize cases where T and H use different textual expressions (words, phrases) while preserving entailment. The EOP platform includes a wide range of knowledge resources, including lexical and syntactic resources, where some of them are grabbed from manual resources, like dictionaries, while others are learned automatically. Many EOP resources are inherited from pre-existing RTE systems migrated into the EOP platform, but now use the same interfaces, which makes them accessible in a uniform fashion.

There are about two dozen lexical (e.g. wordnets) and syntactic resources for three languages (i.e. English, Italian and German). However, since there is still a clear predominance of English resources, the platform includes lexical and syntactic knowledge mining tools to bootstrap resources from corpora, both for other languages and

EDA	Accuracy / F1
Transformation-based English RTE-3	67.13%
Transformation-based English RTE-6	49.55%
Edit-Distance English RTE-3	64.38%
Edit-Distance German RTE-3	59.88%
Edit-Distance Italian RTE-3	63.50%
Classification-based English RTE-3	65.25%
Classification-based German RTE-3	63.75%
Median of RTE-3 (English) submissions	61.75%
Median of RTE-6 (English) submissions	33.72%

Table 1: EDAs results

for specific domains. Particularly, the EOP platform includes a language independent tool to build Wikipedia resources (Shnarch et al., 2009), as well as a language-independent framework for building distributional similarity resources like DIRT (Lin and Pantel, 2002) and Lin similarity(Lin, 1998).

3.3 EOP Evaluation

Results for the three EDAs included in the EOP platform are reported in Table 1. Each line represents an EDA, the language and the dataset on which the EDA was evaluated. For brevity, we omit here the knowledge resources used for each EDA, even though knowledge configuration clearly affects performance. The evaluations were performed on RTE-3 dataset (Giampiccolo et al., 2007), where the goal is to maximize accuracy. We (manually) translated it to German and Italian for evaluations: in both cases the results fix a reference for the two languages. The two new datasets for German and English are available both as part of the EOP distribution and independently[5]. The transformation-based EDA was also evaluated on RTE-6 dataset (Bentivogli et al., 2010), in which the goal is to maximize the F1 measure.

The results of the included EDAs are higher than median values of participated systems in RTE-3, and they are competing with state-of-the-arts in RTE-6 results. To the best of our knowledge, the results of the EDAs as provided in the platform are the highest among those available as open source systems for the community.

4 Use Cases

We see four primary use cases for the EOP. Their requirements were reflected in our design choices.

Use Case 1: Applied Textual Entailment. This category covers users who are not interested in the details of RTE but who are interested in an NLP task in which textual entailment can take over part of or all of the semantic processing, such as Question Answering or Intelligent Tutoring. Such users require a system that is as easy to deploy as possible, which motivates our offer of the EOP platform as a library. They also require a system that provides good quality at a reasonable efficiency as well as guidance as to the best choice of parameters. The latter point is realized through our results archive in the official EOP Wiki on the EOP site.

Use Case 2: Textual Entailment Development. This category covers researchers who are interested in Recognizing Textual Entailment itself, for example with the goal of developing novel algorithms for detecting entailment. In contrast to the first category, this group need to look "under the hood" of the EOP platform and access the source code of the EOP. For this reason, we have spent substantial effort to provide the code in a well-structured and well-documented form.

A subclass of this group is formed by researchers who want to set up a RTE infrastructure for languages in which it does not yet exist (that is, almost all languages). The requirements of this class of users comprises clearly specified procedures to replace the Linguistic Analysis Pipeline, which are covered in our documentation, and simple methods to acquire knowledge resources for these languages (assuming that the EDAs themselves are largely language-independent). These are provided by the language-independent knowledge acquisition tools which we offer alongside the platform (cf. Section 3.2).

Use Case 3: Lexical Semantics Evaluation. A third category consists of researchers whose primary interest is in (lexical) semantics.

As long as their scientific results can be phrased in terms of semantic similarities or inference rules, the EOP platform can be used as a simple and standardized workbench for these results that indicates the impact that the semantic knowledge under consideration has on deciding textual entailment. The main requirement for this user group is the simple integration of new knowledge resources into the EOP platform. This is catered for through the definition of the generic knowledge component interfaces (cf. Section 2.2) and detailed documentation on how to implement these interfaces.

[5] `http://www.excitement-project.eu/index.php/results`

Use Case 4: Educational Use. The fourth and final use case is as an educational tool to support academic courses and projects on Recognizing Textual Entailment and inference more generally. This use case calls, in common with the others, for easy usability and flexibility. Specifically for this use case, we have also developed a series of tutorials aimed at acquainting new users with the EOP platform through a series of increasingly complexity exercises that cover all areas of the EOP. We are also posting proposals for projects to extend the EOP on the EOP Wiki.

5 EOP Distribution

The EOP infrastructure follows state-of-the-art software engineering standards to support both users and developers with a flexible, scalable and easy to use software environment. In addition to communication channels, like the mailing list and the issue tracking system, the EOP infrastructure comprises the following set of facilities.

Version Control System: We use GitHub,[6] a web-based hosting service for code and documentation storage, development, and issue tracking.

Web Site: The GitHub Automatic Page Generator was used to build the EOP web site and Wiki, containing a general introduction to the software platform, the terms of its license, mailing lists to contact the EOP members and links to the code releases.

Documentation: Both user and developer documentation is available from Wiki pages; the pages are written with the GitHub Wiki Editor and hosted on the GitHub repository. The documentation includes a Quick Start guide to start using the EOP platform right away, and a detailed step by step tutorial.

Results Archive: As a new feature for community building, EOP users can, and are encouraged to, share their results: the platform configuration files used to produce results as well as contact information can be saved and archived into a dedicated page on the EOP GitHub repository. That allows other EOP users to replicate experiments under the same condition and/or avoid doing experiments that have already been done.

[6] `https://github.com/`

Build Automation Tool: The EOP has been developed as a Maven[7] multi-modules project, with all modules sharing the same Maven standard structure, making it easier to find files in the project once one is used to Maven.

Maven Artifacts Repository: Using a Maven repository has a twofold goal: (i) to serve as an internal private repository of all software libraries used within the project (libraries are binary files and should not be stored under version control systems, which are intended to be used with text files); (ii) to make the produced EOP Maven artifacts available (i.e., for users who want to use the EOP as a library in their own code). We use Artifactory[8] repository manager to store produced artifacts.

Continuous Integration: The EOP uses Jenkins[9] for Continuous Integration, a software development practice where developers of a team integrate their work frequently (e.g., daily).

Code Quality Tool: Ensuring the quality of the produced software is one of the most important aspects of software engineering. The EOP uses tools like PMD[10] that can automatically be run during development to help the developers check the quality of their software.

5.1 Project Repository

The EOP Java source code is hosted on the EOP Github repository and managed using Git. The repository consists of three main branches: the *release branch* contains the code that is supposed to be in a production-ready state, whereas the *master branch* contains the code to be incorporated into the next release. When the source code in the master branch reaches a stable point and is ready to be released, all of the changes are merged back into release. Finally, the *gh-pages branch* contains the web site pages.

5.2 Licensing

The software of the platform is released under the terms of General Public License (GPL) version 3.[11] The platform contains both components and resources designed by the EOP developers, as well as others that are well known and freely available.

[7] `http://maven.apache.org/`
[8] `http://www.jfrog.com/`
[9] `http://jenkins-ci.org/`
[10] `http://pmd.sourceforge.net`
[11] `http://www.gnu.org/licenses/gpl.html`

in the NLP research community. Additional components and resources whose license is not compatible with the EOP license have to be downloaded and installed separately by the user.

6 Conclusion

This paper has presented the main characteristics of Excitement Open Platform platform, a rich environment for experimenting and evaluating textual entailment systems. On the software side, the EOP is a complex endeavor to integrate tools and resources in Computational Linguistics, including pipelines for three languages, three pre-existing entailment engines, and about two dozens of lexical and syntactic resources. The EOP assumes a clear and modular separation between linguistic annotations, entailment algorithms and knowledge resources which are used by the algorithms. A relevant benefit of the architectural design is that a high level of interoperability is reached, providing a stimulating environment for new research in textual inferences.

The EOP platform has been already tested in several pilot research projects and educational courses, and it is currently distributed as open source software under the GPL-3 license. To the best of our knowledge, the entailment systems and their configurations provided in the platform are the best systems available as open source for the community. As for the future, we are planning several initiatives for the promotion of the platform in the research community, as well as its active experimentation in real application scenarios.

Acknowledgments

This work was partially supported by the EC-funded project EXCITEMENT (FP7ICT-287923).

References

Roy Bar-Haim, Ido Dagan, Iddo Greental, and Eyal Shnarch. 2007. Semantic inference at the lexical-syntactic level. In *Proceedings of AAAI*, pages 871–876, Vancouver, BC.

Luisa Bentivogli, Peter Clark, Ido Dagan, Hoa Trang Dang, and Danilo Giampiccolo. 2010. The Sixth PASCAL Recognizing Textual Entailment Challenge. In *Proceedings of TAC*, Gaithersburg, MD.

Ido Dagan, Bill Dolan, Bernardo Magnini, and Dan Roth. 2009. Recognizing textual entailment: Rational, evaluation and approaches. *Journal of Natural Language Engineering*, 15(4):i–xvii.

Danilo Giampiccolo, Bernardo Magnini, Ido Dagan, and Bill Dolan. 2007. The Third PASCAL Recognising Textual Entailment Challenge. In *Proceedings of the ACL-PASCAL Workshop on Textual Entailment and Paraphrasing*, Prague, Czech Republic.

Iryna Gurevych, Max Mühlhäuser, Christof Müller, Jürgen Steimle, Markus Weimer, and Torsten Zesch. 2007. Darmstadt knowledge processing repository based on UIMA. In *Proceedings of the First Workshop on Unstructured Information Management Architecture (UIMA@GSCL 2007)*, Tübingen, Germany.

Philipp Koehn, Hieu Hoang, Alexandra Birch, Chris Callison-Burch, Marcello Federico, Nicola Bertoldi, Brooke Cowan, Wade Shen, Christine Moran, Richard Zens, Chris Dyer, Ondrej Bojar, Alexandra Constantin, and Evan Herbst. 2007. Moses: Open Source Toolkit for Statistical Machine Translation. In *Proceedings of the ACL demo session*, pages 177–180, Prague, Czech Republic.

Milen Kouylekov and Bernardo Magnini. 2005. Recognizing textual entailment with tree edit distance algorithms. In *Proceedings of the First PASCAL Challenges Workshop on Recognising Textual Entailment*, pages 17–20, Southampton, UK.

Dekang Lin and Patrick Pantel. 2002. Discovery of Inference Rules for Question Answering. *Journal of Natural Language Engineering*, 7(4):343–360.

Dekang Lin. 1998. Automatic retrieval and clustering of similar words. In *Proceedings of ACL/COLING*, pages 768–774, Montréal, Canada.

Tae-Gil Noh and Sebastian Padó. 2013. Using UIMA to structure an open platform for textual entailment. In *Proceedings of the 3rd Workshop on Unstructured Information Management Architecture (UIMA@GSCL 2013)*.

Sebastian Padó, Tae-Gil Noh, Asher Stern, Rui Wang, and Roberto Zanoli. 2014. Design and realization of a modular architecture for textual entailment. *Journal of Natural Language Engineering*. doi: 10.1017/S1351324913000351.

Eyal Shnarch, Libby Barak, and Ido Dagan. 2009. Extracting lexical reference rules from Wikipedia. In *Proceedings of ACL-IJCNLP*, pages 450–458, Singapore.

Asher Stern, Roni Stern, Ido Dagan, and Ariel Felner. 2012. Efficient search for transformation-based inference. In *Proceedings of ACL*, pages 283–291, Jeju Island, South Korea.

Rui Wang and Günter Neumann. 2007. Recognizing textual entailment using a subsequence kernel method. In *Proceedings of AAAI*, pages 937–945, Vancouver, BC.

WELT: Using Graphics Generation in Linguistic Fieldwork

Morgan Ulinski* mulinski@cs.columbia.edu

Anusha Balakrishnan* ab3596@columbia.edu

Daniel Bauer* bauer@cs.columbia.edu

Bob Coyne* coyne@cs.columbia.edu

Julia Hirschberg* julia@cs.columbia.edu

Owen Rambow[†] rambow@ccls.columbia.edu

*Department of Computer Science [†]CCLS
Columbia University
New York, NY, USA

Abstract

We describe the WordsEye Linguistics tool (WELT), a novel tool for the documentation and preservation of endangered languages. WELT is based on WordsEye (Coyne and Sproat, 2001), a text-to-scene tool that automatically generates 3D scenes from written input. WELT has two modes of operation. In the first mode, English input automatically generates a picture which can be used to elicit a description in the target language. In the second mode, the linguist formally documents the grammar of an endangered language, thereby creating a system that takes input in the endangered language and generates a picture according to the grammar; the picture can then be used to verify the grammar with native speakers. We will demonstrate WELT's use on scenarios involving Arrernte and Nahuatl.

1 Introduction

Although languages have appeared and disappeared throughout history, today languages are facing extinction at an unprecedented pace. Over 40% of the estimated 7,000 languages in the world are at risk of disappearing. When languages die out, we lose access to an invaluable resource for studying the culture, history, and experience of peoples around the world (Alliance for Linguistic Diversity, 2013). Efforts to document languages and develop tools in support of collecting data on them become even more important with the increasing rate of extinction. Bird (2009) emphasizes a particular need to make use of computational linguistics during fieldwork.

To address this issue, we are developing the WordsEye Linguistics Tool, or WELT. In the first mode of operation, we provide a field linguist with tools for running custom elicitation sessions based on a collection of 3D scenes. In the second, input in an endangered language generates a picture representing the input's meaning according to a formal grammar.

WELT provides important advantages for elicitation over the pre-fabricated sets of static pictures commonly used by field linguists today. The field worker is not limited to a fixed set of pictures but can, instead, create and modify scenes in real time, based on the informants' answers. This allows them to create additional follow-up scenes and questions on the fly. In addition, since the pictures are 3D scenes, the viewpoint can easily be changed, allowing exploration of linguistic descriptions based on different frames of reference. This will be particularly useful in eliciting spatial descriptions. Finally, since scenes and objects can easily be added in the field, the linguist can customize the images used for elicitation to be maximally relevant to the current informants.

WELT also provides a means to document the semantics of a language in a formal way. Linguists can customize their studies to be as deep or shallow as they wish; however, we believe that a major advantage of documenting a language with WELT is that it enables such studies to be much more precise. The fully functioning text-to-scene system created as a result of this documentation will let linguists easily test the theories they develop with native speakers, making changes to grammars and semantics in real time. The resulting text-to-scene system can be an important tool for language preservation, spreading interest in the language among younger generations of the community and recruiting new speakers.

We will demonstrate the features of WELT for use in fieldwork, including designing elicitation sessions, building scenes, recording audio, and adding descriptions and glosses to a scene. We will use examples from sessions we

Proceedings of 52nd Annual Meeting of the Association for Computational Linguistics: System Demonstrations, pages 49–54,
Baltimore, Maryland USA, June 23-24, 2014.

have conducted with a native speaker of Nahuatl, an endangered language spoken in Mexico. We will demonstrate how to document semantics with WELT, using examples from Arrernte, an Australian aboriginal language spoken in Alice Springs. We will also demonstrate a basic Arrernte text-to-scene system created in WELT.

In the following sections, we will mention related work (Section 2), discuss the WordsEye system that WELT is based on (Section 3), describe WELT in more detail, highlighting the functionality that will appear in our demonstration (Section 4), and briefly mention our future plans for WELT (Section 5).

2 Related Work

One of the most widely-used computer toolkits for field linguistics is SIL Fieldworks. FieldWorks is a collection of software tools; the most relevant for our research is FLEx, Fieldworks Language Explorer. FLEx includes tools for eliciting and recording lexical information, dictionary development, interlinearization of texts, analysis of discourse features, and morphological analysis. An important part of FLEx is its "linguist-friendly" morphological parser (Black and Simons, 2006), which uses an underlying model of morphology familiar to linguists, is fully integrated into lexicon development and interlinear text analysis, and produces a human-readable grammar sketch as well as a machine-interpretable parser.

Several computational tools aim to simplify the formal documentation of syntax by eliminating the need to master particular grammar formalisms. First is the PAWS starter kit (Black and Black, 2012), a system that prompts linguists with a series of guided questions about the target language and uses their answers to produce a PC-PATR grammar (McConnel, 1995). The LinGO Grammar Matrix (Bender et al., 2002) is a similar tool developed for HPSG that uses a type hierarchy to represent cross-linguistic generalizations.

The most commonly used resource for formally documenting semantics across languages is FrameNet (Filmore et al., 2003). FrameNets have been developed for many languages, including Spanish, Japanese, and Portuguese. Most start with English FrameNet and adapt it for the new language; a large portion of the frames end up being substantially the same across languages (Baker, 2008). ParSem (Butt et al., 2002) is a collaboration to develop parallel semantic representations across languages, by developing semantic structures based on LFG. Neither of these resources, however, are targeted at helping non-computational linguists formally document a language, as compared to the morphological parser in FLEx or the syntactic documentation in PAWS.

3 WordsEye Text-to-Scene System

WordsEye (Coyne and Sproat, 2001) is a system for automatically converting natural language text into 3D scenes representing the meaning of that text. WordsEye supports language-based control of spatial relations, textures and colors, collections, facial expressions, and poses; it handles simple anaphora and coreference resolution, allowing for a variety of ways of referring to objects. The system assembles scenes from a library of 2,500 3D objects and 10,000 images tied to an English lexicon of about 15,000 nouns.

The system includes a user interface where the user can type simple sentences that are processed to produce a 3D scene. The user can then modify the text to refine the scene. In addition, individual objects and their parts can be selected and highlighted with a bounding box to focus attention.

Several thousand real-world people have used WordsEye online (http://www.wordseye.com). It has also been used as a tool in education, to enhance literacy (Coyne et al., 2011b). In this paper, we describe how we are using WordsEye to create a comprehensive tool for field linguistics.

Vignette Semantics and VigNet To interpret input text, WordsEye uses a lexical resource called VigNet (Coyne et al., 2011a). VigNet is inspired by and based on FrameNet (Baker et al., 1998), a resource for lexical semantics. In FrameNet, lexical items are grouped together in frames according to their shared semantic structure. Every frame contains a number of frame elements (semantic roles) which are participants in this structure. The English FrameNet defines the mapping between syntax and semantics for a lexical item by providing lists of valence patterns that map syntactic functions to frame elements.

VigNet extends FrameNet in two ways in order to capture "graphical semantics'," the knowledge needed to generate graphical scenes from language. First, graphical semantics are added to the frames by adding primitive graphical (typically, spatial) relations between the frame element fillers. Second, VigNet distinguishes between meanings of words that are distinguished graphically. For example, the specific objects and spatial relations in the graphical semantics for *cook* depend on the object being cooked and on the culture in which it is being cooked (cooking turkey in Baltimore vs. cooking an egg in Alice Springs), even though at an abstract level *cook an egg in Alice Springs* and *cook a turkey in Baltimore* are perfectly compositional semantically. Frames augmented with graphical semantics are called *vignettes*.

4 WordsEye Linguistics Tool (WELT)

In this section, we describe the two modes of WELT, focusing on the aspects of our system that will appear in our demonstration.

4.1 Tools for Linguistic Fieldwork

WELT includes tools that allow linguists to elicit language with WordsEye. Each elicitation session is organized around a set of WordsEye scenes. We will demonstrate how a linguist would use WELT in fieldwork, including (1) creating an elicitation session, either starting from scratch, or by importing scenes from a previous session; (2) building scenes in WordsEye, saving them to a WELT session, and modifying scenes previously added to the session, either overwriting the original scene or saving the changes as a new scene; (3) adding textual descriptions, glosses, and notes to a scene; and (4) recording audio, which is automatically synced to open scenes, and playingit back tto review any given scene. A screen shot of the scene annotation window is included in Figure 1.

To test the fieldwork capabilities of WELT, we created a set of scenes based on the Max Planck topological relations picture series (Bowerman and Pederson, 1992). We used these scenes to elicit descriptions from a native Nahuatl speaker; some examples of scenes and descriptions are included in Figure 2.

4.2 Formal Documentation of a Language

WELT also provides the means to formally document the semantics of a language and create a text-to-scene system for that language. The formal documentation allows precise description of the lexical semantics of a language. We will demonstrate both the user interface for documenting semantics, as well as a text-to-scene system for Ar-

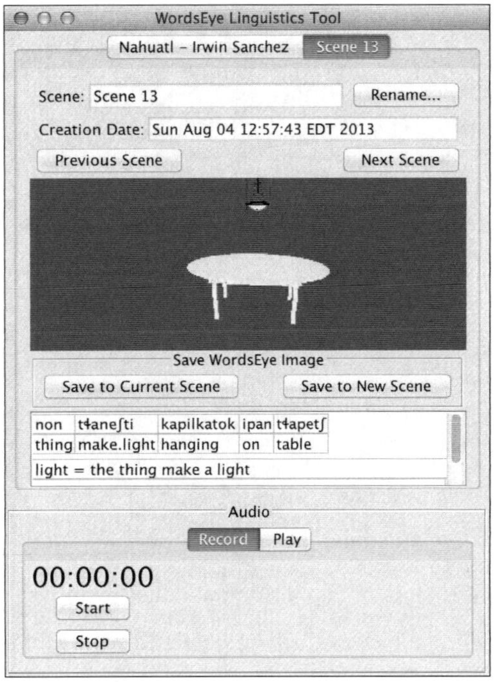

Figure 1: WELT interface for annotating a scene

rernte created with WELT.

When a sentence is processed by WordsEye, it goes through three main stages: (1) morphological analysis and syntactic parsing, (2) semantic analysis, and (3) graphical realization. We will walk through these modules in the context of WELT, discussing (a) the formal documentation required for that component, (b) the processing of an example sentence through that component, and (c) the parts of that component that will feature in our demonstration. We will use the Arrernte sentence shown in (1) as a running example.

(1) artwe le goal arrerneme
man ERG goal put.nonpast
The man kicks a goal.

Morphology and Syntax WELT first parses a sentence into its morphology and syntax. Since the focus of WELT is documentation of semantics, the exact mechanisms for parsing the morphology and syntax may vary. To document Arrernte, we are using XFST (Karttunen et al., 1997) to model the morphology and XLE (Crouch et al., 2006) to model the syntax in the LFG formalism (Kaplan and Bresnan, 1982). These are mature systems that we believe are sufficient for the formal documentation of morphology and syntax. In future, we will provide interfaces to the third-party tools so that common information, like the lexicon, can

(a) in amatɬ tɬakentija se kutʃara
the paper cover one spoon

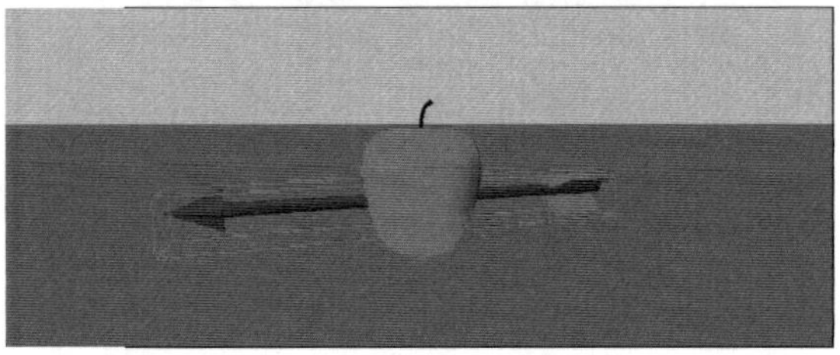

(b) in kwawitɬ tɬapanawi tɬakoja se mansana
the stick pass.thru in.middle one apple

Figure 2: Nahuatl examples elicited with WELT

be shared.

Running each word of the sentence through the morphological analyzer in XFST transforms the verb *arrerneme* into 'arrerne+NONPAST.' The other tokens in the sentence remain unchanged. Parsing the sentence with XLE gives the c-structure shown in Figure 3(a) and the f-structure shown in Figure 3(b). The f-structure will be passed on to the semantics module.

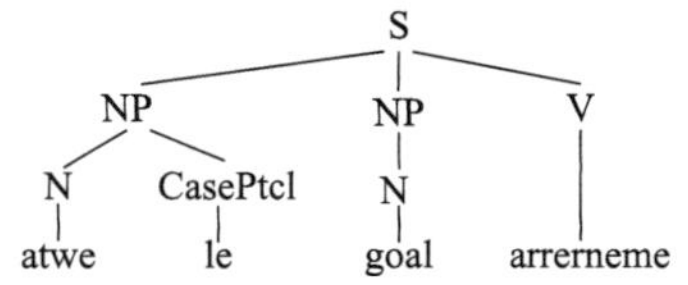

(a)

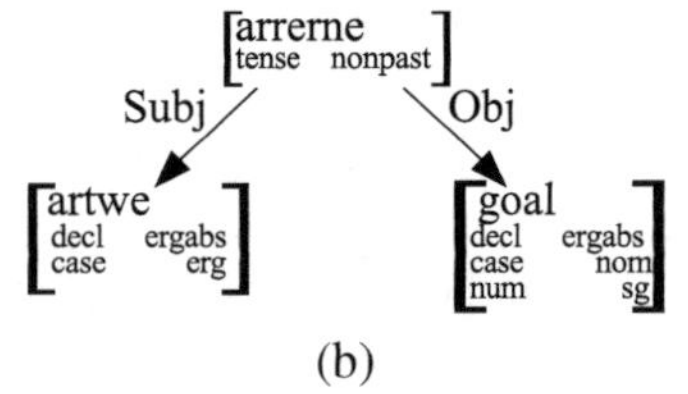

(b)

Figure 3: C-structure (a) and f-structure (b) for *artwe le goal arrerneme*.

We have added one additional feature to the morphology and syntax module of WELT's text-to-scene system: an interface for selecting an f-structure from multiple options produced by XLE, in case the grammar is ambiguous. This way, a linguist can use the WELT text-to-scene system to verify their semantic documentation even if the syntactic documentation is fairly rough. We will demonstrate this feature when demonstrating the Arrernte text-to-scene system.

Semantics The WELT semantics is represented using VigNet, which has been developed for WordsEye based on English. We will assume that large parts of VigNet are language-independent (for instance, the set of low-level graphical relations used to express the graphical semantics is based on physics and human anatomy and does not depend on language). Therefore, it should not be necessary to create a completely new VigNet for every language that will be used in WELT. In future, we will develop tools for modifying VigNet to handle linguistic and cultural differences as they occur.

In order to use VigNet with other languages, we need to map between the formal syntax of the language being studied and the (English) lexical semantics required currently by VigNet. One instance showing why this is necessary occurs in our example Arrrente sentence. When discussing football in English, one would say that someone *kicks a goal* or *makes a goal*. In Arrente, one would say *goal arrerneme*, which translates literally to "put a goal." Although the semantics of both sentences are the same, the entry for "put" in the English VigNet does not include this meaning, but the Arrernte text-to-scene system needs to account for it.

To address such instances, we have created an interface for a linguist to specify a set of rules that map from syntax to semantics. The rules take syntactic f-structures as input and output a high-level semantic representation compatible with VigNet. The left-hand side of a rule consists of a set of conditions on the f-structure elements and the right-hand side consists of the semantic structure that should be returned. Figure 4(a) is an example of a rule mapping Arrernte syntax to semantics, created in WELT.

In addition to these rules, the linguist creates a simple table mapping lexical items into VigNet semantic concepts, so that nouns can be converted to graphical objects. We have created a mapping for the lexical items in the Arrernte grammar; a partial mapping is shown in Table 1.

We now describe the semantic processing of our example Arrernte sentence, assuming a set of rules consisting solely of the one in Figure 4(a) and the noun mapping in Table 1. The f-structure in Fig-

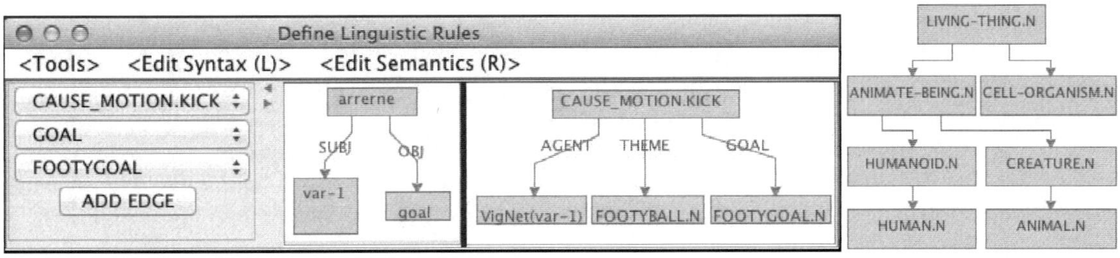

(a) (b)

Figure 4: Syntax-semantics rule (a) and semantic category browser (b) from WELT

Lexical Item	*artwe*	*panikane*	*angepe*	*akngwelye*	*apwerte*	*tipwele*
VigNet Concept	PERSON.N	CUP.N	CROW.N	DOG.N	ROCK-ITEM.N	TABLE.N

Table 1: A mapping from nouns (lexical items) to VigNet semantic concepts

ure 3(b) has main predicate *arrerne* with two arguments; the object is *goal*. Therefore, it matches the left-hand-side of our rule. The output of the rule specifies predicate CAUSE_MOTION.KICK with three arguments. The latter two are straightforward; the Theme is the VigNet object FOOTYBALL.N, and the Goal is FOOTYGOAL.N. To determine the Agent, we need to find the VigNet concept corresponding to `var-1`, which occupies the subject position in the f-structure. The subject in our f-structure is *artwe*, and according to Table 1, it maps to the VigNet concept PERSON.N. The resulting semantic representation is augmented with its graphical semantics, taken from the vignette for CAUSE_MOTION.KICK (vignette definition not shown for lack of space). The final representation is shown in Figure 5, with lexical semantics at the top and graphical semantics below. The WordsEye system then builds the scene from these constraints and renders it in 3D.

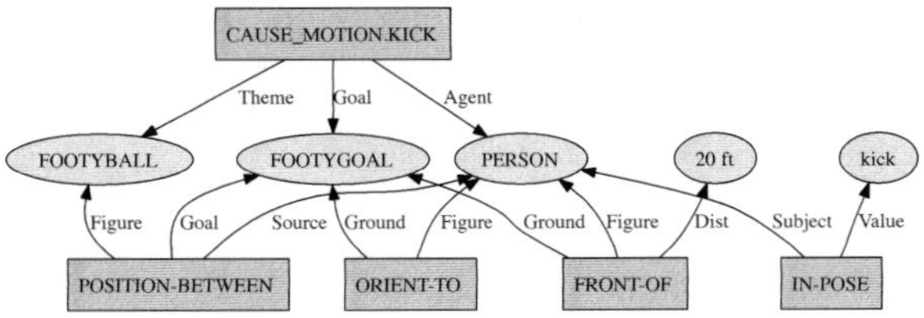

Figure 5: The semantics (lexical and graphical) for sentence (1)

WELT provides an interface for creating rules by defining the tree structures for the left-hand-side and right-hand-side of the rule. Every node on the left-hand-side can optionally contain boolean logic, if for example we want to allow the subject to be [(*artwe* 'man' `OR` *arhele* 'woman') `AND NOT` *ampe* 'child']; so rules can be as simple or complex as desired. Rules need not specify lexical items directly; it is also possible to refer to more general semantic categories. For example, a rule could select for all verbs of motion, or specify a particular constraint on the subject or object. In figure 4(a), for instance, we may want to only allow animate subjects.

Semantic categories are chosen through a browser that allows the user to search through all the semantic categories defined in VigNet. For example, if we want to find the semantic category to use as a constraint on our example subject, we might start by searching for *human*. This takes us to a portion of a tree of semantic concepts centered around HUMAN.N. The semantic categories are displayed one level at a time, so we initially see only the concepts directly above and directly below the word we searched for. From there, it's easy to select the concepts we are interested in, and go up or down the tree until we find the one we want. Below HUMAN.N are HUMAN-FEMALE.N and HUMAN-MALE.N, but we are more interested in the more general categories above the node. A screen shot showing the result of this search is shown in Figure 4(b). Above HUMAN.N is HUMANOID.N; above that, ANIMATE-BEING.N. Doing a quick check of further parents and children, we can see that for the subject of 'put goal,' we would probably want to choose ANIMATE-BEING.N over LIVING-THING.N.

The table mapping lexical items to VigNet concepts is built in a similar way; the lexicon is automatically extracted from the LFG grammar, and the user can search and browse semantic concepts to find the appropriate node for each lexical item.

We will demonstrate the WELT user interface which supports the creation of syntax-to-semantics rules, creates the mapping between nouns in the lexicon and VigNet concepts, and verifies the rules using the WELT text-to-scene system. We will show examples from our documentation of Arrernte and demonstrate entering text into the Arrernte text-to-scene system to generate pictures.

5 Summary and Future Work

We have described a novel tool for linguists working with endangered languages. It provides a new way to elicit data from informants, an interface for formally documenting the lexical semantics of a language, and allows the creation of a text-to-scene system for any language.

This project is in its early stages, so we are planning many additional features and improvements. For both modes of WELT, we want to generate pictures appropriate for the target culture. To handle this, we will add the ability to include custom objects and modify VigNet with new vignettes or new graphical semantics for existing vignettes. We also plan to build tools to import and export the work done in WELT in order to facilitate collaboration among linguists working on similar languages or cultures. Sharing sets of scenes will allow linguists to reuse work and avoid duplicated effort. Importing different versions of VigNet will make it easier to start out with WELT on a new language if it is similar to one that has already been studied. We might expect, for instance, that other Australian aboriginal languages will require the same kinds of cultural modifications to VigNet that we make for Arrernte, or that two languages in the same family might also have similar syntax to semantics rules.

Acknowledgments

This material is based upon work supported by the National Science Foundation under Grant No. 1160700.

References

Alliance for Linguistic Diversity. 2013. The Endangered Languages Project. `http://www.endangeredlanguages.com/`.

C. Baker, J. Fillmore, and J. Lowe. 1998. The Berkeley FrameNet project. In *36th Meeting of the Association for Computational Linguistics and 17th International Conference on Computational Linguistics (COLING-ACL'98)*, pages 86–90, Montréal.

C. Baker. 2008. FrameNet, present and future. In *The First International Conference on Global Interoperability for Language Resources*, pages 12–17.

E. Bender, D. Flickinger, and S. Oepen. 2002. The Grammar Matrix. In J. Carroll, N. Oostdijk, and R. Sutcliffe, editors, *Workshop on Grammar Engineering and Evaluation at the 19th International Conference on Computational Linguistics*, pages 8–14, Taipei, Taiwan.

S. Bird. 2009. Natural language processing and linguistic fieldwork. *Computational Linguistics*, 35(3):469–474.

C. Black and H.A. Black. 2012. Grammars for the people, by the people, made easier using PAWS and XLingPaper. In Sebastian Nordoff, editor, *Electronic Grammaticography*, pages 103–128. University of Hawaii Press, Honolulu.

H.A. Black and G.F. Simons. 2006. The SIL FieldWorks Language Explorer approach to morphological parsing. In *Computational Linguistics for Less-studied Languages: Texas Linguistics Society 10*, Austin, TX, November.

M. Bowerman and E. Pederson. 1992. Topological relations picture series. In S. Levinson, editor, *Space stimuli kit 1.2*, page 51, Nijmegen. Max Planck Institute for Psycholinguistics.

M. Butt, H. Dyvik, T.H. King, H. Masuichi, and C. Rohrer. 2002. The parallel grammar project. In *2002 Workshop on Grammar Engineering and Evaluation - Volume 15*, COLING-GEE '02, pages 1–7, Stroudsburg, PA, USA. Association for Computational Linguistics.

B. Coyne and R. Sproat. 2001. WordsEye: An automatic text-to-scene conversion system. In *SIGGRAPH*.

B. Coyne, D. Bauer, and O. Rambow. 2011a. Vignet: Grounding language in graphics using frame semantics. In *ACL Workshop on Relational Models of Semantics (RELMS)*, Portland, OR.

B. Coyne, C. Schudel, M. Bitz, and J. Hirschberg. 2011b. Evaluating a text-to-scene generation system as an aid to literacy. In *SlaTE (Speech and Language Technology in Education) Workshop at Interspeech*, Venice.

D. Crouch, M. Dalrymple, R. Kaplan, T. King, J. Maxwell, and P. Newman, 2006. *XLE Documentation*. `http://www2.parc.com/isl/groups/nltt/xle/doc/xle`.

C. Filmore, C. Johnson, and M. Petruck. 2003. Background to FrameNet. In *International Journal of Lexicography*, pages 235–250.

R.M. Kaplan and J.W. Bresnan. 1982. Lexical-functional grammar: A formal system for grammatical representation. In J.W. Bresnan, editor, *The Mental Representation of Grammatical Relations*. MIT Press, Cambridge, Mass., December.

L. Karttunen, T. Gaál, and A. Kempe. 1997. Xerox finite-state tool. Technical report, Xerox Research Centre Europe, Grenoble.

S. McConnel, 1995. *PC-PATR Reference Manual*. Summer Institute for Linguistics.

The Stanford CoreNLP Natural Language Processing Toolkit

Christopher D. Manning
Linguistics & Computer Science
Stanford University
manning@stanford.edu

Mihai Surdeanu
SISTA
University of Arizona
msurdeanu@email.arizona.edu

John Bauer
Dept of Computer Science
Stanford University
horatio@stanford.edu

Jenny Finkel
Prismatic Inc.
jrfinkel@gmail.com

Steven J. Bethard
Computer and Information Sciences
U. of Alabama at Birmingham
bethard@cis.uab.edu

David McClosky
IBM Research
dmcclosky@us.ibm.com

Abstract

We describe the design and use of the Stanford CoreNLP toolkit, an extensible pipeline that provides core natural language analysis. This toolkit is quite widely used, both in the research NLP community and also among commercial and government users of open source NLP technology. We suggest that this follows from a simple, approachable design, straightforward interfaces, the inclusion of robust and good quality analysis components, and not requiring use of a large amount of associated baggage.

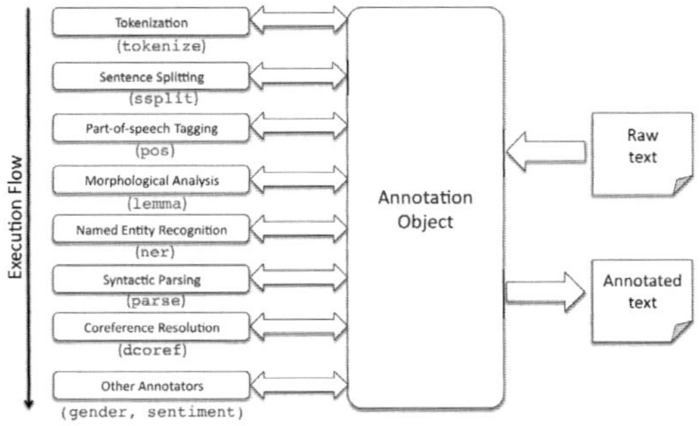

Figure 1: Overall system architecture: Raw text is put into an Annotation object and then a sequence of Annotators add information in an analysis pipeline. The resulting Annotation, containing all the analysis information added by the Annotators, can be output in XML or plain text forms.

1 Introduction

This paper describe the design and development of Stanford CoreNLP, a Java (or at least JVM-based) annotation pipeline framework, which provides most of the common core natural language processing (NLP) steps, from tokenization through to coreference resolution. We describe the original design of the system and its strengths (section 2), simple usage patterns (section 3), the set of provided annotators and how properties control them (section 4), and how to add additional annotators (section 5), before concluding with some higher-level remarks and additional appendices. While there are several good natural language analysis toolkits, Stanford CoreNLP is one of the most used, and a central theme is trying to identify the attributes that contributed to its success.

2 Original Design and Development

Our pipeline system was initially designed for internal use. Previously, when combining multiple natural language analysis components, each with their own ad hoc APIs, we had tied them together with custom glue code. The initial version of the annotation pipeline was developed in 2006 in order to replace this jumble with something better. A uniform interface was provided for an Annotator that adds some kind of analysis information to some text. An Annotator does this by taking in an Annotation object to which it can add extra information. An Annotation is stored as a typesafe heterogeneous map, following the ideas for this data type presented by Bloch (2008). This basic architecture has proven quite successful, and is still the basis of the system described here. It is illustrated in figure 1. The motivations were:

- To be able to quickly and painlessly get linguistic annotations for a text.
- To hide variations across components behind a common API.
- To have a minimal conceptual footprint, so the system is easy to learn.
- To provide a lightweight framework, using plain Java objects (rather than something of heavier weight, such as XML or UIMA's Common Analysis System (CAS) objects).

Proceedings of 52nd Annual Meeting of the Association for Computational Linguistics: System Demonstrations, pages 55–60,
Baltimore, Maryland USA, June 23-24, 2014.

In 2009, initially as part of a multi-site grant project, the system was extended to be more easily usable by a broader range of users. We provided a command-line interface and the ability to write out an Annotation in various formats, including XML. Further work led to the system being released as free open source software in 2010.

On the one hand, from an architectural perspective, Stanford CoreNLP does not attempt to do everything. It is nothing more than a straightforward pipeline architecture. It provides only a Java API.[1] It does not attempt to provide multiple machine scale-out (though it does provide multi-threaded processing on a single machine). It provides a simple concrete API. But these requirements satisfy a large percentage of potential users, and the resulting simplicity makes it easier for users to get started with the framework. That is, the primary advantage of Stanford CoreNLP over larger frameworks like UIMA (Ferrucci and Lally, 2004) or GATE (Cunningham et al., 2002) is that users do not have to learn UIMA or GATE before they can get started; they only need to know a little Java. In practice, this is a large and important differentiator. If more complex scenarios are required, such as multiple machine scale-out, they can normally be achieved by running the analysis pipeline within a system that focuses on distributed workflows (such as Hadoop or Spark). Other systems attempt to provide more, such as the UIUC Curator (Clarke et al., 2012), which includes inter-machine client-server communication for processing and the caching of natural language analyses. But this functionality comes at a cost. The system is complex to install and complex to understand. Moreover, in practice, an organization may well be committed to a scale-out solution which is different from that provided by the natural language analysis toolkit. For example, they may be using Kryo or Google's protobuf for binary serialization rather than Apache Thrift which underlies Curator. In this case, the user is better served by a fairly small and self-contained natural language analysis system, rather than something which comes with a lot of baggage for all sorts of purposes, most of which they are not using.

On the other hand, most users benefit greatly from the provision of a set of stable, robust, high quality linguistic analysis components, which can be easily invoked for common scenarios. While the builder of a larger system may have made overall design choices, such as how to handle scale-out, they are unlikely to be an NLP expert, and are hence looking for NLP components that just work. This is a huge advantage that Stanford CoreNLP and GATE have over the empty toolbox of an Apache UIMA download, something addressed in part by the development of well-integrated component packages for UIMA, such as ClearTK (Bethard et al., 2014), DKPro Core (Gurevych et al., 2007), and JCoRe (Hahn et al., 2008). However, the solution provided by these packages remains harder to learn, more complex and heavier weight for users than the pipeline described here.

These attributes echo what Patricio (2009) argued made Hibernate successful, including: (i) do one thing well, (ii) avoid over-design, and (iii) up and running in ten minutes or less! Indeed, the design and success of Stanford CoreNLP also reflects several other of the factors that Patricio highlights, including (iv) avoid standardism, (v) documentation, and (vi) developer responsiveness. While there are many factors that contribute to the uptake of a project, and it is hard to show causality, we believe that some of these attributes account for the fact that Stanford CoreNLP is one of the more used NLP toolkits. While we certainly have not done a perfect job, compared to much academic software, Stanford CoreNLP has gained from attributes such as clear open source licensing, a modicum of attention to documentation, and attempting to answer user questions.

3 Elementary Usage

A key design goal was to make it very simple to set up and run processing pipelines, from either the API or the command-line. Using the API, running a pipeline can be as easy as figure 2. Or, at the command-line, doing linguistic processing for a file can be as easy as figure 3. Real life is rarely this simple, but the ability to get started using the product with minimal configuration code gives new users a very good initial experience.

Figure 4 gives a more realistic (and complete) example of use, showing several key properties of the system. An annotation pipeline can be applied to any text, such as a paragraph or whole story rather than just a single sentence. The behavior of

[1] Nevertheless, it can call an analysis component written in other languages via an appropriate wrapper Annotator, and in turn, it has been wrapped by many people to provide Stanford CoreNLP bindings for other languages.

```
Annotator pipeline = new StanfordCoreNLP();
Annotation annotation = new Annotation(
    "Can you parse my sentence?");
pipeline.annotate(annotation);
```

Figure 2: Minimal code for an analysis pipeline.

```
export StanfordCoreNLP_HOME /where/installed
java -Xmx2g -cp $StanfordCoreNLP_HOME/*
    edu.stanford.nlp.StanfordCoreNLP
    -file input.txt
```

Figure 3: Minimal command-line invocation.

```
import java.io.*;
import java.util.*;
import edu.stanford.nlp.io.*;
import edu.stanford.nlp.ling.*;
import edu.stanford.nlp.pipeline.*;
import edu.stanford.nlp.trees.*;
import edu.stanford.nlp.trees.TreeCoreAnnotations.*;
import edu.stanford.nlp.util.*;

public class StanfordCoreNlpExample {

  public static void main(String[] args) throws IOException {
    PrintWriter xmlOut = new PrintWriter("xmlOutput.xml");
    Properties props = new Properties();
    props.setProperty("annotators",
        "tokenize, ssplit, pos, lemma, ner, parse");
    StanfordCoreNLP pipeline = new StanfordCoreNLP(props);
    Annotation annotation = new Annotation(
        "This is a short sentence. And this is another.");

    pipeline.annotate(annotation);
    pipeline.xmlPrint(annotation, xmlOut);

    // An Annotation is a Map and you can get and use the
    // various analyses individually. For instance, this
    // gets the parse tree of the 1st sentence in the text.

    List<CoreMap> sentences = annotation.get(
        CoreAnnotations.SentencesAnnotation.class);
    if (sentences != null && sentences.size() > 0) {
      CoreMap sentence = sentences.get(0);
      Tree tree = sentence.get(TreeAnnotation.class);
      PrintWriter out = new PrintWriter(System.out);
      out.println("The first sentence parsed is:");
      tree.pennPrint(out);
    }
  }
}
```

Figure 4: A simple, complete example program.

annotators in a pipeline is controlled by standard Java properties in a Properties object. The most basic property to specify is what annotators to run, in what order, as shown here. But as discussed below, most annotators have their own properties to allow further customization of their usage. If none are specified, reasonable defaults are used. Running the pipeline is as simple as in the first example, but then we show two possibilities for accessing the results. First, we convert the Annotation object to XML and write it to a file. Second, we show code that gets a particular type of information out of an Annotation and then prints it.

Our presentation shows only usage in Java, but the Stanford CoreNLP pipeline has been wrapped by others so that it can be accessed easily from many languages, including Python, Ruby, Perl, Scala, Clojure, Javascript (node.js), and .NET languages, including C# and F#.

4 Provided annotators

The annotators provided with StanfordCoreNLP can work with any character encoding, making use of Java's good Unicode support, but the system defaults to UTF-8 encoding. The annotators also support processing in various human languages, providing that suitable underlying models or resources are available for the different languages. The system comes packaged with models for English. Separate model packages provide support for Chinese and for case-insensitive processing of English. Support for other languages is less complete, but many of the Annotators also support models for French, German, and Arabic (see appendix B), and building models for further languages is possible using the underlying tools. In this section, we outline the provided annotators, focusing on the English versions. It should be noted that some of the models underlying annotators are trained from annotated corpora using supervised machine learning, while others are rule-based components, which nevertheless often require some language resources of their own.

tokenize Tokenizes the text into a sequence of tokens. The English component provides a PTB-style tokenizer, extended to reasonably handle noisy and web text. The corresponding components for Chinese and Arabic provide word and clitic segmentation. The tokenizer saves the character offsets of each token in the input text.

cleanxml Removes most or all XML tags from the document.

ssplit Splits a sequence of tokens into sentences.

truecase Determines the likely true case of tokens in text (that is, their likely case in well-edited text), where this information was lost, e.g., for all upper case text. This is implemented with a discriminative model using a CRF sequence tagger (Finkel et al., 2005).

pos Labels tokens with their part-of-speech (POS) tag, using a maximum entropy POS tagger (Toutanova et al., 2003).

lemma Generates the lemmas (base forms) for all tokens in the annotation.

gender Adds likely gender information to names.

ner Recognizes named (PERSON, LOCATION, ORGANIZATION, MISC) and numerical (MONEY, NUMBER, DATE, TIME, DURATION, SET) entities. With the default annotators, named entities are recognized using a combination of CRF sequence taggers trained on various corpora (Finkel et al., 2005), while numerical entities are recognized using two rule-based systems, one for money and numbers, and a separate state-of-the-art system for processing temporal expressions (Chang and Manning, 2012).

regexner Implements a simple, rule-based NER over token sequences building on Java regular expressions. The goal of this Annotator is to provide a simple framework to allow a user to incorporate NE labels that are not annotated in traditional NL corpora. For example, a default list of regular expressions that we distribute in the models file recognizes ideologies (IDEOLOGY), nationalities (NATIONALITY), religions (RELIGION), and titles (TITLE).

parse Provides full syntactic analysis, including both constituent and dependency representation, based on a probabilistic parser (Klein and Manning, 2003; de Marneffe et al., 2006).

sentiment Sentiment analysis with a compositional model over trees using deep learning (Socher et al., 2013). Nodes of a binarized tree of each sentence, including, in particular, the root node of each sentence, are given a sentiment score.

dcoref Implements mention detection and both pronominal and nominal coreference resolution (Lee et al., 2013). The entire coreference graph of a text (with head words of mentions as nodes) is provided in the Annotation.

Most of these annotators have various options which can be controlled by properties. These can either be added to the Properties object when creating an annotation pipeline via the API, or specified either by command-line flags or through a properties file when running the system from the command-line. As a simple example, input to the system may already be tokenized and presented one-sentence-per-line. In this case, we wish the tokenization and sentence splitting to just work by using the whitespace, rather than trying to do anything more creative (be it right or wrong). This can be accomplished by adding two properties, either to a properties file:

```
tokenize.whitespace: true
ssplit.eolonly:      true
```

in code:

```
/** Simple annotator for locations stored in a gazetteer. */
package org.foo;
public class GazetteerLocationAnnotator implements Annotator {
  // this is the only method an Annotator must implement
  public void annotate(Annotation annotation) {
    // traverse all sentences in this document
    for (CoreMap sentence:annotation.get(SentencesAnnotation.class)) {
      // loop over all tokens in sentence (the text already tokenized)
      List<CoreLabel> toks = sentence.get(TokensAnnotation.class);
      for (int start = 0; start < toks.size(); start++) {
        // assumes that the gazetteer returns the token index
        // after the match or -1 otherwise
        int end = Gazetteer.isLocation(toks, start);
        if (end > start) {
          for (int i = start; i < end; i ++) {
            toks.get(i).set(NamedEntityTagAnnotation.class,"LOCATION");
          }
        }
      }
    }
  }
}
```

Figure 5: An example of a simple custom annotator. The annotator marks the words of possibly multi-word locations that are in a gazetteer.

```
props.setProperty("tokenize.whitespace", "true");
props.setProperty("ssplit.eolonly", "true");
```

or via command-line flags:

```
-tokenize.whitespace -ssplit.eolonly
```

We do not attempt to describe all the properties understood by each annotator here; they are available in the documentation for Stanford CoreNLP. However, we note that they follow the pattern of being *x.y*, where *x* is the name of the annotator that they apply to.

5 Adding annotators

While most users work with the provided annotators, it is quite easy to add additional custom annotators to the system. We illustrate here both how to write an Annotator in code and how to load it into the Stanford CoreNLP system. An Annotator is a class that implements three methods: a single method for analysis, and two that describe the dependencies between analysis steps:

```
public void annotate(Annotation annotation);
public Set<Requirement> requirementsSatisfied();
public Set<Requirement> requires();
```

The information in an Annotation is updated in place (usually in a non-destructive manner, by adding new keys and values to the Annotation). The code for a simple Annotator that marks locations contained in a gazetteer is shown in figure 5.[2] Similar code can be used to write a wrapper Annotator, which calls some pre-existing analysis component, and adds its results to the Annotation.

[2]The functionality of this annotator is already provided by the regexner annotator, but it serves as a simple example.

While building an analysis pipeline, Stanford CoreNLP can add additional annotators to the pipeline which are loaded using reflection. To provide a new Annotator, the user extends the class `edu.stanford.nlp.pipeline.Annotator` and provides a constructor with the signature `(String, Properties)`. Then, the user adds the property

```
customAnnotatorClass.FOO: BAR
```

to the properties used to create the pipeline. If FOO is then added to the list of annotators, the class BAR will be loaded to instantiate it. The Properties object is also passed to the constructor, so that annotator-specific behavior can be initialized from the Properties object. For instance, for the example above, the properties file lines might be:

```
customAnnotatorClass.locgaz: org.foo.GazetteerLocationAnnotator
annotators: tokenize,ssplit,locgaz
locgaz.maxLength: 5
```

6 Conclusion

In this paper, we have presented the design and usage of the Stanford CoreNLP system, an annotation-based NLP processing pipeline. We have in particular tried to emphasize the properties that we feel have made it successful. Rather than trying to provide the largest and most engineered kitchen sink, the goal has been to make it as easy as possible for users to get started using the framework, and to keep the framework small, so it is easily comprehensible, and can easily be used as a component within the much larger system that a user may be developing. The broad usage of this system, and of other systems such as NLTK (Bird et al., 2009), which emphasize accessibility to beginning users, suggests the merits of this approach.

A Pointers

Website: `http://nlp.stanford.edu/software/corenlp.shtml`
Github: `https://github.com/stanfordnlp/CoreNLP`
Maven: `http://mvnrepository.com/artifact/edu.stanford.nlp/stanford-corenlp`
License: GPL v2+

Stanford CoreNLP keeps the models for machine learning components and miscellaneous other data files in a separate models jar file. If you are using Maven, you need to make sure that you list the dependency on this models file as well as the code jar file. You can do that with code like the following in your `pom.xml`. Note the extra dependency with a `classifier` element at the bottom.

```
<dependency>
  <groupId>edu.stanford.nlp</groupId>
  <artifactId>stanford-corenlp</artifactId>
  <version>3.3.1</version>
</dependency>
<dependency>
  <groupId>edu.stanford.nlp</groupId>
  <artifactId>stanford-corenlp</artifactId>
  <version>3.3.1</version>
  <classifier>models</classifier>
</dependency>
```

B Human language support

We summarize the analysis components supported for different human languages in early 2014.

Annotator	Arabic	Chinese	English	French	German
Tokenize	✓	✓	✓	✓	✓
Sent. split	✓	✓	✓	✓	✓
Truecase			✓		
POS	✓	✓	✓	✓	✓
Lemma			✓		
Gender			✓		
NER		✓	✓		✓
RegexNER	✓	✓	✓	✓	✓
Parse	✓	✓	✓	✓	✓
Dep. Parse		✓	✓		
Sentiment			✓		
Coref.			✓		

C Getting the sentiment of sentences

We show a command-line for sentiment analysis.

```
$ cat sentiment.txt
I liked it.
It was a fantastic experience.
The plot move rather slowly.
$ java -cp "*" -Xmx2g edu.stanford.nlp.pipeline.StanfordCoreNLP -annotators
      tokenize,ssplit,pos,lemma,parse,sentiment -file sentiment.txt
Adding annotator tokenize
Adding annotator ssplit
Adding annotator pos
Reading POS tagger model from edu/stanford/nlp/models/pos-tagger/
english-left3words/english-left3words-distsim.tagger ... done [1.0 sec].
Adding annotator lemma
Adding annotator parse
Loading parser from serialized file edu/stanford/nlp/models/lexparser/
englishPCFG.ser.gz ... done [1.4 sec].
Adding annotator sentiment

Ready to process: 1 files, skipped 0, total 1
Processing file /Users/manning/Software/stanford-corenlp-full-2014-01-04/
sentiment.txt ... writing to /Users/manning/Software/
stanford-corenlp-full-2014-01-04/sentiment.txt.xml {
  Annotating file /Users/manning/Software/stanford-corenlp-full-2014-01-04/
sentiment.txt [0.583 seconds]
} [1.219 seconds]
Processed 1 documents
Skipped 0 documents, error annotating 0 documents
Annotation pipeline timing information:
PTBTokenizerAnnotator: 0.0 sec.
WordsToSentencesAnnotator: 0.0 sec.
POSTaggerAnnotator: 0.0 sec.
```

```
MorphaAnnotator: 0.0 sec.
ParserAnnotator: 0.4 sec.
SentimentAnnotator: 0.1 sec.
TOTAL: 0.6 sec. for 16 tokens at 27.4 tokens/sec.
Pipeline setup: 3.0 sec.
Total time for StanfordCoreNLP pipeline: 4.2 sec.
$ grep sentiment sentiment.txt.xml
      <sentence id="1" sentimentValue="3" sentiment="Positive">
      <sentence id="2" sentimentValue="4" sentiment="Verypositive">
      <sentence id="3" sentimentValue="1" sentiment="Negative">
```

D Use within UIMA

The main part of using Stanford CoreNLP within the UIMA framework (Ferrucci and Lally, 2004) is mapping between CoreNLP annotations, which are regular Java classes, and UIMA annotations, which are declared via XML type descriptors (from which UIMA-specific Java classes are generated). A wrapper for CoreNLP will typically define a subclass of JCasAnnotator_ImplBase whose process method: (i) extracts UIMA annotations from the CAS, (ii) converts UIMA annotations to CoreNLP annotations, (iii) runs CoreNLP on the input annotations, (iv) converts the CoreNLP output annotations into UIMA annotations, and (v) saves the UIMA annotations to the CAS.

To illustrate part of this process, the ClearTK (Bethard et al., 2014) wrapper converts CoreNLP token annotations to UIMA annotations and saves them to the CAS with the following code:

```
int begin = tokenAnn.get(CharacterOffsetBeginAnnotation.class);
int end = tokenAnn.get(CharacterOffsetEndAnnotation.class);
String pos = tokenAnn.get(PartOfSpeechAnnotation.class);
String lemma = tokenAnn.get(LemmaAnnotation.class);
Token token = new Token(jCas, begin, end);
token.setPos(pos);
token.setLemma(lemma);
token.addToIndexes();
```

where Token is a UIMA type, declared as:

```
<typeSystemDescription>
 <name>Token</name>
 <types>
   <typeDescription>
     <name>org.cleartk.token.type.Token</name>
     <supertypeName>uima.tcas.Annotation</supertypeName>
     <features>
       <featureDescription>
         <name>pos</name>
         <rangeTypeName>uima.cas.String</rangeTypeName>
       </featureDescription>
       <featureDescription>
         <name>lemma</name>
         <rangeTypeName>uima.cas.String</rangeTypeName>
       </featureDescription>
     </features>
   </typeDescription>
 </types>
</typeSystemDescription>
```

References

Steven Bethard, Philip Ogren, and Lee Becker. 2014. ClearTK 2.0: Design patterns for machine learning in UIMA. In *LREC 2014*.

Steven Bird, Ewan Klein, and Edward Loper. 2009. *Natural Language Processing with Python*. O'Reilly Media.

Joshua Bloch. 2008. *Effective Java*. Addison Wesley, Upper Saddle River, NJ, 2nd edition.

Angel X. Chang and Christopher D. Manning. 2012. SUTIME: A library for recognizing and normalizing time expressions. In *LREC 2012*.

James Clarke, Vivek Srikumar, Mark Sammons, and Dan Roth. 2012. An NLP Curator (or: How I learned to stop worrying and love NLP pipelines). In *LREC 2012*.

Hamish Cunningham, Diana Maynard, Kalina Bontcheva, and Valentin Tablan. 2002. GATE: an architecture for development of robust HLT applications. In *ACL 2002*.

Marie-Catherine de Marneffe, Bill MacCartney, and Christopher D. Manning. 2006. Generating typed dependency parses from phrase structure parses. In *LREC 2006*, pages 449–454.

David Ferrucci and Adam Lally. 2004. UIMA: an architectural approach to unstructured information processing in the corporate research environment. *Natural Language Engineering*, 10:327–348.

Jenny Rose Finkel, Trond Grenager, and Christopher Manning. 2005. Incorporating non-local information into information extraction systems by Gibbs sampling. In *ACL 43*, pages 363–370.

I. Gurevych, M. Mühlhäuser, C. Müller, J. Steimle, M. Weimer, and T. Zesch. 2007. Darmstadt knowledge processing repository based on UIMA. In *First Workshop on Unstructured Information Management Architecture at GLDV 2007*, Tübingen.

U. Hahn, E. Buyko, R. Landefeld, M. Mühlhausen, Poprat M, K. Tomanek, and J. Wermter. 2008. An overview of JCoRe, the Julie lab UIMA component registry. In *LREC 2008*.

Dan Klein and Christopher D. Manning. 2003. Fast exact inference with a factored model for natural language parsing. In Suzanna Becker, Sebastian Thrun, and Klaus Obermayer, editors, *Advances in Neural Information Processing Systems*, volume 15, pages 3–10. MIT Press.

Heeyoung Lee, Angel Chang, Yves Peirsman, Nathanael Chambers, Mihai Surdeanu, and Dan Jurafsky. 2013. Deterministic coreference resolution based on entity-centric, precision-ranked rules. *Computational Linguistics*, 39(4).

Anthony Patricio. 2009. Why this project is successful? `https://community.jboss.org/wiki/WhyThisProjectIsSuccessful`.

Richard Socher, Alex Perelygin, Jean Wu, Jason Chuang, Christopher D. Manning, Andrew Ng, and Christopher Potts. 2013. Recursive deep models for semantic compositionality over a sentiment treebank. In *EMNLP 2013*, pages 1631–1642.

Kristina Toutanova, Dan Klein, Christopher D. Manning, and Yoram Singer. 2003. Feature-rich part-of-speech tagging with a cyclic dependency network. In *NAACL 3*, pages 252–259.

DKPro TC: A Java-based Framework for Supervised Learning Experiments on Textual Data

Johannes Daxenberger†, **Oliver Ferschke**†‡, **Iryna Gurevych**†‡ **and Torsten Zesch**§‡

† UKP Lab, Technische Universität Darmstadt
‡ Information Center for Education, DIPF, Frankfurt
§ Language Technology Lab, University of Duisburg-Essen
http://www.ukp.tu-darmstadt.de

Abstract

We present DKPro TC, a framework for supervised learning experiments on textual data. The main goal of DKPro TC is to enable researchers to focus on the actual research task behind the learning problem and let the framework handle the rest. It enables rapid prototyping of experiments by relying on an easy-to-use workflow engine and standardized document preprocessing based on the Apache Unstructured Information Management Architecture (Ferrucci and Lally, 2004). It ships with standard feature extraction modules, while at the same time allowing the user to add customized extractors. The extensive reporting and logging facilities make DKPro TC experiments fully replicable.

1 Introduction

Supervised learning on textual data is a ubiquitous challenge in Natural Language Processing (NLP). Applying a machine learning classifier has become the standard procedure, as soon as there is annotated data available. Before a classifier can be applied, relevant information (referred to as *features*) needs to be extracted from the data. A wide range of tasks have been tackled in this way including language identification, part-of-speech (POS) tagging, word sense disambiguation, sentiment detection, and semantic similarity.

In order to solve a supervised learning task, each researcher needs to perform the same set of steps in a predefined order: *reading input data*, *preprocessing*, *feature extraction*, *machine learning*, and *evaluation*. Standardizing this process is quite challenging, as each of these steps might vary a lot depending on the task at hand. To complicate matters further, the experimental process is usually embedded in a series of configuration changes. For example, introducing a new feature often requires additional preprocessing. Researchers should not need to think too much about such details, but focus on the actual research task. DKPro TC is our take on the standardization of an inherently complex problem, namely the implementation of supervised learning experiments for new datasets or new learning tasks.

We will make some simplifying assumptions wherever they do not harm our goal that the framework should be applicable to the widest possible range of supervised learning tasks. For example, DKPro TC only supports a limited set of machine learning frameworks, as we argue that differences between frameworks will mainly influence runtime, but will have little influence on the final conclusions to be drawn from the experiment. The main goal of DKPro TC is to enable the researcher to quickly find an optimal experimental configuration. One of the major contributions of DKPro TC is the modular architecture for preprocessing and feature extraction, as we believe that the focus of research should be on a meaningful and expressive feature set. DKPro TC has already been applied to a wide range of different supervised learning tasks, which makes us confident that it will be of use to the research community.

DKPro TC is mostly written in Java and freely available under an open source license.[1]

2 Requirements

In the following, we give a more detailed overview of the requirements and goals we have identified for a general-purpose text classification system. These requirements have guided the development of the DKPro TC system architecture.

[1] http://dkpro-tc.googlecode.com

Proceedings of 52nd Annual Meeting of the Association for Computational Linguistics: System Demonstrations, pages 61–66,
Baltimore, Maryland USA, June 23-24, 2014.

		Single-label	Multi-label	Regression
	Document Mode	· Spam Detection · Sentiment Detection	· Text Categorization · Keyphrase Assignment	· Text Readability
	Unit/Sequence Mode	· Named Entity Recognition · Part-of-Speech Tagging	· Dialogue Act Tagging	· Word Difficulty
	Pair Mode	· Paraphrase Identification · Textual Entailment	· Relation Extraction	· Text Similarity

Table 1: Supervised learning scenarios and feature modes supported in DKPro TC, with example NLP applications.

Flexibility Users of a system for supervised learning on textual data should be able to choose between different machine learning approaches depending on the task at hand. In supervised machine learning, we have to distinguish between approaches based on classification and approaches based on regression. In classification, given a document $d \in D$ and a set of labels $C = \{c_1, c_2, ..., c_n\}$, we want to label each document d with $L \subset C$, where L is the set of relevant or true labels. In single-label classification, each document d is labeled with exactly one label, i.e. $|L| = 1$, whereas in multi-label classification, a set of labels is assigned, i.e. $|L| \geq 1$. Single-label classification can further be divided into binary classification ($|C| = 2$) and multi-class classification ($|C| > 2$). In regression, real numbers instead of labels are assigned.

Feature extraction should follow a modular design in order to facilitate reuse and to allow seamless integration of new features. However, the way in which features need to be extracted from the input documents depends on the the task at hand. We have identified several typical scenarios in supervised learning on textual data and propose the following *feature modes*:

- In *document mode*, each input document will be used as its own entity to be classified, e.g. an email classified as wanted or unwanted (spam).
- In *unit/sequence mode*, each input document contains several units to be classified. The units in the input document cannot be divided into separate documents, either because the context of each unit needs to be preserved (e.g. to disambiguate named entities) or because they form a sequence which needs to be kept (in sequence tagging).
- The *pair mode* is intended for problems which require a pair of texts as input, e.g. a pair of sentences to be classified as paraphrase or non-paraphrase. It represents a special case of multi-instance learning (Surdeanu et al., 2012), in which a document contains exactly two instances.

Considering the outlined learning approaches and feature modes, we have summarized typical scenarios in supervised learning on textual data in Table 1 and added example applications in NLP.

Replicability and Reusability As it has been recently noted by Fokkens et al. (2013), NLP experiments are not replicable in most cases. The problem already starts with undocumented preprocessing steps such as tokenization or sentence boundary detection that might have heavy impact on experimental results. In a supervised learning setting, this situation is even worse, as e.g. feature extraction is usually only partially described in the limited space of a research paper. For example, a paper might state that "n-gram features" were used, which encompasses a very broad range of possible implementations.

In order to make NLP experiments replicable, a text classification framework should (i) encourage the user to reuse existing components which they can refer to in research papers rather than writing their own components, (ii) document all performed steps, and (iii) make it possible to re-run experiments with minimal effort.

Apart from helping the replicability of experiments, reusing components allows the user to concentrate on the new functionality that is specific to the planned experiment instead of having to reinvent the wheel. The parts of a text classification system which can typically be reused are preprocessing components, generic feature extractors, machine learning algorithms, and evaluation.

3 Architecture

We now give an overview of the DKPro TC architecture that was designed to take into account the requirements outlined above. A core design decision is to model each of the typical steps in text classification (reading input data and preprocessing, feature extraction, machine learning and evaluation) as separate *tasks*. This modular architecture helps the user to focus on the main problem, i.e. developing and selecting good features.

In the following, we describe each module in more detail, starting with the workflow engine that is used to assemble the tasks into an experiment.

3.1 Configuration and Workflow Engine

We rely on the DKPro Lab (Eckart de Castilho and Gurevych, 2011) workflow engine, which allows fine-grained control over the dependencies between single tasks, e.g. the pre-processing of a document obviously needs to happen before the feature extraction. In order to shield the user from the complex "wiring" of tasks, DKPro TC currently provides three pre-defined workflows: *Train/Test*, *Cross-Validation*, and *Prediction* (on unseen data). Each workflow supports the feature modes described above: document, unit/sequence, and pair.

The user is still able to control the behavior of the workflow by setting parameters, most importantly the sources of input data, the set of feature extractors, and the classifier to be used. Internally, each parameter is treated as a single dimension in the global *parameter space*. Users may provide more than one value for a certain parameter, e.g. specific feature sets or several classifiers. The workflow engine will automatically run all possible parameter value combinations (a process called *parameter sweeping*).

3.2 Reading Input Data

Input data for supervised learning tasks comes in myriad different formats which implies that reading data cannot be standardized, but needs to be handled individually for each data set. However, the internal processing should not be dependent on the input format. We therefore use the Common Analysis Structure (CAS), provided by the Apache Unstructured Information Management Architecture (UIMA), to represent input documents and annotations in a standardized way.

Under the UIMA model, reading input data means to transform arbitrary input data into a CAS representation. DKPro TC already provides a wide range of readers from UIMA component repositories such as DKPro Core.[2] The reader also needs to assign to each classification unit an *outcome* attribute that represents the relevant label (single-label), labels (multi-label), or a real value (regression). In unit/sequence mode, the reader additionally needs to mark the units in the CAS. In pair mode, a pair of texts (instead of a single document) is stored within one CAS.

3.3 Preprocessing

In this step, additional information about the document is added to the CAS, which efficiently stores large numbers of stand-off annotations. In pair mode, the preprocessing is automatically applied to both documents.

DKPro TC allows the user to run arbitrary UIMA-based preprocessing components as long as they are compatible with the DKPro type system that is currently used by DKPro Core and EOP.[3] Thus, a large set of ready-to-use preprocessing components for more than ten languages is available, containing e.g. sentence boundary detection, lemmatization, POS-tagging, or parsing.

3.4 Feature Extraction

DKPro TC ships a constantly growing number of feature extractors. Feature extractors have access to the document text as well as all the additional information that has been added in the form of UIMA stand-off annotations during the preprocessing step. Users of DKPro TC can add customized feature extractors for particular use cases on demand.

Among the ready-to-use feature extractors contained in DKPro TC, there are several ones extracting grammatical information, e.g. the plural-singular ratio or the ratio of modal to all verbs. Other features collect information about stylistic cues of a document, e.g. the number of exclamations or the type-token-ratio. DKPro TC is able to extract n-grams or skip n-grams of tokens, characters, and POS tags.

Some feature extractors need access to information about the entire document collection, e.g. in

[2] http://dkpro-core-asl.googlecode.com

[3] http://hltfbk.github.io/Excitement-Open-Platform/

order to weigh lexical features with tf.idf scores. Such extractors have to declare that they depend on collection level information and DKPro TC will automatically include a special task that is executed before the actual features are extracted. Depending on the feature mode which has been configured, DKPro TC will extract information on document level, unit- and/or sequence-level, or document pair level.

DKPro TC stores extracted features in its internal feature store. When the extraction process is finished, a configurable *data writer* converts the content from the feature store into a format which can be handled by the utilized machine learning tool. DKPro TC currently ships data writers for the Weka (Hall et al., 2009), Meka[4], and Mallet (McCallum, 2002) frameworks. Users can also add dedicated data writers that output features in the format used by the machine learning framework of their choice.

3.5 Supervised Learning

For the actual machine learning, DKPro TC currently relies on Weka (single-label and regression), Meka (multi-label), and Mallet (sequence labeling). It contains a task which trains a freely configurable classifier on the training data and evaluates the learned model on the test data.

Before training and evaluation, the user may apply dimensionality reduction to the feature set, i.e. select a limited number of (expectedly meaningful) features to be included for training and evaluating the classifier. DKPro TC uses the feature selection capabilities of Weka (single-label and regression) and Mulan (multi-label) (Tsoumakas et al., 2010).

DKPro TC can also predict labels on unseen (i.e. unlabeled) data, using a trained classifier. In that case, no evaluation will be carried out, but the classifier's prediction for each document will be written to a file.

3.6 Evaluation and Reporting

DKPro TC calculates common evaluation scores including accuracy, precision, recall, and F_1-score. Whenever sensible, scores are reported for each individual label as well as aggregated over all labels. To support users in further analyzing the performance of a classification workflow, DKPro TC outputs the confusion matrix, the actual predictions assigned to each document, and a ranking of the most useful features based on the configured feature selection algorithm. Additional task-specific reporting can be added by the user.

As mentioned before, a major goal of DKPro TC is to increase the replicability of NLP experiments. Thus, for each experiment, all configuration parameters are stored and will be reported together with the classification results.

4 Tweet Classification: A Use Case

We now give a brief summary of what a supervised learning task might look like in DKPro TC using a simple Twitter sentiment classification example. Assuming that we want to classify a set of tweets either as "emotional" or "neutral", we can use the setup shown in Listing 1. The example uses the Groovy programming language which yields better readable code, but pure Java is also supported. Likewise, a DKPro TC experiment can also be set up with the help of a configuration file, e.g. in JSON or via Groovy scripts.

First, we create a workflow as a `BatchTask-CrossValidation` which can be used to run a cross-validation experiment on the data (using 10 folds as configured by the corresponding parameter). The workflow uses `LabeledTweet-Reader` in order to import the experiment data from source text files into the internal document representation (one document per tweet). This reader adds a UIMA annotation that specifies the gold standard classification outcome, i.e. the relevant label for the tweet. In this use case, preprocessing consists of a single step: running the `ArkTweetTagger` (Gimpel et al., 2011), a specialized Twitter tokenizer and POS-tagger that is integrated in DKPro Core. The feature mode is set to document (one tweet per CAS), and the learning mode to single-label (each tweet is labeled with exactly one label), cf. Table 1.

Two feature extractors are configured: One for returning the number of hashtags and another one returning the ratio of emoticons to tokens in the tweet. Listing 2 shows the Java code for the second extractor. Two things are noteworthy: (i) document text and UIMA annotations are readily available through the JCas object, and (ii) this is really all that the user needs to write in order to add a new feature extractor.

The next item to be configured is the `Weka-DataWriter` which converts the internal fea-

[4] http://meka.sourceforge.net

```
BatchTaskCrossValidation batchTask = [
    experimentName: "Twitter-Sentiment",
    preprocessingPipeline: createEngineDescription(ArkTweetTagger), // Preprocessing
    parameterSpace: [ // multi-valued parameters in the parameter space will be swept
        Dimension.createBundle("reader", [
            readerTrain: LabeledTweetReader,
            readerTrainParams: [LabeledTweetReader.PARAM_CORPUS_PATH, "src/main/resources/tweets.txt"]]),
        Dimension.create("featureMode", "document"),
        Dimension.create("learningMode", "singleLabel"),
        Dimension.create("featureSet", [EmoticonRatioExtractor.name, NumberOfHashTagsExtractor.name]),
        Dimension.create("dataWriter", WekaDataWriter.name),
        Dimension.create("classificationArguments", [NaiveBayes.name, RandomForest.name])],
    reports: [BatchCrossValidationReport], // collects results from folds
    numFolds: 10];
```

Listing 1: Groovy code to configure a DKPro TC cross-validation BatchTask on Twitter data.

```
public class EmoticonRatioFeatureExtractor
extends FeatureExtractorResource_ImplBase implements DocumentFeatureExtractor
{
    @Override
    public List<Feature> extract(JCas annoDb) throws TextClassificationException {
        int nrOfEmoticons = JCasUtil.select(annoDb, EMO.class).size();
        int nrOfTokens = JCasUtil.select(annoDb, Token.class).size();
        double ratio = (double) nrOfEmoticons / nrOfTokens;
        return new Feature("EmoticonRatio", ratio).asList();
    }
}
```

Listing 2: A DKPro TC document mode feature extractor measuring the ratio of emoticons to tokens.

ture representation into the Weka ARFF format. For the classification, two machine learning algorithms will be iteratively tested: a Naive Bayes classifier and a Random Forest classifier. Passing a list of parameters into the parameter space will automatically make DKPro TC test all possible parameter combinations. The classification task automatically trains a model on the training data and stores the results of the evaluation on the test data for each fold on the disk. Finally, the evaluation scores for each fold are collected by the `BatchCrossValidationReport` and written to a single file using a tabulated format.

5 Related Work

This section will give a brief overview about tools with a scope similar to DKPro TC. We only list freely available software, most of which is open-source. Unless otherwise indicated, all of the tools are written in Java.

ClearTK (Ogren et al., 2008) is conceptually closest to DKPro TC and shares many of its distinguishing features like the modular feature extractors. It provides interfaces to machine learning libraries such as Mallet or libsvm, offers wrappers for basic NLP components, and comes with a feature extraction library that facilitates the development of custom feature extractors within the UIMA framework. In contrast to DKPro TC, it is rather designed as a programming library than a customizable research environment for quick experiments and does not provide predefined text classification setups. Furthermore, it does not support parameter sweeping and has no explicit support for creating experiment reports.

Argo (Rak et al., 2013) is a web-based workbench with support for manual annotation and automatic analysis of mainly bio-medical data. Like DKPro TC, Argo is based on UIMA, but focuses on sequence tagging, and it lacks DKPro TC's parameter sweeping capabilities.

NLTK (Bird et al., 2009) is a general-purpose NLP toolkit written in Python. It offers components for a wide range of preprocessing tasks and also supports feature extraction and machine learning for supervised text classification. Like DKPro TC, it can be used to quickly setup baseline experiments. As opposed to DKPro TC, NLTK lacks a modular structure with respect to preprocessing and feature extraction and does not support parameter sweeping.

Weka (Hall et al., 2009) is a machine learning framework that covers only the last two steps of DKPro TC's experimental process, i.e. machine learning and evaluation. However, it offers no dedicated support for preprocessing and feature generation. Weka is one of the machine learning frameworks that can be used within DKPro TC for actual machine learning.

Mallet (McCallum, 2002) is another machine

learning framework implementing several supervised and unsupervised learning algorithms. As opposed to Weka, is also supports sequence tagging, including Conditional Random Fields, as well as topic modeling. Mallet can be used as machine learning framework within DKPro TC.

Scikit-learn (Pedregosa et al., 2011) is a machine learning framework written in Python. It offers basic functionality for preprocessing, feature selection, and parameter tuning. It provides some methods for preprocessing such as converting documents to tf.idf vectors, but does not offer sophisticated and customizable feature extractors for textual data like DKPro TC.

6 Summary and Future Work

We have presented DKPro TC, a comprehensive and flexible framework for supervised learning on textual data. DKPro TC makes setting up experiments and creating new features fast and simple, and can therefore be applied for rapid prototyping. Its extensive logging capabilities emphasize the replicability of results. In our own research lab, DKPro TC has successfully been applied to a wide range of tasks including author identification, text quality assessment, and sentiment detection.

There are some limitations to DKPro TC which we plan to address in future work. To reduce the runtime of experiments with very large document collections, we want to add support for parallel processing of documents. While the current main goal of DKPro TC is to bootstrap experiments on new data sets or new applications, we also plan to make DKPro TC workflows available as resources to other applications, so that a model trained with DKPro TC can be used to automatically label textual data in different environments.

Acknowledgments

This work has been supported by the Volkswagen Foundation as part of the Lichtenberg-Professorship Program under grant No. I/82806, and by the Hessian research excellence program "Landes-Offensive zur Entwicklung Wissenschaftlich-ökonomischer Exzellenz" (LOEWE) as part of the research center "Digital Humanities". The authors would like give special thanks to Richard Eckhart de Castilho, Nicolai Erbs, Lucie Flekova, Emily Jamison, Krish Perumal, and Artem Vovk for their contributions to the DKPro TC framework.

References

S. Bird, E. Loper, and E. Klein. 2009. *Natural Language Processing with Python*. O'Reilly Media Inc.

R. Eckart de Castilho and I. Gurevych. 2011. A Lightweight Framework for Reproducible Parameter Sweeping in Information Retrieval. In *Proc. of the Workshop on Data Infrastructures for Supporting Information Retrieval Evaluation*, pages 7–10.

D. Ferrucci and A. Lally. 2004. UIMA: An Architectural Approach to Unstructured Information Processing in the Corporate Research Environment. *Natural Language Engineering*, 10(3-4):327–348.

A. Fokkens, M. van Erp, M. Postma, T. Pedersen, P. Vossen, and N. Freire. 2013. Offspring from Reproduction Problems: What Replication Failure Teaches Us. In *Proc. ACL*, pages 1691–1701.

K. Gimpel, N. Schneider, B. O'Connor, D. Das, D. Mills, J. Eisenstein, M. Heilman, D. Yogatama, J. Flanigan, and N. Smith. 2011. Part-of-speech tagging for Twitter: annotation, features, and experiments. In *Proc. ACL*, pages 42–47.

M. Hall, E. Frank, G. Holmes, B. Pfahringer, P. Reutemann, and I. Witten. 2009. The WEKA Data Mining Software: An Update. *SIGKDD Explorations*, 11(1):10–18.

A. McCallum. 2002. MALLET: A Machine Learning for Language Toolkit.

P. Ogren, P. Wetzler, and S. Bethard. 2008. ClearTK: A UIMA toolkit for statistical natural language processing. In *Towards Enhanced Interoperability for Large HLT Systems: UIMA for NLP workshop at LREC*, pages 32–38.

F. Pedregosa, G. Varoquaux, A. Gramfort, V. Michel, B. Thirion, O. Grisel, M. Blondel, P. Prettenhofer, R. Weiss, V. Dubourg, J. Vanderplas, A. Passos, D. Cournapeau, M. Brucher, M. Perrot, and E. Duchesnay. 2011. Scikit-learn: Machine Learning in Python. *Journal of Machine Learning Research*, 12:2825–2830.

R. Rak, A. Rowley, J. Carter, and S. Ananiadou. 2013. Development and Analysis of NLP Pipelines in Argo. In *Proc. ACL*, pages 115–120.

M. Surdeanu, J. Tibshirani, R. Nallapati, and C. Manning. 2012. Multi-instance multi-label learning for relation extraction. In *Proc. EMNLP-CoNLL*, pages 455–465.

G. Tsoumakas, I. Katakis, and I. Vlahavas. 2010. Mining Multi-label Data. *Transformation*, 135(2):1–20.

WoSIT: A Word Sense Induction Toolkit for Search Result Clustering and Diversification

Daniele Vannella, Tiziano Flati and **Roberto Navigli**
Dipartimento di Informatica
Sapienza Università di Roma
{vannella,flati,navigli}@di.uniroma1.it

Abstract

In this demonstration we present WoSIT, an API for Word Sense Induction (WSI) algorithms. The toolkit provides implementations of existing graph-based WSI algorithms, but can also be extended with new algorithms. The main mission of WoSIT is to provide a framework for the extrinsic evaluation of WSI algorithms, also within end-user applications such as Web search result clustering and diversification.

1 Introduction

The Web is by far the world's largest information archive, whose content – made up of billions of Web pages – is growing exponentially. Unfortunately the retrieval of any given piece of information is an arduous task which challenges even prominent search engines such as those developed by Google, Yahoo! and Microsoft. Even today, such systems still find themselves up against the lexical ambiguity issue, that is, the linguistic property due to which a single word may convey different meanings.

It has been estimated that around 4% of Web queries and 16% of the most frequent queries are ambiguous (Sanderson, 2008). A major issue associated with the lexical ambiguity phenomenon on the Web is the low number of query words submitted by Web users to search engines. A possible solution to this issue is the diversification of search results obtained by maximizing the dissimilarity of the top-ranking Web pages returned to the user (Agrawal et al., 2009; Ashwin Swaminathan and Kirovski, 2009). Another solution consists of clustering Web search results by way of clustering engines such as Carrot[1] and Yippy[2] and presenting them to the user grouped by topic.

[1] http://search.carrot2.org

[2] http://yippy.com

Diversification and Web clustering algorithms, however, do not perform any semantic analysis of search results, clustering them solely on the basis of their lexical similarity. Recently, it has been shown that the automatic acquisition of the meanings of a word of interest, a task referred to as Word Sense Induction, can be successfully integrated into search result clustering and diversification (Navigli and Crisafulli, 2010; Di Marco and Navigli, 2013) so as to outperform non-semantic state-of-the-art Web clustering systems.

In this demonstration we describe a new toolkit for Word Sense Induction, called WoSIT, which i) provides ready implementations of existing WSI algorithms; ii) can be extended with additional WSI algorithms; iii) enables the integration of WSI algorithms into search result clustering and diversification, thereby providing an extrinsic evaluation tool. As a result the toolkit enables the objective comparison of WSI algorithms within an end-user application in terms of the degree of diversification of the search results of a given ambiguous query.

2 WoSIT

In Figure 1 we show the workflow of the WoSIT toolkit, composed of three main phases: WSI; semantically-enhanced search result clustering and diversification; evaluation. Given a target query q whose meanings we want to automatically acquire, the toolkit first builds a graph for q, obtained either from a co-occurrence database, or constructed programmatically by using any user-provided input. The co-occurrence graph is then input to a WSI algorithm, chosen from among those available in the toolkit or implemented by the user. As a result, a set of word clusters is produced. This concludes the first phase of the WoSIT workflow. Then, the word clusters produced are used for assigning meanings to the search results returned by a search engine for the query q, i.e. search result disambiguation. The

Proceedings of 52nd Annual Meeting of the Association for Computational Linguistics: System Demonstrations, pages 67–72,
Baltimore, Maryland USA, June 23-24, 2014.

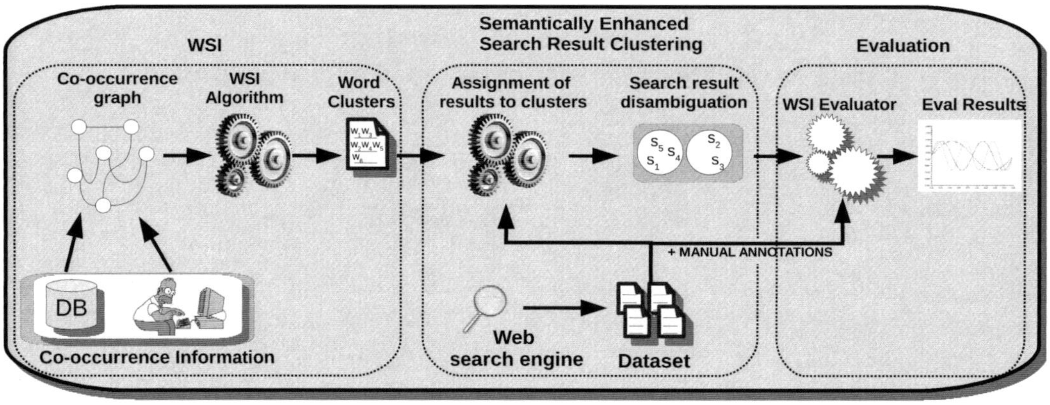

Figure 1: The WoSIT workflow.

outcome is that we obtain a clustering of search results. Finally, during the third phase, we apply the evaluation module which performs an evaluation of the search result clustering quality and the diversification performance.

We now describe in detail the three main phases of WoSIT.

2.1 Word Sense Induction

The first phase of WoSIT consists of the automatic identification of the senses of a query of interest, i.e. the task of Word Sense Induction. Although WoSIT enables the integration of custom implementations which can potentially work with any WSI paradigm, the toolkit provides ready-to-use implementations of several graph-based algorithms that work with word co-occurrences. All these algorithms carry out WSI in two steps: co-occurrence graph construction (Section 2.1.1) and discovery of word senses (Section 2.1.2).

2.1.1 Co-occurrence graph construction

Given a target query q, we build a co-occurrence graph $G_q = (V, E)$ such that V is the set of words co-occurring with q and E is the set of undirected edges, each denoting a co-occurrence between pairs of words in V. In Figure 2 we show an example of a co-occurrence graph for the target word *excalibur*.

WoSIT enables the creation of the co-occurrence graph either programmatically, by adding edges and vertices according to any user-specific algorithm, or starting from the statistics for co-occurring words obtained from a co-occurrence database (created, e.g., from a text corpus, as was done by Di Marco and Navigli (2013)). In either case, weights for edges have to be provided in terms of the correlation strength between pairs of words (e.g. using Dice, Jaccard or other co-occurrence measures).

The information about the co-occurrence database, e.g. a MySQL database, is provided programmatically or via parameters in the properties configuration file (`db.properties`). The co-occurrence database has to follow a given schema provided in the toolkit documentation. An additional configuration file (`wosit.properties`) also allows the user to specify additional constraints, e.g. the minimum weight value of co-occurrence (the `wordGraph.minWeight` parameter) to be added as edges to the graph.

The graphs produced can also be saved to binary (i.e. serialized) or text file:

```
g.saveToSer(fileName);
g = WordGraph.loadFromSer(fileName);
```

```
g.saveToTxt(fileName);
g = WordGraph.loadFromTxt(fileName);
```

We are now ready to provide our co-occurrence graph, created with just a few lines of code, as input to a WSI algorithm, as will be explained in the next section.

2.1.2 Discovery of Word Senses

Once the co-occurrence graph for the query q is built, it can be input to any WSI algorithm which extends the `GraphClusteringAlgorithm` class in the toolkit. WoSIT comes with a number of ready-to-use such algorithms, among which:

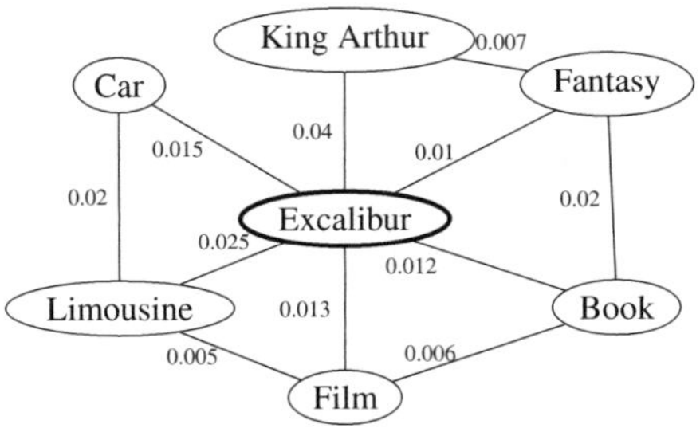

Figure 2: Example of a co-occurrence graph for the word *excalibur*.

- **Balanced Maximum Spanning Tree (B-MST)** (Di Marco and Navigli, 2013), an extension of a WSI algorithm based on the calculation of a Maximum Spanning Tree (Di Marco and Navigli, 2011) aimed at balancing the number of co-occurrences in each sense cluster.
- **HyperLex** (Véronis, 2004), an algorithm which identifies hubs in co-occurrence graphs, thereby identifying basic meanings for the input query.
- **Chinese Whispers** (Biemann, 2006), a randomized algorithm which partitions nodes by means of the iterative transfer of word sense information across the co-occurrence graph (Biemann, 2006).
- **Squares, Triangles and Diamonds (SquaT++)** (Di Marco and Navigli, 2013), an extension of the SquaT algorithm (Navigli and Crisafulli, 2010) which exploits three cyclic graph patterns to determine and discard those vertices (or edges) with weak degree of connectivity in the graph.

We also provide an implementation of a word clustering algorithm, i.e. **Lin98** (Lin, 1998), which does not rely on co-occurrence graphs, but just on the word co-occurrence information to iteratively refine word clusters on the basis of their "semantic" relationships.

A programmatic example of use of the B-MST WSI algorithm is as follows:

```
BMST mst = new BMST(g);
mst.makeClustering();
Clustering wordClusters =
                    mst.getClustering();
```

where `g` is a co-occurrence graph created as explained in Section 2.1.1, provided as input to the constructor of the algorithm's class. The `makeClustering` method implements the induction algorithm and creates the word clusters, which can then be retrieved calling the `getClustering` method. As a result an instance of the `Clustering` class is provided.

As mentioned above, WoSIT also enables the creation of custom WSI implementations. This can be done by extending the `GraphClusteringAlgorihm` abstract class. The new algorithm just has to implement two methods:

```
public void makeClustering();
public Clustering getClustering();
```

As a result, the new algorithm is readily integrated into the WoSIT toolkit.

2.2 Semantically-enhanced Search Result Clustering and Diversification

We now move to the use of the induced senses of our target query q within an application, i.e. search result clustering and diversification.

Search result clustering. The next step (cf. Figure 1) is the association of the search results returned by a search engine for query q with the most suitable word cluster (i.e. meaning of q). This can be done in two lines:

```
SnippetAssociator associator =
        SnippetAssociator.getInstance();
SnippetClustering clustering =
     associator.associateSnippet(
        targetWord,
        searchResults,
        wordClusters,
        AssociationMetric.DEGREE_OVERLAP);
```

The first line obtains an instance of the class which performs the association between search result snippets and the word clusters obtained from the WSI algorithm. The second line calls the association method `associateSnippet` which inputs the target word, the search results obtained from the search engine, the word clusters and, finally, the kind of metric to use for the association. Three different association metrics are implemented in the toolkit:

- `WORD_OVERLAP` performs the association by maximizing the size of the intersection between the word sets in each snippet and the word clusters;
- `DEGREE_OVERLAP` performs the association by calculating for each word cluster the sum

of the vertex degrees in the co-occurrence graph of the words occurring in each snippet;

- `TOKEN_OVERLAP` is similar in spirit to `WORD_OVERLAP`, but takes into account each token occurrence in the snippet bag of words.

Search result diversification. The above two lines of code return a set of snippet clusters and, as a result, semantically-enhanced search result clustering is performed. At the end, the resulting clustering can be used to provide a diversified reranking of the results:

```
List<Snippet> snippets =
        clustering.diversify(sorter);
```

The `diversify` method returns a flat list of snippet results obtained according to the `Sorter` object provided in input. The `Sorter` abstract class is designed to rerank the snippet clusters according to some predefined rule. For instance, the `CardinalitySorter` class, included in the toolkit, sorts the clusters according to the size of each cluster. Once a sorting order has been established, an element from each snippet cluster is added to an initially-empty list; next, a second element from each cluster is added, and so on, until all snippets are added to the list.

The sorting rules implemented in the toolkit are:

- `CardinalitySorter`: sorts the clusters according to their size, i.e. the number of vertices in the cluster;
- `MeanSimilaritySorter`: sorts the clusters according to the average association score between the snippets in the cluster and the backing word cluster (defined by the selected association metrics).

Notably, the end user can then implement his or her own custom sorting procedure by simply extending the `Sorter` class.

2.2.1 Search Result Datasets

The framework comes with two search result datasets of ambiguous queries: the AMBIENT+MORESQUE dataset made available by Bernardini et al. (2009) and Navigli and Crisafulli (2010), respectively, and the SemEval-2013-Task11 dataset.[3] New result datasets can be provided by users complying with the dataset format described below.

[3] For details visit `http://lcl.uniroma1.it/wosit/`.

A search result dataset in WoSIT is made up of at least two files:

- `topics.txt`, which contains the queries (topics) of interest together with their numeric ids. For instance:

```
id   description
1    polaroid
2    kangaroo
3    shakira
...  ...
```

- `results.txt`, which lists the search results for each given query, in terms of URL, page title and page snippet:

```
ID  url    title    snippet
1.1 http://www.polaroid.com/ Polaroid | Home ...
1.2 http://www.polaroid.com/products products...
1.3 http://en.wikipedia.org/wiki/Polaroid_Cor...
... ...
```

Therefore, the two files provide the queries and the corresponding search results returned by a search engine. In order to enable an automatic evaluation of the search result clustering and diversification output, two additional files have to be provided:

- `subTopics.txt`, which for each query provides the list of meanings for that query, e.g.:

```
ID  description
1.1 Polaroid Corporation, a multinational con...
1.2 Instant film photographs are sometimes kn...
1.3 Instant camera (or Land camera), sometime...
... ...
```

- `STRel.txt`, which provides the manual associations between each search result and the most suitable meaning as provided in the `subTopics.txt` file. For instance:

```
subTopicID   resultID
1.1          1.1
1.1          1.2
1.1          1.3
...          ...
```

2.3 WSI Evaluator

As shown in Figure 1 the final component of our workflow is the evaluation of WSI when integrated into search result clustering and diversification (already used by Navigli and Vannella (2013)). This component, called the WSI Evaluator, takes as input the snippet clusters obtained for a given query together with the fully annotated search result dataset, as described in the previous section. Two kinds of evaluations are carried out, described in what follows.

```
1  Dataset searchResults = Dataset.getInstance();
2  DBConfiguration db = DBConfiguration.getInstance();
3  for(String targetWord : dataset.getQueries())
4  {
5     WordGraph g = WordGraph.createWordGraph(targetWord, searchResults, db);
6     BMST mst = new BMST(g);
7     mst.makeClustering();
8     SnippetAssociator snippetAssociator = SnippetAssociator.getInstance();
9     SnippetClustering snippetClustering = snippetAssociator.associateSnippet(
10     targetWord, searchResults, mst.getClustering(), AssociationMetric.WORD_OVERLAP);
11    snippetClustering.export("output/outputMST.txt", true);
12 }
13 WSIEvaluator.evaluate(searchResults, "output/outputMST.txt");
```

Figure 3: An example of evaluation code for the B-MST clustering algorithm.

2.3.1 Evaluation of the clustering quality

The quality of the output produced by semantically-enhanced search result clustering is evaluated in terms of Rand Index (Rand, 1971, RI), Adjusted Rand Index (Hubert and Arabie, 1985, ARI), Jaccard Index (JI) and, finally, precision and recall as done by Crabtree et al. (2005), together with their F1 harmonic mean.

2.3.2 Evaluation of the clustering diversity

To evaluate the snippet clustering diversity the measures of S-recall@K and S-precision@r (Zhai et al., 2003) are calculated. These measures determine how many different meanings of a query are covered in the top-ranking results shown to the user. We calculate these measures on the output of the three different association metrics illustrated in Section 2.2.

3 A Full Example

We now show a full example of usage of the WoSIT API. The code shown in Figure 3 initially obtains a search result dataset (line 1), selects a database (line 2) and iterates over its queries (line 3). Next, a co-occurrence graph for the current query is created from a co-occurrence database (line 5) and an instance of the B-MST WSI algorithm is created with the graph as input (line 6). After executing the algorithm (line 7), the snippets for the given query are clustered (lines 8-10). The resulting snippet clustering is appended to an output file (line 11). Finally, the WSI evaluator is run on the resulting snippet clustering using the given dataset (line 13).

3.1 Experiments

We applied the WoSIT API to the AMBIENT+MORESQUE dataset using 4 induction algorithms among those available in the toolkit, where co-occurrences were obtained from the Google Web1T corpus (Brants and Franz, 2006). In Table 1 we show the clustering quality results output by the WoSIT evaluator, whereas in Figure 4 we show the diversification performance in terms of S-recall@K.

Algorithm	Assoc. metr.	Web1T ARI	JI	F1	# cl.
SquaT++	WO	69.65	75.69	59.19	2.1
	DO	69.21	75.45	59.19	2.1
	TO	69.67	75.69	59.19	2.1
B-MST	WO	60.76	71.51	64.56	5.0
	DO	66.48	69.37	64.84	5.0
	TO	63.17	71.21	64.04	5.0
HyperLex	WO	60.86	72.05	65.41	13.0
	DO	66.27	68.00	71.91	13.0
	TO	62.82	70.87	65.08	13.0
Chinese Whispers	WO	67.75	75.37	60.25	12.5
	DO	65.95	69.49	70.33	12.5
	TO	67.57	74.69	60.50	12.5

Table 1: Results of WSI algorithms with a Web1T co-occurrence database and the three association metrics (Word Overlap, Degree Overlap and Token Overlap). The reported measures are Adjusted Rand Index (ARI), Jaccard Index (JI) and F1. We also show the average number of clusters per query produced by each algorithm.

3.2 Conclusions

In this demonstration we presented WoSIT, a full-fledged toolkit for Word Sense Induction algorithms and their integration into search result clustering and diversification. The main contributions are as follows: first, we release a Java API for performing Word Sense Induction which includes several ready-to-use implementations of existing algorithms; second, the API enables the use of the acquired senses for a given query for enhancing

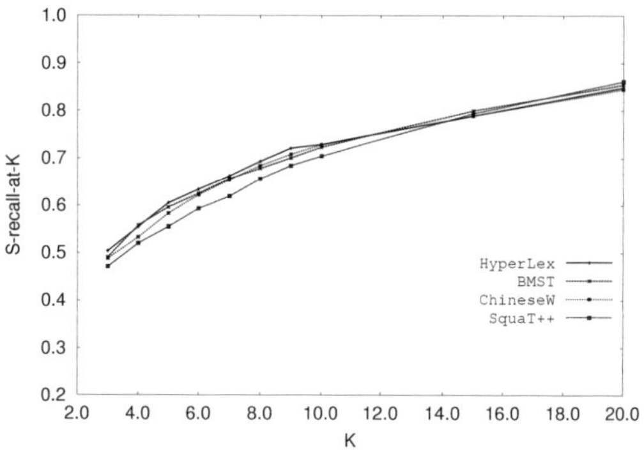

Figure 4: S-recall@K performance.

search result clustering and diversification; third, we provide an evaluation component which, given an annotated dataset of search results, carries out different kinds of evaluation of the snippet clustering quality and diversity.

WoSIT is the first available toolkit which provides an end-to-end approach to the integration of WSI into a real-world application. The toolkit enables an objective comparison of WSI algorithms as well as an evaluation of the impact of applying WSI to clustering and diversifying search results. As shown by Di Marco and Navigli (2013), this integration is beneficial and allows outperformance of non-semantic state-of-the-art Web clustering systems.

The toolkit, licensed under a Creative Commons Attribution-Non Commercial-Share Alike 3.0 License, is available at `http://lcl.uniroma1.it/wosit/`.

References

Rakesh Agrawal, Sreenivas Gollapudi, Alan Halverson, and Samuel Ieong. 2009. Diversifying search results. In *Proc. of the Second International Conference on Web Search and Web Data Mining (WSDM 2009)*, pages 5–14, Barcelona, Spain.

Cherian V. Mathew Ashwin Swaminathan and Darko Kirovski. 2009. Essential Pages. In *Proc. of the 2009 IEEE/WIC/ACM International Joint Conference on Web Intelligence and Intelligent Agent Technology*, volume 1, pages 173–182.

Andrea Bernardini, Claudio Carpineto, and Massimiliano D'Amico. 2009. Full-Subtopic Retrieval with Keyphrase-Based Search Results Clustering. In *Proc. of Web Intelligence 2009*, volume 1, pages 206–213, Los Alamitos, CA, USA.

Chris Biemann. 2006. Chinese Whispers - an Efficient Graph Clustering Algorithm and its Application to Natural Language Processing Problems. In *Proc. of TextGraphs: the First Workshop on Graph Based Methods for Natural Language Processing*, pages 73–80, New York City.

Thorsten Brants and Alex Franz. 2006. Web 1T 5-gram, ver. 1, LDC2006T13. In *Linguistic Data Consortium*, Philadelphia, USA.

Daniel Crabtree, Xiaoying Gao, and Peter Andreae. 2005. Improving web clustering by cluster selection. In *Proc. of the 2005 IEEE/WIC/ACM International Conference on Web Intelligence*, pages 172–178, Washington, DC, USA.

Antonio Di Marco and Roberto Navigli. 2011. Clustering Web Search Results with Maximum Spanning Trees. In *Proc. of the XIIth International Conference of the Italian Association for Artificial Intelligence (AI*IA)*, pages 201–212, Palermo, Italy.

Antonio Di Marco and Roberto Navigli. 2013. Clustering and Diversifying Web Search Results with Graph-Based Word Sense Induction. *Computational Linguistics*, 39(3):709–754.

Lawrence Hubert and Phipps Arabie. 1985. Comparing Partitions. *Journal of Classification*, 2(1):193–218.

Dekang Lin. 1998. Automatic Retrieval and Clustering of Similar Words. In *Proc. of the 17th International Conference on Computational linguistics (COLING)*, pages 768–774, Montreal, Canada.

Roberto Navigli and Giuseppe Crisafulli. 2010. Inducing Word Senses to Improve Web Search Result Clustering. In *Proc. of the 2010 Conference on Empirical Methods in Natural Language Processing*, pages 116–126, Boston, USA.

Roberto Navigli and Daniele Vannella. 2013. SemEval-2013 Task 11: Evaluating Word Sense Induction & Disambiguation within An End-User Application. In *Proc. of the 7th International Workshop on Semantic Evaluation (SemEval 2013), in conjunction with the Second Joint Conference on Lexical and Computational Semantics (*SEM 2013)*, pages 193–201, Atlanta, USA.

William M. Rand. 1971. Objective criteria for the evaluation of clustering methods. *Journal of the American Statistical association*, 66(336):846–850.

Mark Sanderson. 2008. Ambiguous queries: test collections need more sense. In *Proc. of the 31st annual international ACM SIGIR conference on Research and development in information retrieval*, pages 499–506, Singapore.

Jean Véronis. 2004. HyperLex: lexical cartography for information retrieval. *Computer, Speech and Language*, 18(3):223–252.

ChengXiang Zhai, William W. Cohen, and John Lafferty. 2003. Beyond independent relevance: Methods and evaluation metrics for subtopic retrieval. In *Proc. of the 26th annual international ACM SIGIR conference on Research and development in information retrieval*, pages 10–17, Toronto, Canada.

A Rule-Augmented Statistical Phrase-based Translation System

Cong Duy Vu Hoang[†], **AiTi Aw**[†] **and Nhung T. H. Nguyen**[‡*]
[†]Human Language Technology Dept.
Institute for Infocomm Research (I[2]R), A*STAR, Singapore
{cdvhoang, aaiti}@i2r.a-star.edu.sg
[‡]School of Information Science
Japan Advanced Institute of Science and Technology (JAIST), Japan
nthnhung@jaist.ac.jp

Abstract

Interactive or Incremental Statistical Machine Translation (IMT) aims to provide a mechanism that allows the statistical models involved in the translation process to be incrementally updated and improved. The source of knowledge normally comes from users who either post-edit the entire translation or just provide the translations for wrongly translated domain-specific terminologies. Most of the existing work on IMT uses batch learning paradigm which does not allow translation systems to make use of the new input instantaneously. We introduce an adaptive MT framework with a Rule Definition Language (RDL) for users to amend MT results through translation rules or patterns. Experimental results show that our system acknowledges user feedback via RDL which improves the translations of the baseline system on three test sets for Vietnamese to English translation.

1 Introduction

In current Statistical Machine Translation (SMT) framework, users are often seen as passive contributors to MT performance. Even if there is a collaboration between the users and the system, it is carried out in a batch learning paradigm (Ortiz-Martinez et al., 2010), where the training of the SMT system and the collaborative process are carried out in different stages. To increase the productivity of the whole translation process, one has to incorporate human correction activities within the translation process. Barrachina et al. (2009) proposed an iterative process in which the translator activity is used by the system to compute its best (or n-best) translation suffix hypotheses to complete the prefix. Ortiz-Martinez et al. (2011) proposed an IMT framework that includes stochastic error-correction models in its statistical formalization to address the prefix coverage problems in Barrachina et al. (2009). Gonzalez-Rubio et al. (2013) proposed a similar approach with a specific error-correction model based on a statistical interpretation of the Levenshtein distance (Levenshtein, 1966). On the other hand, Ortiz-Martinez et al. (2010) presented an IMT system that is able to learn from user feedback by incrementally updating the statistical models used by the system. The key aspect of this proposed system is the use of HMM-based alignment models trained by an incremental EM algorithm.

Here, we present a system similar to Ortiz-Martinez et al. (2010). Instead of updating the translation model given a new sentence pair, we provide a framework for users to describe translation rules using a Rule Definition Language (RDL). Our RDL borrows the concept of the rule-based method that allows users to control the translation output by writing rules using their linguistic and domain knowledge. Although statistical methods pre-dominate the machine translation research currently, rule-based methods are still promising in improving the translation quality. This approach is especially useful for low resource languages where large training corpus is not always available. The advantage of rule-based methods is that they can well handle particular linguistic phenomena which are peculiar to languages and domains. For example, the TCH MT system at IWSLT 2008 (Wang et al., 2008) used dictionary and hand-crafted rules (e.g. regular expression) to process NEs. Their experiments showed that handling NE separately (e.g., person name, location name, date, time, digit) results in translation quality improvement.

In this paper, we present an adaptive and in-

*Work done during an internship at I[2]R, A*STAR.

Proceedings of 52nd Annual Meeting of the Association for Computational Linguistics: System Demonstrations, pages 73–78,
Baltimore, Maryland USA, June 23-24, 2014. ©2014 Association for Computational Linguistics

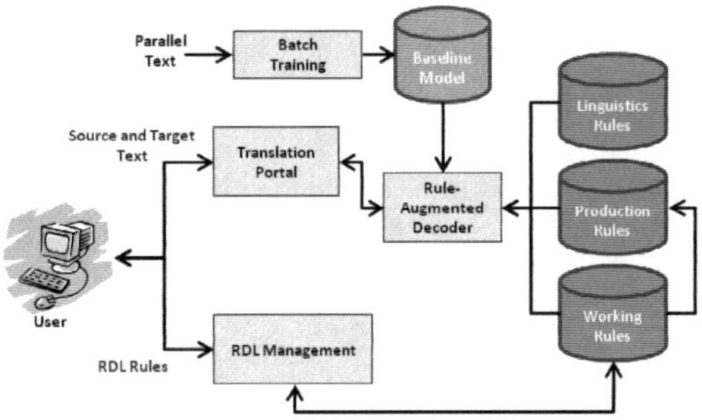

Figure 1: The proposed rule-augmented SMT framework.

teractive MT system that allows users to correct the translation and integrate the adaptation into the next translation cycle. Our experiments show that the system is specifically effective in handling translation errors related to out of vocabulary words (OOVs), language expressions, name entities (NEs), abbreviations, terminologies, idioms, etc. which cannot be easily addressed in the absence of in-domain parallel data.

2 System Overview

Figure 1 shows the translation and interactive process of our system. The system is trained with a batch of parallel texts to create a baseline model. Users improve the translation by adding RDL rules to change or correct the unsatisfactory translation. New RDL rules are tested in a working environment before uploading to the production environment where they would be used by subsequent translation requests.

In our system, RDL Management checks, validates and indexes the translation rules. The Rule-Augmented Decoder has two components: (1) the RDL Matcher to find applicable RDL rules for a given source text to create dynamic translation hypotheses; and (2) the Augmented Decoder to produce the final consensus translation using both dynamic hypotheses and static hypotheses from the baseline model.

3 Rule Definition Language (RDL)

The Rule Definition Language (RDL) comprises a RDL grammar, a RDL parser and a RDL matching algorithm.

3.1 RDL Grammar

Our RDL grammar is represented with a Backus-Naur Form (BNF)s syntax. The major feature of RDL grammar is the support of pre-defined identifiers and meta-operators which go beyond the normal framework of regular expression. We also included a set of pre-defined functions to further constraint the application and realization of the rules. This framework allows us to incorporate semantic information into the rule definition and derive translation hypotheses using both semantic and lexical information. A RDL rule is identified by a unique rule ID and five constituents, including **S**ource pattern, rule **C**ondition, **T**arget translation, **R**eordering rule and user **C**on**F**idence. The source pattern and target translation can be constructed using different combination of node types as described in Table 1. The rules can be further conditioned by using some pre-defined functions and the system allows users to reorder the translation of the target node. Figure 2 gives an example of a RDL rule where identifier @Num is used.

Node Type	Description
Token	Any string of characters in the defined basic processing unit of the language.
String	A constant string of characters.
Identifier	A term represents a pre-defined role (e.g. integer, date, sequence, ...).
Meta-node	A term executes a specific function (e.g. casing, selection/option, connection).
Context cue	A term describes source context's existence.
Function	A term executes a pre-defined task.

Table 1: A brief description of RDL nodes.

```
rule DATE5_1 //rule info
{
#s [!"Vào"] (!"Năm tài khoá"|!" Năm tài chính") @Num //source
#c ~inRangeOf(@Num, "1000", "9999") //condition
#t [!"Vào"] -> ["in"] //target
#r [["in"] "the fiscal year" @Num] //reordering
#cf false //user confidence
}
```

Figure 2: An Example of RDL Rule.

3.2 RDL Parsing and Indexing

The RDL Parser checks the syntax of the rules before indexing and storing them into the rule database. We utilize the compiler generator (WoB et al., 2003) to generate a RDL template parser and then embed all semantic parsing components into the template to form our RDL Parser.

As rule matching is performed during translation, searching of the relevant rules have to be very fast and efficient. We employed the modified version of an inverted index scheme (Zobel and Moffat, 2006) for our rule indexing. The algorithm is

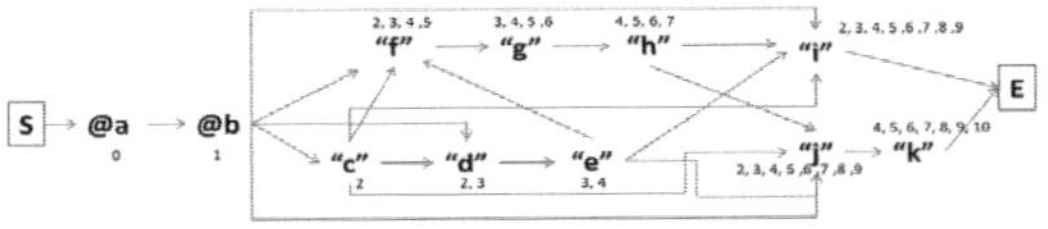

Figure 3: A linked item chain for a rule source (@a @b [c] ["d e"] ["f g h"] ("i" | "j k")).

represented in Algorithm 1.

Data: ruleID & srcPatn
Result: idxTbl
// To build data structure – Forward Step
doForward(srcPatn, linkedItmChain);
// To create index table – Backward Step
doBackward(linkedItmChain, ruleID, idxTbl);
Algorithm 1: Algorithm for RDL rule indexing.

The main idea of the rule indexing algorithm is to index all string-based nodes in the source pattern of the RDL rule. Each node is represented using 3-tuple. They are ruleID, number of nodes in source pattern and all plausible positions of the node during rule matching. The indexing is carried out via a Forward Step and Backward Step. The Forward Step builds a linked item chain which traverses all possible position transitions from one node to another as illustrated in Figure 3. Note that S and E are the Start and End Node. The link indicates the order of transition from a node to another. The numbers refer to the possible positions of an item in source. The Backward Step starts at the end of the source pattern; traverses back the link to index each node using the 3-tuple constructed in the Forward Step. This data structure allows us to retrieve, add or update RDL rules efficiently and incrementally without re-indexing.

3.3 RDL Matching Algorithm

Each word in the source string will be matched against the index table to retrieve relevant RDL rules during decoding. The aim is to retrieve all RDL rules in which the word is used as part of the context in the source pattern. We sort all the rules based on the word positions recorded during indexing, match their source patterns against the input string within the given span, check the conditions and generate the hypotheses if the rules fulfill all the constraints.

4 Rule-Augmented Decoder

The rule-augmented decoder integrates the dynamic hypotheses generated during rule matching with the baseline hypotheses during decoding. Given a sentence *f* from a source language *F*, the fundamental equation of SMT (Brown et al., 1993) to translate it into a target sentence *e* of a target language *E* is stated in Equation 1.

$$\begin{aligned} e_{best} &= argmax_e P_r(e|f) \\ &= argmax_e P_r(f|e)P_r(e) \\ &= argmax_e \sum_{n=1}^{N} \lambda_n h_n(e,f) \end{aligned} \tag{1}$$

Here, $P_r(f|e)$ is approximated by a translation model that represents the correlation between the source and the target sentence and $P_r(e)$ is approximated by a language model presenting the well-formedness of the candidate translation e. Most of the SMT systems follow a log-linear approach (Och and Ney, 2002), where direct modelling of the posterior probability $P_r(f|e)$ of Equation 1 is used. The decoder searches for the best translation given a set of model $h_m(e,f)$ by maximizing the log-linear feature score (Och and Ney, 2004) as in Equation 1.

For each hypothesis generated by the RDL rule, an appropriate feature vector score is needed to ensure that it will not disturb the probability distribution of each model and contributes to hypothesis selection process of SMT decoder.

4.1 Model Score Estimation

The aim of the RDL implementation is to address the translation of language-specific expressions (such as date-time, number, title, etc.) and domain-specific terminologies. Sometimes, translation rules and bilingual phrases can be easily observed and obtained from experienced translators or linguists. However, it is difficult to estimate the probability of the RDL rules manually to reflect the correct word or phrase distribution in real data. Many approaches have been proposed to solve the OOV problem and estimate word translation probabilities without using parallel data. Koehn et al. (2000) estimated word translation probabilities from unrelated monolingual corpora using the EM algorithm. Habash et al. (2008) presented different techniques to extend the phrase table for online handling of OOV. In their approach, the extended phrases are added to the baseline phrase table with a default weight. Arora et al. (2008) extended the phrase table by adding new phrase translations for all source language words that do not have a single-word entry in the original phrase-table, but appear in the context of larger phrases. They adjusted the probabilities of each entry in the extended phase table.

We performed different experiments to estimate the lexical translation feature vector for each dynamic hypothesis generated by our RDL rules. We obtain the best performance by estimating the feature vector score using the baseline phrase table through context approximation. For each hypothesis generated by the RDL rule, we retrieve entries from the phrase table which have at least one similar word with the source of the generated hypothesis. We sort the entries based on the similarities between the generated and retrieved hypotheses using both source and target phrase. The medium score of the sorted list is assigned to the generated hypothesis.

5 System Features

The main features of our system are (1) the flexibilities provided to the user to create different levels of translation rules, from simple one-to-one bilingual phrases to complex generalization rules for capturing the translation of specific linguistic phenomena; and (2) the ability to validate and manage translation rules online and incrementally.

5.1 RDL Rule Management

Our system framework is language independent and has been implemented on a Vietnamese to English translation project. Figure 4 shows the RDL Management Screen where a user can add, modify or delete a translation rule using RDL. A RDL rule can be created using nodes. Each node can be defined using string or system predefined meta-identifiers with or without meta-operators as described in Table 1. Based on the node type selected by the user, the system further restricts the user to appropriate conditions and translation functions. The user can define the order of the translation output of each node and at the same time, inform the system whether to use a specific RDL exclusively during decoding, in which any phrases from the baseline phrase table overlapping with that span will be ignored[1]. The system also provides an editor for expert users to code the rules using the RDL controlled language. Each rule is validated by the RDL parser (discussed in section 3.2), which will display errors or warning messages when an invalid syntax is encountered.

Figure 4: RDL Management screen with identifiers & meta-functions supported.

5.2 RDL Rule Validation

Our decoder manages two types of phrase table. One is the static phrase-table obtained through the SMT training in parallel texts; the other is the dynamic table that comprises of the hypotheses generated on-the-fly during RDL rule matching. To ensure only fully tested rules are used in the production environment, the system supports two types of dynamic phrase table. The working phrase-table holds the latest updates made by the users. The users can test the translation with these latest modifications using a specific translation protocol. When users are satisfied with these modifications, they can perform an operation to upload the RDL rules to the production phrase-table, where the RDLs are used for all translation

[1]Similar to Moses XML markup exclusive feature `http://www.statmt.org/moses/?n=Moses.AdvancedFeatures#ntoc9`

Named Entity Category	Number of Rules
Date-time	120
Measurement	92
Title	13
Designation	12
Number	19
Terminology	178
Location	13
Organization	48
Total	**495**

Table 2: Statistics of created RDL rules for Vietnamese-to-English NE Translation.

requests. Uploaded rules can be deleted, modified and tested again in the working environment before updated to the production environment. Figure 5b and Figure 5c show the differences in translation output before and after applied the RDL rule in Figure 5a.

6 A Case Study for Vietnamese–English Translation

We performed an experiment using the proposed RDL framework for a Vietnamese to English translation system. As named entity (NE) contributes to most of the OOV occurrences and impacts the system performance for out-of-domain test data in our system, we studied the NE usage in a large Vietnamese monolingual corpus comprising 50M words to extract RDL rules. We created RDL rules for 8 popular NE types including title, designation, date-time, measurement, location, organization, number and terminology. We made use of a list of anchor words for each NE category and compiled our RDL rules based on these anchor words. As a result, we compiled a total of 495 rules for 8 categories and it took about 3 months for the rule creation. Table 2 shows the coverage of our compiled rules.

6.1 Experiment & Results

Our experiments were performed on a training set of about 875K parallel sentences extracted from web news and revised by native linguists over 2 years. The corpus has 401K and 225K unique English and Vietnamese tokens. We developed 1008 and 2548 parallel sentences, each with 4 references, for development and testing, respectively. All the reference sentences are created and revised by different native linguists at different times. We also trained a very large English language model using data from Gigaword, Europarl and English

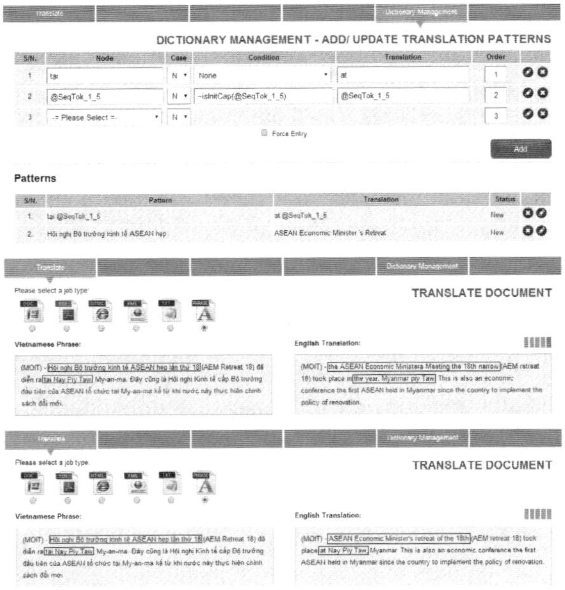

Figure 5: Translation Demo with RDL rules.

Data Set	nS	nT	nMR
TrainFull (VN)	875,579	28,251,775	627,125
TrainFull (EN)	875,579	20,191,526	-
Test1 (VN)	1009	34,717	737
Test1 (4 refs) (EN)	1009	≈25,713	-
Test2 (VN)	1033	29,546	603
Test2 (4 refs) (EN)	1033	≈22,717	-
Test3 (VN)	506	16,817	344
Test3 (4 refs) (EN)	506	≈12,601	-
Dev (VN)	1008	34,803	-
Dev (4 refs) (EN)	1008	≈25,631	-

Table 3: Statistics of Vietnamese-to-English parallel data. nS, nT, and nMR are number of sentence pairs and tokens, and count of matched rules, respectively.

web texts of Vietnamese authors to validate the impact of RDL rules on large-scale and domain-rich corpus. The experimental results show that created RDL rules improve the translation performance on all 3 test sets. Table 3 and Table 4 show respective data statistics and results of our evaluation. More specifically, the BLEU scores increase 3%, 3.6% and 1.4% on the three sets, respectively.

7 Conclusion

We have presented a system that provides a control language (Kuhn, 2013) specialized for MT for users to create translation rules. Our RDL differs from Moses's XML mark-up in that it offers fea-

Data Set	System	BLEU	NIST	METEOR
Set 1	Baseline	39.21	9.2323	37.81
	+RDL (all)	39.51	9.2658	37.98
Set 2	Baseline	40.25	9.5174	38.24
	+RDL (all)	40.61	9.6092	38.84
Set 3	Baseline	36.77	8.6953	37.65
	+RDL (all)	36.91	8.7062	37.69

Table 4: Experimental results with RDL rules.

tures that go beyond the popular regular expression framework. Without restricting the mark-up on the source text, we allow multiple translations to be specified for the same span or overlapping span.

Our experimental results show that RDL rules improve the overall performance of the Vietnamese-to-English translation system. The framework will be tested for other language pairs (e.g. Chinese-to-English, Malay-to-English) in the near future. We also plan to explore advanced methods to identify and score *"good"* dynamic hypotheses on-the-fly and integrate them into current SMT translation system (Simard and Foster, 2013).

Acknowledgments

We would like to thank the reviewers of the paper for their helpful comments.

References

Paul M. Sumita E. Arora, K. 2008. Translation of unknown words in phrase-based statistical machine translation for languages of rich morphology. In *In Proceedings of the Workshop on Spoken Language Technologies for Under-Resourced Languages, SLTU 2008.*

Sergio Barrachina, Oliver Bender, Francisco Casacuberta, Jorge Civera, Elsa Cubel, Shahram Khadivi, Antonio Lagarda, Hermann Ney, Jesús Tomás, Enrique Vidal, and Juan-Miguel Vilar. 2009. Statistical approaches to computer-assisted translation. *Comput. Linguist.*, 35(1):3–28, March.

Peter F. Brown, Vincent J. Della Pietra, Stephen A. Della Pietra, and Robert L. Mercer. 1993. The mathematics of statistical machine translation: Parameter estimation. *Comput. Linguist.*, 19(2):263–311, June.

Jesús González-Rubio, Daniel Ortíz-Martinez, José-Miguel Benedí, and Francisco Casacuberta. 2013. Interactive machine translation using hierarchical translation models. In *Proceedings of the 2013 Conference on Empirical Methods in Natural Language Processing*, pages 244–254, Seattle, Washington, USA, October.

Nizar Habash. 2008. Four techniques for online handling of out-of-vocabulary words in arabic-english statistical machine translation. In *Proceedings of ACL: Short Papers*, HLT-Short '08, pages 57–60, Stroudsburg, PA, USA.

Philipp Koehn and Kevin Knight. 2000. Estimating word translation probabilities from unrelated monolingual corpora using the em algorithm. In *Proceedings of the Seventeenth National Conference on Artificial Intelligence and Twelfth Conference on Innovative Applications of Artificial Intelligence*, pages 711–715. AAAI Press.

Tobias Kuhn. 2013. A survey and classification of controlled natural languages. *Computational Linguistics.*

VI Levenshtein. 1966. Binary codes capable of correcting deletions, insertions and reversals. *Soviet Physics Doklady*, 10:707.

Franz Josef Och and Hermann Ney. 2002. Discriminative training and maximum entropy models for statistical machine translation. In *In Proceedings of ACL*, pages 295–302, Stroudsburg, PA, USA.

Franz Josef Och and Hermann Ney. 2004. The alignment template approach to statistical machine translation. *Comput. Linguist.*, 30(4):417–449, December.

Daniel Ortiz-Martinez, Ismael Garcia-Varea, and Francisco Casacuberta. 2010. Online learning for interactive statistical machine translation. In *In Proceedings of NAACL*, HLT '10, pages 546–554, Stroudsburg, PA, USA.

Daniel Ortiz-Martínez, Luis A. Leiva, Vicent Alabau, Ismael García-Varea, and Francisco Casacuberta. 2011. An interactive machine translation system with online learning. In *In Proceedings of ACL: Systems Demonstrations*, HLT '11, pages 68–73, Stroudsburg, PA, USA.

Michel Simard and George Foster. 2013. Pepr: Post-edit propagation using phrase-based statistical machine translation. *Proceedings of the XIV Machine Translation Summit*, pages 191–198.

Haifeng Wang, Hua Wu, Xiaoguang Hu, Zhanyi Liu, Jianfeng Li, Dengjun Ren, and Zhengyu Niu. 2008. The tch machine translation system for iwslt 2008. In *In Proceedings of IWSLT 2008, Hawaii, USA.*

Albrecht WoB, Markus Loberbauer, and Hanspeter Mossenbock. 2003. Ll(1) conflict resolution in a recursive descent compiler generator. In *Modular Programming Languages*, volume 2789 of *Lecture Notes in Computer Science*, pages 192–201.

Justin Zobel and Alistair Moffat. 2006. Inverted files for text search engines. *ACM Comput. Surv.*, 38, July.

KyotoEBMT: An Example-Based Dependency-to-Dependency Translation Framework

John Richardson[†] **Fabien Cromières**[‡] **Toshiaki Nakazawa**[‡] **Sadao Kurohashi**[†]
[†]Graduate School of Informatics, Kyoto University, Kyoto 606-8501
[‡]Japan Science and Technology Agency, Kawaguchi-shi, Saitama 332-0012
john@nlp.ist.i.kyoto-u.ac.jp, {fabien, nakazawa}@pa.jst.jp,
kuro@i.kyoto-u.ac.jp

Abstract

This paper introduces the KyotoEBMT Example-Based Machine Translation framework. Our system uses a *tree-to-tree* approach, employing syntactic dependency analysis for both source and target languages in an attempt to preserve non-local structure. The effectiveness of our system is maximized with online example matching and a flexible decoder. Evaluation demonstrates BLEU scores competitive with state-of-the-art SMT systems such as Moses. The current implementation is intended to be released as open-source in the near future.

1 Introduction

Corpus-based approaches have become a major focus of Machine Translation research. We present here a fully-fledged Example-Based Machine Translation (EBMT) platform making use of both source-language and target-language dependency structure. This paradigm has been explored comparatively less, as studies on Syntactic-based SMT/EBMT tend to focus on constituent trees rather than dependency trees, and on tree-to-string rather than tree-to-tree approaches. Furthermore, we employ separate dependency parsers for each language rather than projecting the dependencies from one language to another, as in (Quirk et. al, 2005).

The dependency structure information is used end-to-end: for improving the quality of the alignment of the translation examples, for constraining the translation rule extraction and for guiding the decoding. We believe that dependency structure, which considers more than just local context, is important in order to generate fluent and accurate translations of complex sentences across distant language pairs.

Our experiments focus on technical domain translation for Japanese-Chinese and Japanese-English, however our implementation is applicable to any domain and language pair for which there exist translation examples and dependency parsers.

A further unique characteristic of our system is that, again contrary to the majority of similar systems, it does not rely on precomputation of translation rules. Instead it matches each input sentence to the full database of translation examples before extracting translation rules online. This has the merit of maximizing the information available when creating and combining translation rules, while retaining the ability to produce excellent translations for input sentences similar to an existing translation example.

The system is mostly developed in C++ and incorporates a web-based translation interface for ease of use. The web interface (see Figure 1) also displays information useful for error analysis such as the list of translation examples used. Experiments are facilitated through the inclusion of a curses-based graphical interface for performing tuning and evaluation. The decoder supports multiple threads.

We are currently making preparations for the project to be released with an open-source license. The code will be available at http://nlp.ist.i.kyoto-u.ac.jp/kyotoebmt/.

2 System Overview

Figure 2 shows the basic structure of the proposed translation pipeline.

The training process begins with parsing and aligning parallel sentences from the train-

Proceedings of 52nd Annual Meeting of the Association for Computational Linguistics: System Demonstrations, pages 79–84,
Baltimore, Maryland USA, June 23-24, 2014.

Figure 1: A screenshot of the web interface showing a Japanese-English translation. The interface provides the source and target side dependency tree, as well as the list of examples used with their alignments. The web interface facilitates easy and intuitive error analysis, and can be used as a tool for computer-aided translation.

ing corpus. Alignment uses a Bayesian subtree alignment model based on dependency trees. This contains a tree-based reordering model and can capture non-local reorderings, which sequential word-based models often cannot handle effectively. The alignments are then used to build an example database ('translation memory') containing 'examples' or 'treelets' that form the hypotheses to be combined during decoding.

Translation is performed by first parsing an input sentence then searching for treelets matching entries in the example database. The retrieved treelets are combined by a decoder that optimizes a log linear model score. The example retrieval and decoding steps are explained in more detail in sections 3 and 4 respectively. The choice of features and the tuning of the log linear model is described in section 5.

Figure 3 shows the process of combining examples matching the input tree to create an output sentence.

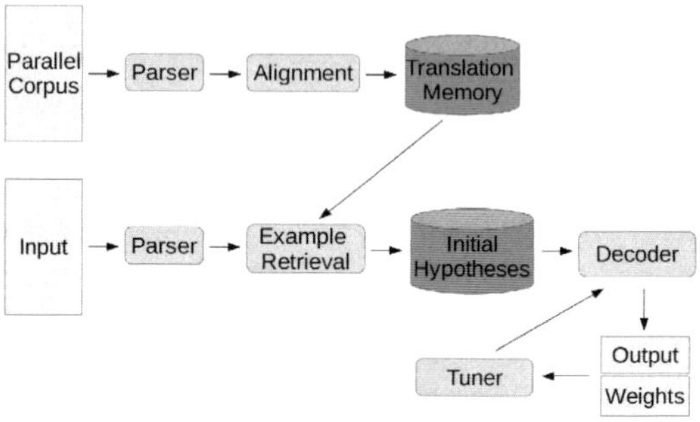

Figure 2: Translation pipeline. An example database is first trained from a parallel corpus. Translation is performed by the decoder, which combines initial hypotheses generated by the example retrieval module. Weights can be improved with batch tuning.

3 Example retrieval and translation hypothesis construction

An important characteristic of our system is that we do not extract and store translation rules in advance: the alignment of translation examples is performed offline. However, for a given input sentence i, the steps for finding examples partially matching i and extracting their translation hypotheses is an online process. This approach could be considered to be more faithful to the original EBMT approach advocated by Nagao (1984). It has already been proposed for phrase-based (Callison-Burch et al., 2005), hierarchical (Lopez, 2007), and syntax-based (Cromières and Kurohashi, 2011) systems. It does not however, seem to be very commonly integrated in syntax-based MT.

This approach has several benefits. The first is that we are not required to impose a limit on the size of translation hypotheses. Systems extracting rules in advance typically restrict the size and number of extracted rules for fear of becoming unmanageable. In particular, if an input sentence is the same or very similar to one of our translation examples, we will be able to retrieve a perfect translation. A second advantage is that we can make use of the full context of the example to assign features and scores to each translation hypothesis.

The main drawback of our approach is that it can be computationally more expensive to retrieve arbitrarily large matchings in the ex-

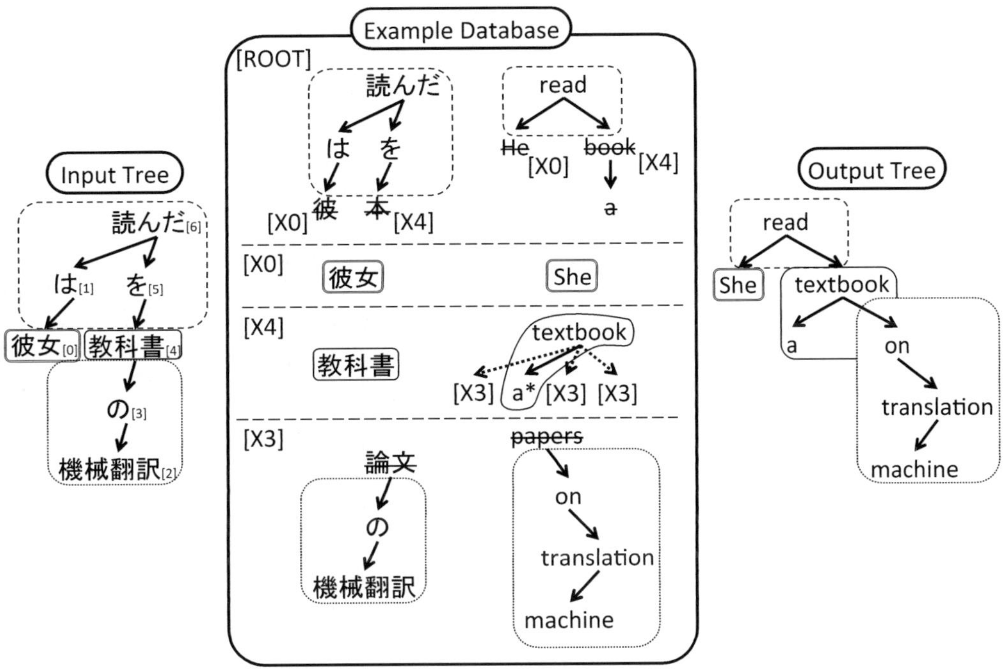

Figure 3: The process of translation. The source sentence is parsed and matching subtrees from the example database are retrieved. From the examples, we extract translation hypotheses than can contain optional target words and several position for each non-terminals. For example the translation hypothesis containing "textbook" has three possible position for the non-terminal X3 (as a left-child before "a", as a left-child after "a" or as a right-child). The translation hypotheses are then combined during decoding. Choice of optional words and final Non-Terminal positions is also done during decoding.

ample database online than it is to match precomputed rules. We use the techniques described in (Cromières and Kurohashi, 2011) to perform this step as efficiently as possible.

Once we have found an example translation (s, t) for which s partially matches i, we proceed to extract a translation hypothesis from it. A translation hypothesis is defined as a generic translation rule for a part p of the input sentence that is represented as a target-language treelet, with non-terminals representing the insertion positions for the translations of other parts of the sentence. A translation hypothesis is created from a translation example as follows:

1. We project the part of s that is matched into the target side t using the alignment of s and t. This is trivial if each word of s and t is aligned, but this is not typically the case. Therefore our translation hypotheses will often have some target words/nodes marked as *optionals*: this means that we will decide if they should be added to the final translation only at the moment of combination.

2. We insert the non-terminals as child nodes of the projected subtree. This is simple if i, s and t have the same structure and are perfectly aligned, but again this is not typically the case. A consequence is that we will sometimes have *several possible insertion positions* for each non-terminal. The choice of insertion position is again made during combination.

4 Decoding

After having extracted translation hypotheses for as many parts of the input tree as possible, we need to decide how to select and combine them. Our approach here is similar to what

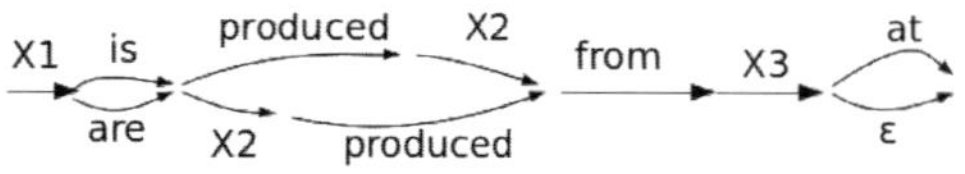

Figure 4: A translation hypothesis endoded as a lattice. This representation allows us to handle efficiently the ambiguities of our translation rules. Note that each path in this lattice corresponds to different choices of insertion position for X2, morphological forms of "be", and the optional insertion of "at".

has been proposed for Corpus-Based Machine Translation. We first choose a number of features and create a linear model scoring each possible combination of hypotheses (see Section 5). We then attempt to find the combination that maximizes this model score.

The combination of rules is constrained by the structure of the input dependency tree. If we only consider local features[1], then a simple bottom-up dynamic programming approach can efficiently find the optimal combination with linear $O(|\mathcal{H}|)$ complexity[2]. However, non-local features (such as language models) will force us to prune the search space. This pruning is done efficiently through a variation of cube-pruning (Chiang, 2007). We use KenLM[3] (Heafield, 2011) for computing the target language model score. Decoding is made more efficient by using some of the more advanced features of KenLM such as state-reduction ((Li and Khudanpur, 2008), (Heafield et al., 2011)) and rest-cost estimations(Heafield et al., 2012).

Compared with the original cube-pruning algorithm, our decoder is designed to handle an arbitrary number of non-terminals. In addition, as we have seen in Section 3, the translation hypotheses we initially extract from examples are ambiguous in term of which target word is going to be used and which will be the final position of each non-terminal. In order to handle such ambiguities, we use a lattice-based internal representation that can encode them efficiently (see Figure 4). This lattice representation also allows the decoder to make choices between various morphological variations of a word (e.g. be/is/are).

5 Features and Tuning

During decoding we use a linear model to score each possible combination of hypotheses. This linear model is based on a linear combination of both local features (local to each translation hypothesis) and non-local features (such as a 5-gram language model score of the final translation). The decoder considers in total a combination of 34 features, a selection of which are given below.

- Example penalty and example size
- Translation probability
- Language model score
- Optional words added/removed

The optimal weights for each feature are estimated using the Pairwise Ranking Optimization (PRO) algorithm (Hopkins and May, 2011) and parameter optimization with MegaM[4]. We use the implementation of PRO that is provided with the Moses SMT system and the default settings of MegaM.

6 Experiments

In order to evaluate our system, we conducted translation experiments on four language pairs: Japanese-English (JA–EN), English-Japanese (EN–JA), Japanese-Chinese (JA–ZH) and Chinese-Japanese (ZH–JA).

For Japanese-English, we evaluated on the NTCIR-10 PatentMT task data (patents) (Goto et al., 2013) and compared our system with the official baseline scores. For Japanese-Chinese, we used parallel scientific paper excerpts from the ASPEC[5] corpus and compared against the same baseline system as for Japanese-English. The corpora contain 3M parallel sentences for Japanese-English and 670K for Japanese-Chinese.

The two baseline systems are based on the open-source GIZA++/Moses pipeline. The baseline labeled "Moses" uses the classic phrase-based engine, while "Moses-Hiero" uses the Hierarchical Phrase-Based decoder. These

[1]The score of a combination will be the sum of the local scores of each translation hypothesis.

[2]$\mathcal{H}$ = set of translation hypotheses

[3]http://kheafield.com/code/kenlm/

[4]http://www.umiacs.umd.edu/~hal/megam/

[5]http://orchid.kuee.kyoto-u.ac.jp/ASPEC/

System	JA–EN	EN–JA	JA–ZH	ZH–JA
Moses	28.86	**33.61**	32.90	**42.79**
Moses-Hiero	28.56	32.98	—	—
Proposed	**29.00**	32.15	**32.99**	37.64

Table 1: Scores

System	BLEU	Translation
Moses	31.09	Further, the expansion stroke, the sectional area of the inner tube 12, and the oil is supplied to the lower oil chamber S2 from the oil reservoir chamber R × stroke.
Moses-Hiero	21.49	Also, the expansion stroke, the cross-sectional area of the inner tube 12 × stroke of oil supplied from the oil reservoir chamber R lower oil chamber S2.
Proposed	44.99	Further in this expansion stroke, the oil at an amount obtained by multiplying cross sectional area of the inner tube 12 from the oil reservoir chamber R is resupplied to the lower oil chamber S2.
Reference	100.00	In this expansion stroke, oil in an amount obtained by multiplying the cross sectional area of the inner tube 12 by the stroke is resupplied from the upper oil reservoir chamber R to the lower oil chamber S2.

Table 2: Example of JA–EN translation with better translation quality than baselines.

correspond to the highest performing official baselines for the NTCIR-10 PatentMT task.

As it appeared Moses was giving similar and slightly higher BLEU scores than Moses-Hiero for Japanese-English, we restricted evaluation to the standard settings for Moses for our Japanese-Chinese experiments.

The following dependency parsers were used. The scores in parentheses are the approximate parsing accuracies (micro-average), which were evaluated by hand on a random subset of sentences from the test data. The parsers were trained on domains different to those used in the experiments.

- English: NLParser[6] (92%) (Charniak and Johnson, 2005)
- Japanese: KNP (96%) (Kawahara and Kurohashi, 2006)
- Chinese: SKP (88%) (Shen et al., 2012)

6.1 Results

The results shown are for evaluation on the test set after tuning. Tuning was conducted over 50 iterations on the development set using an n-best list of length 500.

Table 2 shows an example sentence showing significant improvement over the baseline. In particular, non-local structure has been preserved by the proposed system, such as the modification of 'oil' by the 'in an amount... by the stroke' phrase. Another example is the incorrect location of '× stroke' in the Moses output. The proposed system produces a much more fluent output than the hierarchical-based baseline Moses-Hiero.

The proposed system also outperforms the baseline for JA–ZH, however falls short for ZH–JA. We believe this is due to the low quality of parsing for Chinese input.

The decoder requires on average 0.94 seconds per sentence when loading from precompiled hypothesis files. As a comparison, Moses (default settings) takes 1.78 seconds per sentence, loading from a binarized and filtered phrase table.

7 Conclusion

This paper introduces an example-based translation system exploiting both source and target dependency analysis and online example retrieving, allowing the availability of full translation examples at translation time.

We believe that the use of dependency parsing is important for accurate translation across distant language pairs, especially in settings such as ours with many long sentences. We have designed a complete translation frame-

[6] Converted to dependency parses with in-house tool.

work around this idea, using dependency-parsed trees at each step from alignment to example retrieval to example combination.

The current performance (BLEU) of our system is similar to (or even slightly better than) state-of-the-art open-source SMT systems. As we have been able to obtain steady performance improvements during development, we are hopeful that this trend will continue and we will shortly obtain even better results. Future plans include enriching the feature set, adding a tree-based language model and considering forest input for multiple parses to provide robustness against parsing errors. When the code base is sufficiently stable, we intend to release the entire system as open-source, in the hope of providing a more syntactically-focused alternative to existing open-source SMT engines.

Acknowledgements

This work was partially supported by the Japan Science and Technology Agency. The first author is supported by a Japanese Government (MEXT) research scholarship. We would like to thank the anonymous reviewers.

References

Eugene Charniak and Mark Johnson. 2005. Coarse-to-Fine n-Best Parsing and MaxEnt Discriminative Reranking. In *Proceedings of the 43rd Annual Meeting of the Association for Computational Linguistics, ACL 2005.*

Fabien Cromières and Sadao Kurohashi. 2011. Efficient retrieval of tree translation examples for syntax-based machine translation. In *Proceedings of the 2011 Conference on Empirical Methods in Natural Language Processing.*

Isao Goto, Ka Po Chow, Bin Lu, Eiichiro Sumita and Benjamin Tsou. 2013. Overview of the Patent Machine Translation Task at the NTCIR-10 Workshop. In *Proceedings of the 10th NTCIR Workshop Meeting on Evaluation of Information Access Technologies (NTCIR-10).*

Mark Hopkins and Jonathan May. 2011. Tuning as Ranking. In *Proceedings of the 2011 Conference on Empirical Methods in Natural Language Processing.*

Daisuke Kawahara and Sadao Kurohashi. 2006. A Fully-Lexicalized Probabilistic Model for Japanese Syntactic and Case Structure Analysis. In *Proceedings of the Human Language Technology Conference of the NAACL.*

Makoto Nagao. 1984. A framework of a mechanical translation between Japanese and English by analogy principle. In *A. Elithorn and R. Banerji. Artificial and Human Intelligence.*

Toshiaki Nakazawa and Sadao Kurohashi. 2012. Alignment by bilingual generation and monolingual derivation. In *Proceedings of COLING 2012.*

Mo Shen, Daisuke Kawahara and Sadao Kurohashi. 2012. A Reranking Approach for Dependency Parsing with Variable-sized Subtree Features. In *Proceedings of 26th Pacific Asia Conference on Language Information and Computing.*

Chris Callison-Burch, Colin Bannard, and Josh Schroeder. Scaling phrase-based statistical machine translation to larger corpora and longer phrases. In *Proceedings of the 43rd Annual Meeting on Association for Computational Linguistics*, pages 255–262. Association for Computational Linguistics, 2005.

David Chiang. 2007. Hierarchical phrase-based translation. In *Computational Linguistics.*

Kenneth Heafield. 2011. KenLM: faster and smaller language model queries. In *Proceedings of the EMNLP 2011 Sixth Workshop on Statistical Machine Translation*, 2011.

Kenneth Heafield, Hieu Hoang, Philipp Koehn, Tetsuo Kiso, and Marcello Federico. 2011. Left language model state for syntactic machine translation. In *Proceedings of the International Workshop on Spoken Language Translation*, 2011.

Kenneth Heafield, Philipp Koehn, and Alon Lavie. 2012. Language model rest costs and space-efficient storage. In *Proceedings of the Joint Conference on Empirical Methods in Natural Language Processing and Computational Natural Language Learning*, 2012.

Zhifei Li and Sanjeev Khudanpur. 2008. A scalable decoder for parsing-based machine translation with equivalent language model state maintenance. In *Proceedings of the Second Workshop on Syntax and Structure in Statistical Translation.* Association for Computational Linguistics, 2008.

Adam Lopez. 2007. Hierarchical phrase-based translation with suffix arrays. In *EMNLP-CoNLL* 2007.

Chris Quirk, Arul Menezes, and Colin Cherry. 2005. Dependency Treelet Translation: Syntactically Informed Phrasal SMT. In *Proceedings of the 43rd Annual Meeting on Association for Computational Linguistics.* Association for Computational Linguistics, 2005.

kLogNLP: Graph Kernel–based Relational Learning of Natural Language

Mathias Verbeke◇ **Paolo Frasconi**♠ **Kurt De Grave**◇ **Fabrizio Costa**♣ **Luc De Raedt**◇

◇ Department of Computer Science, KU Leuven, Belgium
{mathias.verbeke, kurt.degrave, luc.deraedt}@cs.kuleuven.be
♠ Dipartimento di Sistemi e Informatica, Università degli Studi di Firenze, Italy,
p-f@dsi.unifi.it
♣ Institut für Informatik, Albert-Ludwigs-Universität, Germany,
costa@informatik.uni-freiburg.de

Abstract

kLog is a framework for kernel-based learning that has already proven successful in solving a number of relational tasks in natural language processing. In this paper, we present *kLogNLP*, a natural language processing module for kLog. This module enriches kLog with NLP-specific preprocessors, enabling the use of existing libraries and toolkits within an elegant and powerful declarative machine learning framework. The resulting relational model of the domain can be extended by specifying additional relational features in a declarative way using a logic programming language. This declarative approach offers a flexible way of experimentation and a way to insert domain knowledge.

1 Introduction

kLog (Frasconi et al., 2012) is a logical and relational language for kernel-based learning. It has already proven successful for several tasks in computer vision (Antanas et al., 2012; Antanas et al., 2013) and natural language processing. For example, in the case of binary sentence classification, we have shown an increase of 1.2 percent in F1-score on the best performing system in the CoNLL 2010 Shared Task on hedge cue detection (Wikipedia dataset) (Verbeke et al., 2012a). On a sentence labeling task for evidence-based medicine, a multi-class multi-label classification problem, kLog showed improved results over both the state-of-the-art CRF-based system of Kim et al. (2011) and a memory-based benchmark (Verbeke et al., 2012b). Also for spatial relation extraction from natural language, kLog has shown to provide a flexible relational representation to model the task domain (Kordjamshidi et al., 2012).

kLog has two distinguishing features. First, it is able to transform relational into graph-based representations, which allows to incorporate structural features into the learning process. Subsequently, kernel methods are used to work in an extended high-dimensional feature space, which is much richer than most of the direct propositionalisation approaches. Second, it uses the logic programming language Prolog for defining and using (additional) background knowledge, which renders the model very interpretable and provides more insights into the importance of individual (structural) features.

These properties prove especially advantageous in the case of NLP. The graphical approach of kLog is able to exploit the full relational representation that is often a natural way to express language structures, and in this way allows to fully exploit contextual features. On top of this relational learning approach, the declarative feature specification allows to include additional background knowledge, which is often essential for solving NLP problems.

In this paper, we present *kLogNLP*[1], an NLP module for kLog. Starting from a dataset and a declaratively specified model of the domain (based on entity-relationship modeling from database theory), it transforms the dataset into a graph-based relational format. We propose a general model that fits most tasks in NLP, which can be extended by specifying additional relational features in a declarative way. The resulting relational representation then serves as input for kLog, and thus results in a full relational learning pipeline for NLP.

kLogNLP is most related to Learning-Based Java (LBJ) (Rizzolo and Roth, 2010) in that it offers a declarative pipeline for modeling and learning tasks in NLP. The aims are similar, namely abstracting away the technical details from the programmer, and leaving him to reason about the modeling. However, whereas LBJ focuses more on the learning side (by the specification of constraints on features which are reconciled at inference time, using the constrained conditional

[1] Software available at http://dtai.cs.kuleuven.be/klognlp

Proceedings of 52nd Annual Meeting of the Association for Computational Linguistics: System Demonstrations, pages 85–90,
Baltimore, Maryland USA, June 23-24, 2014.

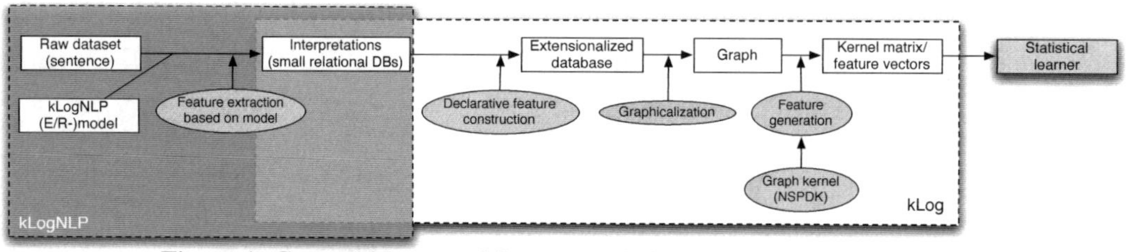

Figure 1: General kLog workflow extended with the kLogNLP module

model framework), due to its embedding in kLog, kLogNLP focuses on the relational modeling, in addition to declarative feature construction and feature generation using graph kernels. kLog in itself is related to several frameworks for relational learning, for which we refer the reader to (Frasconi et al., 2012).

The remainder of this paper is organized according to the general kLog workflow, preceded with the kLogNLP module, as outlined in Figure 1. In Section 2, we discuss the modeling of the data, and present a general relational data model for NLP tasks. Also the option to declaratively construct new features using logic programming is outlined. In the subsequent parts, we will illustrate the remaining steps in the kLog pipeline, namely graphicalization and feature generation (Section 3), and learning (Section 4) in an NLP setting. The last section draws conclusions and presents ideas for future work.

2 Data Modeling

kLog employs a learning from interpretations setting (De Raedt et al., 2008). In learning from interpretations, each interpretation is a set of tuples that are true in the example, and can be seen as a small relational database. Listing 3, to be discussed later, shows a concise example. In the NLP setting, an interpretation most commonly corresponds to a document or a sentence. The scope of an interpretation is either determined by the task (e.g., for document classification, the interpretations will at least need to comprise a single document), or by the amount of context that is taken into account (e.g., in case the task is sentence classification, the interpretation can either be a single sentence, or a full document, depending on the scope of the context that you want to take into account).

Since kLog is rooted in database theory, the modeling of the problem domain is done using an entity-relationship (E/R) model (Chen, 1976). It gives an abstract representation of the interpretations. E/R models can be seen as a tool that is tailored to model the domain at hand. As the name indicates, E/R models consist of entities, which we will represent as purple rectangles, and relations, represented as orange diamonds. Both entities and relations can have several attributes (yellow ovals). Key attributes (green ovals) uniquely identify an instance of an entity. We will now discuss the E/R model we propose as a starting point in the kLogNLP pipeline.

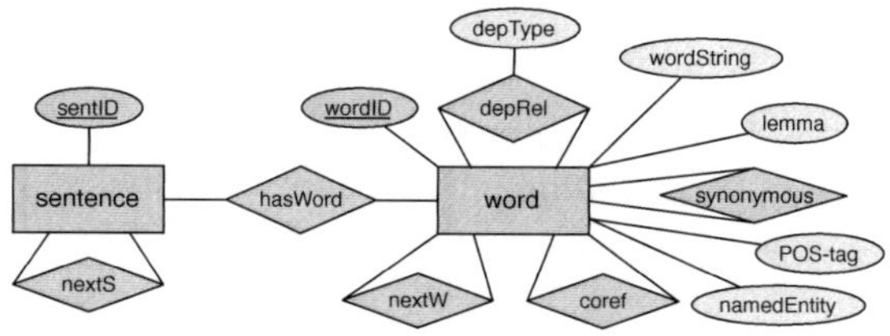

Figure 2: Entity-relationship diagram of the kLogNLP model

2.1 kLogNLP model

Since in NLP, most tasks are situated at either the document, sentence, or token level, we propose the E/R model in Figure 2 as a general domain model suitable for most settings. It is able to represent interpretations of documents as a sequence (`nextS`) of `sentence` entities, which are composed of a sequence (`nextW`) of `word` entities. Next to the sequence relations, also the dependency relations between words (`depRel`) are taken into account, where each relation has its type (`depType`) as a property. Furthermore, also the coreference relationship between words or phrases (`coref`) and possibly synonymy relations (`synonymous`) are taken into account. The entities in our model also have a primary key, namely `wordID` and `sentID` for words and sentences respectively. Additional properties can be attached to words such as the `wordString` itself, its `lemma` and `POS-tag`, and an indication whether the word is a `namedEntity`.

This E/R model of Figure 2 is coded declaratively in kLog as shown in Listing 1. The kLog syntax is an extension of the logical programming language Prolog. In the next step this script will be used for feature extraction and generation. Every entity or relationship is declared with the keyword `signature`. Each signature is of a certain type; either `extensional` or `intensional`. kLogNLP only acts at the extensional level. Each signature is characterized by a name and a list of typed arguments. There are three possible argument types. First of all, the type can be the name of an entity set which has been declared in another signature (e.g., line 4 in Listing 1; the `nextS` signature represents the sequence relation between two entities of type `sentence`, namely `sent_1` and `sent_2`). The type `self` is used to denote the primary key of an entity. An example is `word_id` (line 6), which denotes the unique identifier of a certain word in the interpretation. The last possible type is `property`, in case the argument is neither a reference to another entity nor a primary key (e.g., `postag`, line 9).

We will first discuss extensional signatures, and the automated extensional feature extraction provided by kLogNLP, before illustrating how the user can further enrich the model with intensional predicates.

```
1  begin_domain.
2  signature sentence(sent_id::self)::
       extensional.
3
4  signature nextS(sent_1::sentence, sent_2
       ::sentence)::extensional.
5
6  signature word(word_id::self,
7          word_string::property,
8          lemma::property,
9          postag::property,
10         namedentity::property
11         )::extensional.
12
13 signature nextW(word_1::word, word_2::
       word)::extensional.
14
15 signature corefPhrase(coref_id::self)::
       extensional.
16 signature isPartOfCorefPhrase(
       coref_phrase::corefPhrase, word::
       word)::extensional.
17 signature coref(coref_phrase_1::
       corefPhrase, coref_phrase_2::
       corefPhrase)::extensional.
18
19 signature synonymous(word_1::word,
       word_2::word)::extensional.
20
21 signature dependency(word_1::word,
22          word_2::word,
23          dep_rel::property
24          )::extensional.
25
26 kernel_points([word]).
27 end_domain.
```

Listing 1: Declarative representation of the kLogNLP model

2.2 Extensional Feature Extraction

kLog assumes a closed-world, which means that atoms that are not known to be true, are assumed to be false. For extensional signatures, this entails that all ground atoms need to be listed explicitly in the relational database of interpretations. These atoms are generated automatically by the kLogNLP module based on the kLog script and the input dataset. Considering the defined attributes and relations in the model presented in Listing 1, the module interfaces with NLP toolkits to preprocess the data to the relational format. The user can remove unnecessary extensional signatures or modify the number of attributes given in the standard kLogNLP script as given in Listing 1 according to the needs of the task under consideration.

An important choice is the inclusion of the `sentence` signature. By inclusion, the granularity of the interpretation is set to the document level, which implies that more context can be taken into account. By excluding this signature, the granularity of the interpretation is set to the sentence level.

Currently, kLogNLP interfaces with the following NLP toolkits:

NLTK The Python Natural Language Toolkit (NLTK) (Bird et al., 2009) offers a suite of text processing libraries for tokenization, stemming, tagging and parsing, and offers an interface to WordNet.

Stanford CoreNLP Stanford CoreNLP[2] provides POS tagging, NER, parsing and coreference resolution functionality.

The preprocessing toolkit to be used can be set using the kLogNLP flags mechanism, as illustrated by line 3 of Listing 2. Subsequently, the `dataset` predicate (illustrated in line 4 of Listing 2) calls kLogNLP to preprocess a given dataset[3]. This is done according to the specified kLogNLP model, i.e., the necessary preprocessing modules to be called in the preprocessing toolkit are determined based on the presence of the entities, relationships, and their attributes in the kLogNLP script. For example, the presence

[2] http://nlp.stanford.edu/software/corenlp.shtml

[3] Currently supported dataset formats are directories consisting of (one or more) plain text files or XML files consisting of sentence and/or document elements.

of `namedentity` as a property of `word` results in the addition of a named entity recognizer in the preprocessing toolkit. The resulting set of interpretations is output to a given file. In case several instantiations of a preprocessing module are available in the toolkit, the preferred one can be chosen by setting the name of the property accordingly. The names as given in Listing 1 outline the standard settings for each module. For instance, in case the Snowball stemmer is preferred above the standard (Wordnet) lemmatizer in NLTK, it can be selected by changing `lemma` into `snowball` as name for the word lemma property (line 8).

```
experiment :-
    % kLogNLP
    klognlp_flag(preprocessor,
        stanfordnlp),
    dataset('/home/hedgecuedetection/
        train/','trainingset.pl'),
    attach('trainingset.pl'),
    % Kernel parametrization
    new_feature_generator(my_fg,nspdk),
    klog_flag(my_fg,radius,1),
    klog_flag(my_fg,distance,1),
    klog_flag(my_fg,match_type, hard),
    % Learner parametrization
    new_model(my_model,libsvm_c_svc),
    klog_flag(my_model,c,0.1),
    kfold(target, 10, my_model, my_fg).
```

Listing 2: Full predicate for 10-fold classification experiment

Each interpretation can be regarded as a small relational database. We will illustrate the extensional feature extraction step on the CoNLL-2010 dataset on hedge cue detection, a binary classification task where the goal is to detect uncertainty in sentences. This task is situated at the sentence level, so we left out the `sentence` and `nextS` signatures, as no context from other sentences was taken into account. A part of a resulting interpretation is shown in Listing 3.

```
word(w1,often,often,rb,0,1).
depRel(w1,w5,adv).
nextW(w1,w2).
word(w2,the,the,dt,0,2).
depRel(w2,w4,nmod).
nextW(w2,w3).
word(w3,response,response,nn,0,3).
nextW(w3,w4).
depRel(w3,w4,nmod).
word(w4,may,may,md,0,5).
nextW(w4,w5).
```

Listing 3: Part of an interpretation

Optionally, additional extensional signatures can easily be added to the knowledge base by the user, as deemed suitable for the task under consideration. At each level of granularity (document, sentence, or word level), the user is given the corresponding interpretation and entity IDs, with which additional extensional facts can be added using the dedicated Python classes. We will now turn to declarative feature construction. The following steps are inherently part of the kLog framework. We will briefly illustrate their use in the context of NLP.

2.3 Declarative Feature Construction

The kLog script presented in Listing 1 can now be extended using declarative feature construction with *intensional* signatures. In contrast to extensional signatures, intensional signatures introduce novel relations using a mechanism resembling deductive databases. This type of signatures is mostly used to add domain knowledge about the task at hand. The ground atoms are defined implicitly using Prolog definite clauses.

For example, in case of sentence labeling for evidence-based medicine, the lemma of the root word proved to be a distinguishing feature (Verbeke et al., 2012b), which can be expressed as

```
signature lemmaRoot(sent_id::sentence,
    lemmaOfRoot::property)::intensional.
lemmaRoot(S,L) :-
    hasWord(S, I),
    word(I,_,L,_,_,_),
    depRel(I,_,root).
```

Also more complex features can be constructed. For example, section headers in documents (again in the case of sentence labeling using document context) can be identified as follows:

```
hasHeaderWord(S,X) :-
    word(W,X,_,_,_,_),
    hasWord(S,W),
    (atom(X) -> name(X,C) ; C = X),
    length(C,Len),
    Len > 4,
    all_upper(C).

signature isHeaderSentence(sent_id::
    sentence)::intensional.
isHeaderSentence(S) :-
    hasHeaderWord(S,_).

signature hasSectionHeader(sent_id::
    sentence, header::property)::
    intensional.
hasSectionHeader(S,X) :-
    nextS(S1,S),
    hasHeaderWord(S1,X).
hasSectionHeader(S,X) :-
    nextS(S1,S),
    not isHeaderSentence(S),
    once(hasSectionHeader(S1,X)).
```

In this case, first the sentences that contain a header word are identified using the helper pred-

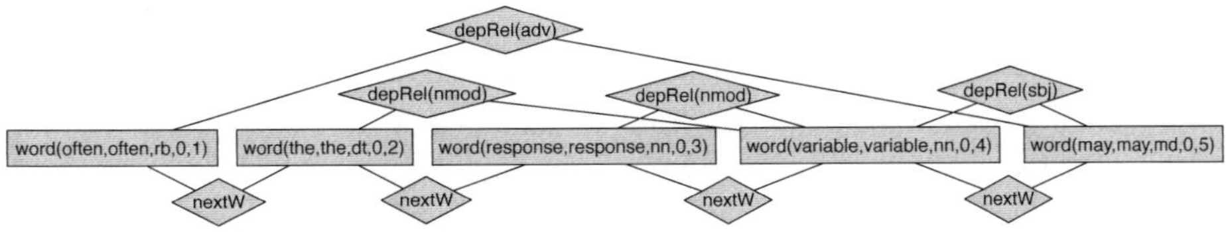

Figure 3: Graphicalization of the (partial) interpretation in Listing 3. For the sake of clarity, attributes of entities and relationships are depicted inside the respective entity or relationship.

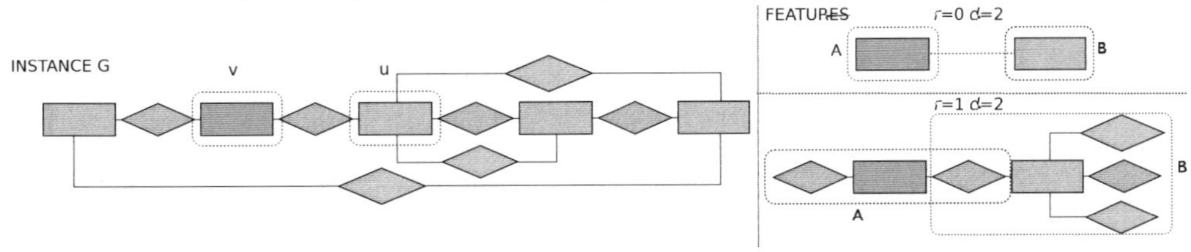

Figure 4: Illustration of the NSPDK feature concept. Left: instance G with 2 vertices v, u as roots for neighborhood subgraphs (A, B) at distance 2. Right: some of the neighborhood pairs, which form the NSPDK features, at distance $d = 2$ and radius $r = 0$ and 1 respectively. Note that neighborhood subgraphs can overlap.

icate `hasHeaderWord`, where a header word is defined as an upper case string that has more than four letters (lines 1-7). Next, all sentences that represent a section header are identified using the intensional signature `isHeaderSentence` (lines 9-11), and each sentence in the paragraphs following a particular section header is labeled with this header, using the `hasSectionHeader` predicate (lines 13-20).

Due to the relational approach, the span can be very large. Furthermore, since these features are defined declaratively, there is no need to reprocess the dataset each time a new feature is introduced, which renders experimentation very flexible[4].

3 Graphicalization and Feature Generation

In this step, a technique called *graphicalization* transforms the relational representations from the previous step into graph-based ones and derives features from a grounded entity/relationship diagram using graph kernels. This can be interpreted as unfolding the E/R diagram over the data. An example of the graphicalization of the interpretation part in Listing 3 can be found in Figure 3.

From the resulting graphs, features can be extracted using a feature generation technique that is based on Neighborhood Subgraph Pairwise Distance Kernel (NSPDK) (Costa and De Grave, 2010), a particular type of graph kernel. Informally the idea of this kernel is to decompose a graph into small neighborhood subgraphs of increasing radii $r \leq r_{max}$. Then, all pairs of such subgraphs whose roots are at a distance not greater than $d \leq d_{max}$ are considered as individual features. The kernel notion is finally given as the fraction of features in common between two graphs.

Formally, the kernel is defined as:

$$\kappa_{r,d}(G, G') = \sum_{\substack{A,B \in R^{-1}_{r,d}(G) \\ A',B' \in R^{-1}_{r,d}(G')}} \mathbf{1}_{A \cong A'} \cdot \mathbf{1}_{B \cong B'} \quad (1)$$

where $R^{-1}_{r,d}(G)$ indicates the multiset of all pairs of neighborhoods of radius r with roots at distance d that exist in G, and where $\mathbf{1}$ denotes the indicator function and $\cong$ the isomorphism between graphs. For the full details, we refer the reader to (Costa and De Grave, 2010). The neighborhood pairs are illustrated in Figure 4 for a distance of 2 between two arbitrary roots (v and u).

In kLog, the feature set is generated in a combinatorial fashion by explicitly enumerating all pairs of neighborhood subgraphs; this yields a high-dimensional feature space that is much richer than most of the direct propositionalization approaches. The result is an extended high-dimensional feature space on which a statistical learning algorithm can be applied. The feature generator is initialized using the `new_feature_generator` predicate and hyperparameters (e.g., maximum distance and radius, and match type) can be set using the kLog flags mechanism (Listing 2, lines 6-10).

[4]Note that changes in the *extensional* signatures do require reprocessing the dataset. However, for different runs of an experiment with varying parameters for the feature generator or the learner, kLogNLP uses a caching mechanism to check if the extensional signatures have changed, when calling the `dataset` predicate.

4 Learning

In the last step, different learning tasks can be performed on the resulting extended feature space. To this end, kLog interfaces with several solvers, including LibSVM (Chang and Lin, 2011) and SVM SGD (Bottou, 2010). Lines 11-15 (Listing 2) illustrate the initialization of LibSVM and its use for 10-fold cross-validation.

5 Conclusions and Future Work

In this paper, we presented kLogNLP, a natural language processing module for kLog. Based on an entity-relationship representation of the domain, it transforms a dataset into the graph-based relational format of kLog. The basic kLogNLP model can be easily extended with additional background knowledge by adding relations using the declarative programming language Prolog. This offers a more flexible way of experimentation, as new features can be constructed on top of existing ones without the need to reprocess the dataset. In future work, interfaces will be added to other (domain-specific) NLP frameworks (e.g., the BLLIP parser with the self-trained biomedical parsing model (McClosky, 2010)) and additional dataset formats will be supported.

Acknowledgments

This research is funded by the Research Foundation Flanders (FWO project G.0478.10 - Statistical Relational Learning of Natural Language). KDG was supported by ERC StG 240186 "MiGraNT".

References

Laura Antanas, Paolo Frasconi, Fabrizio Costa, Tinne Tuytelaars, and Luc De Raedt. 2012. A relational kernel-based framework for hierarchical image understanding. In *Lecture Notes in Computer Science,*, pages 171–180. Springer, November.

Laura Antanas, McElory Hoffmann, Paolo Frasconi, Tinne Tuytelaars, and Luc De Raedt. 2013. A relational kernel-based approach to scene classification. *IEEE Workshop on Applications of Computer Vision*, 0:133–139.

Steven Bird, Ewan Klein, and Edward Loper. 2009. *Natural Language Processing with Python*. O'Reilly Media, Inc., 1st edition.

Léon Bottou. 2010. Large-scale machine learning with stochastic gradient descent. In *Proc. of the 19th International Conference on Computational Statistics (COMPSTAT'2010)*, pages 177–187. Springer.

Chih-Chung Chang and Chih-Jen Lin. 2011. LIBSVM: A library for support vector machines. *ACM Transactions on Intelligent Systems and Technology*, 2:27:1–27:27. Software available at `http://www.csie.ntu.edu.tw/~cjlin/libsvm`.

Peter Pin-Shan Chen. 1976. The entity-relationship model - toward a unified view of data. *ACM Trans. Database Syst.*, 1(1):9–36, March.

Fabrizio Costa and Kurt De Grave. 2010. Fast neighborhood subgraph pairwise distance kernel. In *Proc. of the 26th International Conference on Machine Learning,*, pages 255–262. Omnipress.

Luc De Raedt, Paolo Frasconi, Kristian Kersting, and Stephen Muggleton, editors. 2008. *Probabilistic Inductive Logic Programming - Theory and Applications*, volume 4911 of *Lecture Notes in Computer Science*. Springer.

Paolo Frasconi, Fabrizio Costa, Luc De Raedt, and Kurt De Grave. 2012. klog: A language for logical and relational learning with kernels. *CoRR*, abs/1205.3981.

Su Kim, David Martinez, Lawrence Cavedon, and Lars Yencken. 2011. Automatic classification of sentences to support evidence based medicine. *BMC Bioinformatics*, 12(Suppl 2):S5.

Parisa Kordjamshidi, Paolo Frasconi, Martijn van Otterlo, Marie-Francine Moens, and Luc De Raedt. 2012. Relational learning for spatial relation extraction from natural language. In *Inductive Logic Programming*, pages 204–220. Springer.

David McClosky. 2010. *Any Domain Parsing: Automatic Domain Adaptation for Natural Language Parsing*. Ph.D. thesis, Brown University, Providence, RI, USA. AAI3430199.

N. Rizzolo and D. Roth. 2010. Learning based java for rapid development of nlp systems. In *LREC*, Valletta, Malta, 5.

Mathias Verbeke, Paolo Frasconi, Vincent Van Asch, Roser Morante, Walter Daelemans, and Luc De Raedt. 2012a. Kernel-based logical and relational learning with kLog for hedge cue detection. In *Proc. of the 21st International Conference on Inductive Logic Programming*, pages 347–357. Springer, March.

Mathias Verbeke, Vincent Van Asch, Roser Morante, Paolo Frasconi, Walter Daelemans, and Luc De Raedt. 2012b. A statistical relational learning approach to identifying evidence based medicine categories. In *Proc. of the 2012 Joint Conference on Empirical Methods in Natural Language Processing and Computational Natural Language Learning*, pages 579–589. ACL.

Automatic Annotation Suggestions and Custom Annotation Layers in WebAnno

Seid Muhie Yimam[1] Richard Eckart de Castilho[2] Iryna Gurevych[2,3] Chris Biemann[1]
(1) FG Language Technology, Dept. of Computer Science, Technische Universität Darmstadt
(2) Ubiquitous Knowledge Processing Lab (UKP-TUDA)
Dept. of Computer Science, Technische Universität Darmstadt
(3) Ubiquitous Knowledge Processing Lab (UKP-DIPF)
German Institute for Educational Research and Educational Information
`http://www.{lt,ukp}.tu-darmstadt.de`

Abstract

In this paper, we present a flexible approach to the efficient and exhaustive manual annotation of text documents. For this purpose, we extend WebAnno (Yimam et al., 2013) an open-source web-based annotation tool.[1] While it was previously limited to specific annotation layers, our extension allows adding and configuring an arbitrary number of layers through a web-based UI. These layers can be annotated separately or simultaneously, and support most types of linguistic annotations such as spans, semantic classes, dependency relations, lexical chains, and morphology. Further, we tightly integrate a generic machine learning component for automatic annotation suggestions of span annotations. In two case studies, we show that automatic annotation suggestions, combined with our split-pane UI concept, significantly reduces annotation time.

1 Introduction

The annotation of full text documents is a costly and time-consuming task. Thus, it is important to design annotation tools in such a way that the annotation process can happen as swiftly as possible. To this end, we extend WebAnno with the capability of suggesting annotations to the annotator.

A general-purpose web-based annotation tool can greatly lower the entrance barrier for linguistic annotation projects, as tool development costs and preparatory work are greatly reduced. WebAnno 1.0 only partially fulfilled desires regarding generality: Although it covered already more kinds of annotations than most other tools, it supported only a fixed set of customizable annotation layers (named entities, part-of-speech, lemmata, coreference, dependencies). Thus, we also remove a limitation of the tool, which was previously bound to specific, hardcoded annotation layers.

We have generalized the architecture to support three configurable generic structures: *spans*, *relations*, and *chains*. These support all of the original layers and allow the user to define arbitrary custom annotation layers based on either of these structures. Additionally, our approach allows maintaining multiple properties on annotations, e.g. to support morphological annotations, while previously only one property per annotation was supported.

Automatic suggestion of annotations is based on machine learning, which is common practice in annotation tools. However, most of existing web-based annotation tools, such as GATE (Cunningham et al., 2011) or brat (Stenetorp et al., 2012), depend on external preprocessing and postprocessing plugins or on web services. These tools have limitations regarding adaptability (difficulty to adapt to other annotation tasks), reconfigurability (generating a classifier when new features and training documents are available is complicated), and reusability (requires manual intervention to add newly annotated documents into the iteration).

For our approach, we assume that an annotator actually does manually verify all annotations to produce a completely labeled dataset. This task can be sped up by automatically suggesting annotations that the annotator may then either accept or correct. Note that this setup and its goal differs from an active learning scenario, where a system actively determines the most informative yet unannotated example to be labeled, in order to quickly arrive at a high-quality classifier that is then to be applied to large amounts of unseen data.

Our contribution is the integration of machine learning into the tool to support exhaustive an-

[1]WebAnno is open-source software under the terms of the Apache Software License 2.0. This paper describes v1.2: `http://webanno.googlecode.com`

Proceedings of 52nd Annual Meeting of the Association for Computational Linguistics: System Demonstrations, pages 91–96,
Baltimore, Maryland USA, June 23-24, 2014.

notation of documents providing a shorter loop than comparable tools (Cunningham et al., 2011; Stenetorp et al., 2012), because new documents are added to the training set as soon as they are completed by the annotators. The machine learning support currently applies to sequence classification tasks only. It is complemented by our extension allowing to define custom annotation layers, making it applicable to a wide range of annotation tasks with only little configuration effort.

Section 2 reviews related work about the utilization of automatic supports and customization of annotation schemes in existing annotation tools. The integration of automatic suggestions into WebAnno, the design principles followed, and two case studies are explained in Section 3. Section 4 presents the implementation of customizable annotation layers into the tool. Finally, Section 5 summarizes the main contributions and future directions of our work.

2 Related Work

Automatic annotation support The impact of using lexical and statistical resources to produce pre-annotation automatically to increase the annotation speed has been studied widely for various annotation tasks. For the task of medical named entity labeling, Lingren et al. (2013) investigate the impact of automatic suggestions on annotation speed and potential biases using dictionary-based annotations. This technique results in 13.83% to 21.5% time saving and in an inter-annotator agreement (IAA) increase by several percentage points.

WordFreak (Morton and LaCivita, 2003) includes an automation component, where instances with a low machine learning confidence are presented for annotation in an active learning setup. Beck et al. (2013) demonstrate that the use of active learning for machine translation reduces the annotation effort and show a reduced annotation load on three out of four datasets.

The GoldenGATE editor (Sautter et al., 2007) integrates NLP tools and assistance features for manual XML editing. The tool is used in correcting/editing an automatically annotated document with an editor where both text and XML markups are modified. GoldenGATE is merely used to facilitate the correction of an annotation while pre-annotation is conducted outside of the tool.

Automatic annotation support in brat (Stenetorp et al., 2012) was carried out for a semantic class disambiguation task to investigate how such automation facilitates the annotators' progress. They report a 15.4% reduction in total annotation time. However, the automation process in brat 1) depends on bulk annotation imports and web service configurations, which is labor intensive, 2) is task specific so that it requires a lot of effort to adapt it to different annotation tasks, 3) there is no way of using the corrected result for the next iteration of training the automatic tool.

The GATE Teamware (Bontcheva et al., 2013) automation component is most similar to our work. It is based either on plugins and externally trained classification models, or uses web services. Thus, it is highly task specific and requires extensive configuration. The automatic annotation suggestion component in our tool, in contrast, is easily configurable and adaptable to different annotation tasks and allows the use of annotations from the current annotation project.

Custom annotation layers Generic annotation data models are typically directed graph models (e.g. GATE, UIMA CAS (Götz and Suhre, 2004), GrAF (Ide and Suderman, 2007)). In addition, an annotation schema defines possible kinds of annotations, their properties and relations. While these models offer great expressiveness and flexibility, it is difficult to adequately transfer their power into a convenient annotation editor. For example, one schema may prescribe that the part-of-speech tag is a property on a *Token* annotation, another one may prescribe that the tag is a separate annotation, which is linked to the token. An annotator should not be exposed to these details in the UI and should be able to just edit a part-of-speech tag, ignorant of the internal representation.

This problem is typically addressed in two ways. Either, the full complexity of the annotation model is exposed to the annotator, or the annotation editor uses a simplified model. The first approach can easily lead to an unintuitive UI and make the annotation an inconvenient task. The second approach (e.g. as advocated by brat) requires the implementation of specific import and export filters to transform between the editor data model and the generic annotation data models.

We propose a third approach integrating a configurable mapping between a generic annotation model (UIMA CAS) and a simplified editing model (brat) directly into the annotation tool. Thus, we avoid exposing the full complexity of the generic model to the user and also avoid the necessity for implementing import/export filters. Similar approaches have already been used to map annotation models to visualization modules (cf. (Zeldes et al., 2009)), but have, to our knowledge, not been used in an annotation editor. Our approach is different from schema-based annotation editors (e.g. GATE), which employ a schema as a template of properties and controlled vocabularies that can be used to annotate documents, but which do not allow to map structures inherent in annotations, like relations or chains, to respective concepts in the UI.

3 Automatic Annotation Suggestions

It is the purpose of the automatic annotation suggestion component to increase the annotation efficiency, while maintaining the quality of annotations. The key design principle of our approach is a split-pane (Figure 1) that displays automatic annotation suggestions in the *suggestion pane* (lower part) and only verified or manual ones in the *annotation pane* (upper part). In this way, we force the annotators to review each automatic suggestion as to avoid overlooking wrong suggestions.

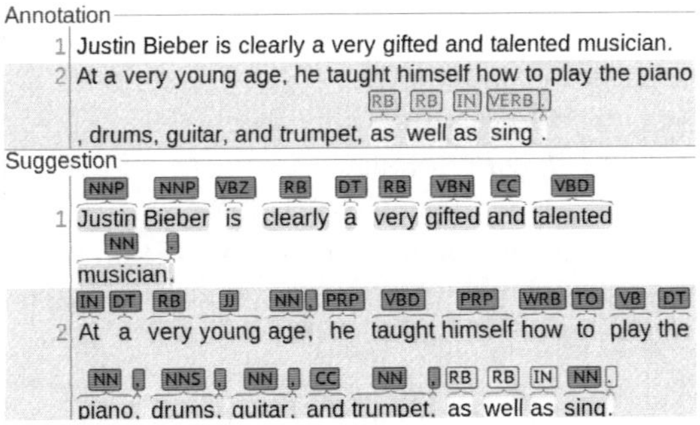

Figure 1: Split-pane UI. Upper: the *annotation pane*, which should be completed by the annotator. Lower: the *suggestion pane*, displaying predictions or automatic suggestions, and coding their status in color. This examples shows automatic suggestions for parts-of-speech. Unattended annotations are rendered in blue, accepted annotations in grey and rejected annotations in red. Here, the last five POS annotations have been attended, four have been accepted by clicking on the suggestion, and one was rejected by annotating it in the annotation pane.

3.1 Suggestion modes

We distinguish three modes of automatic annotation suggestion:

Correction mode In this mode, we import documents annotated by arbitrary external tools and present them to the user in the suggestion pane of the annotation page. This mode is specifically appropriate for annotation tasks where a pre-annotated document contains several possibilities for annotations in parallel, and the user's task is to select the correct annotation. This allows to leverage specialized external automatic annotation components, thus the tool is not limited to the integrated automation mechanism.

Repetition mode In this mode, further occurrences of a word annotated by the user are highlighted in the suggestion pane. To accept suggestions, the user can simply click on them in the suggestion pane. This basic – yet effective – suggestion is realized using simple string matching.

Learning mode For this mode, we have integrated MIRA (Crammer and Singer, 2003), an extension of the perceptron algorithm for online machine learning which allows for the automatic suggestions of span annotations. MIRA was selected because of its relatively lenient licensing, its good performance even on small amounts of data, and its capability of allowing incremental classifier updates. Results of automatic tagging are displayed in the suggestion pane. Our architecture is flexible to integrate further machine learning tools.

3.2 Suggestion Process

The workflow to set up an automatically supported annotation project consists of the following steps.

Importing annotation documents We can import documents with existing annotations (manual or automatic). The *annotation pane* of the automation page allows users to annotate documents and the *suggestion pane* is used for the automatic suggestion as shown in Figure 1. The suggestion pane facilitates accepting correct pre-annotations with minimal effort.

Configuring features For the machine learning tool, it is required to define classification features to train a classifier. We have designed a UI where a range of standard classification features for sequence tagging can be configured. The features include morphological features (prefixes, suffixes, and capitalization), n-grams, and other layers as a feature (for example POS annotation as a feature

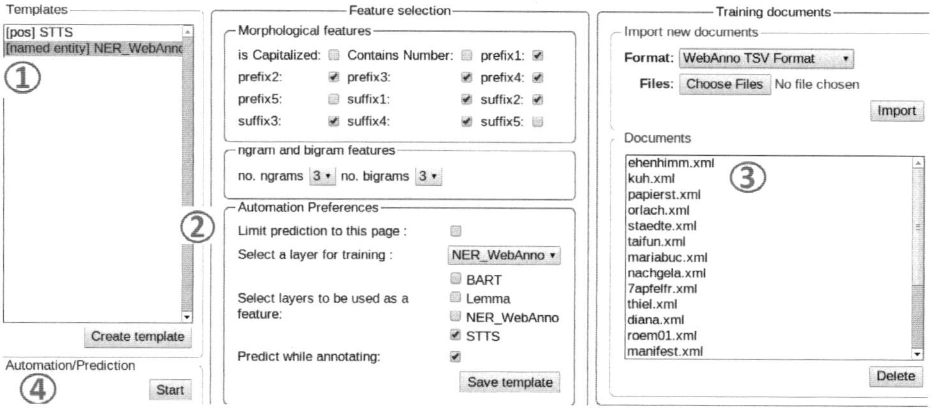

Figure 2: Configuring an annotation suggestion: 1) layers for automation, 2) different features, 3) training documents, 4) start training classifier.

for named entity recognition). While these standard features do not lead to state-of-the-art performance on arbitrary tasks, we have found them to perform very well for POS tagging, named entity recognition, and chunking. Figure 2 shows the feature configuration in the project settings.

Importing training documents We offer two ways of providing training documents: importing an annotated document in one of the supported file formats, such as CoNLL, TCF, or UIMA XMI; or using existing annotation documents in the same project that already have been annotated.

Starting the annotation suggestion Once features for a training layer are configured and training documents are available, automatic annotation is possible. The process can be started manually by the administrator from the automation settings page, and it will be automatically re-initiated when additional documents for training become available in the project. While the automatic annotation is running in the background, users still can work on the annotation front end without being affected. Training and creating a classifier will be repeated only when the feature configuration is changed or when a new training document is available.

Display results on the monitoring page After the training and automatic annotation are completed, detailed information about the training data such as the number of documents (sentence, tokens), features used for each layer, F-score on held-out data, and classification errors are displayed on the monitoring page, allowing an estimation whether the automatic suggestion is useful. The UI also shows the status of the training process (*not started, running, or finished*).

3.3 Case Studies

We describe two case studies that demonstrate language independence and flexibility with respect to sequence label types of our automatic annotation suggestions. In the first case study, we address the task of POS tagging for Amharic as an example of an under-resourced language. Second, we explore German named entity recognition.

3.3.1 Amharic POS tagging

Amharic is an under-resourced language in the Semitic family, mainly spoken in Ethiopia. POS tagging research for Amharic is mostly conducted as an academic exercise. The latest result reported by Gebre (2009) was about 90% accuracy using the Walta Information Center (WIC) corpus of about 210,000 tokens (1065 news documents). We intentionally do not use the corpus as training data because of the reported inconsistencies in the tagging process (Gebre, 2009). Instead, we manually annotate Amharic documents for POS tagging both to test the performance of the automation module and to produce POS-tagged corpora for Amharic. Based upon the work by Petrov et al. (2012) and Ethiopian Languages Research Center (ELRC) tagset, we have designed 11 POS tags equivalent to the Universal POS tags. The tag *DET* is not included as Amharic denotes definiteness as noun suffixes.

We collected some Amharic documents from an online news portal.[2] Preprocessing of Amharic documents includes the normalization of characters and tokenization (sentence and word bound-

[2] http://www.ethiopianreporter.com/

Figure 3: Example Amharic document. The red tags in the suggestion pane have not been confirmed by the annotator.

Figure 4: UI for custom annotation layers.

ary detection). Initially, we manually annotated 21 sentences. Using these, an iterative automatic annotation suggestion process was started until 300 sentences were fully annotated. We obtained an F-score of 0.89 with the final model. Hence the automatic annotation suggestion helps in decreasing the total annotation time, since the user has to manually annotate only one out of ten words, while being able to accept most automatic suggestions. Figure 3 shows such an Amharic document in WebAnno.

3.3.2 German Named Entity Recognition

A pilot Named Entity Recognition (NER) project for German was conducted by Benikova et al. (2014). We have used the dataset – about 31,000 sentences, over 41,000 NE annotations – for training NER. Using this dataset, an F-score of about 0.8 by means of automatic suggestions was obtained, which leads to an increase in annotation speed of about 21% with automatic suggestion.

4 Customs Annotation Layers

The tasks in which an annotation editor can be employed depends on the expressiveness of the underlying annotation model. However, fully exposing the expressive power in the UI can make the editor inconvenient to use.

We propose an approach that allows the user to configure a mapping of an annotation model to concepts well-supported in a web-based UI. In this way, we can avoid to expose all details of the annotation model in the UI, and remove the need to implement custom import/export filters.

WebAnno 1.0 employs a variant of the annotation UI provided by brat, which offers the concepts of *spans* and *arcs*. Based on these, WebAnno 1.2 implements five annotation layers: *named entity*, *part-of-speech*, *lemmata*, *co-reference*, and *dependencies*. In the new WebAnno version, we generalized the support for these five layers into three structural categories: *span*, *relation* (arc), and *chain*. Each of these categories is handled by a generic *adapter* which can be configured to simulate any of the original five layers. Based on this generalization, the user can now define custom layers (Figure 4).

Additionally, we introduced a new concept of constraints. For example, NER spans should not cross sentence boundaries and attach to whole tokens (not substrings of tokens). Such constraints not only help preventing the user from making invalid annotations, but can also offer extra convenience. We currently support four hard-coded constraints:

Lock to token offsets Defines if annotation boundaries must coincide with token boundaries, e.g. named entities, lemmata, part-of-speech, etc. For the user's convenience, the annotation is automatically expanded to include the full token, even if only a part of a token is selected during annotation (span/chain layers only).

Allow multiple tokens Some kinds of annotations may only cover a single token, e.g. part-of-speech, while others may cover multiple tokens, e.g. named entities (span/chain layers only).

Allow stacking Controls if multiple annotations of the same kind can be at the same location, e.g. if multiple lemma annotations are allowed per token. For the user's convenience, an existing annotation is replaced if a new annotation is created when stacking is not allowed.

Allow crossing sentence boundaries Certain annotations, e.g. named entities or dependency delations, may not cross sentence boundaries, while others need to, e.g. coreference chains.

Finally, we added the ability to define multiple properties for annotations to WebAnno. For example, this can be use to define a custom span-based *morphology* layer with multiple annotation properties such as *gender*, *number*, *case*, etc.

5 Conclusion and Outlook

We discussed two extensions of WebAnno: the tight and generic integration of automatic annotation suggestions for reducing the annotation time, and the web-based addition and configuration of custom annotation layers.

While we also support the common practice of using of external tools to automatically pre-annotate documents, we go one step further by tightly integrating a generic sequence classifier into the tool that can make use of completed annotation documents from the same project. In two case studies, we have shown quick convergence for Amharic POS tagging and a substantial reduction in annotation time for German NER. The key concept here is the split-pane UI that allows to display automatic suggestions, while forcing the annotator to review all of them.

Allowing the definition of custom annotation layers in a web-based UI is greatly increasing the number of annotation projects that potentially could use our tool. While it is mainly an engineering challenge to allow this amount of flexibility and to hide its complexity from the user, it is a major contribution in the transition from specialized tools towards general-purpose tools.

The combination of both – custom layers and automatic suggestions – gives rise to the rapid setup of efficient annotation projects. Adding to existing capabilities in WebAnno, such as curation, agreement computation, monitoring and fine-grained annotation project definition, our contributions significantly extend the scope of annotation tasks in which the tool can be employed.

In future work, we plan to support annotation suggestions for non-span structures (arcs and chains), and to include further machine learning algorithms.

Acknowledgments

The work presented in this paper was funded by a German BMBF grant to the CLARIN-D project, the Hessian LOEWE research excellence program as part of the research center "Digital Humanities" and by the Volkswagen Foundation as part of the Lichtenberg-Professorship Program under grant No. I/82806.

References

Daniel Beck, Lucia Specia, and Trevor Cohn. 2013. Reducing annotation effort for quality estimation via active learning. In *Proc. ACL 2013 System Demonstrations*, Sofia, Bulgaria.

Darina Benikova, Chris Biemann, and Marc Reznicek. 2014. NoSta-D Named Entity Annotation for German: Guidelines and Dataset. In *Proc. LREC 2014*, Reykjavik, Iceland.

Kalina Bontcheva, H. Cunningham, I. Roberts, A. Roberts, V. Tablan, N. Aswani, and G. Gorrell. 2013. GATE Teamware: a web-based, collaborative text annotation framework. *Language Resources and Evaluation*, 47(4):1007–1029.

Koby Crammer and Yoram Singer. 2003. Ultraconservative online algorithms for multiclass problems. In *Journal of Machine Learning Research 3*, pages 951 – 991.

Hamish Cunningham, D. Maynard, K. Bontcheva, V. Tablan, N. Aswani, I. Roberts, G. Gorrell, A. Funk, A. Roberts, D. Damljanovic, T. Heitz, M. A. Greenwood, H. Saggion, J. Petrak, Y. Li, and W. Peters. 2011. *Text Processing with GATE (Version 6)*. University of Sheffield Department of Computer Science, ISBN 978-0956599315.

Binyam Gebrekidan Gebre. 2009. Part-of-speech tagging for Amharic. In *ISMTCL Proceedings, International Review Bulag, PUFC*.

T. Götz and O. Suhre. 2004. Design and implementation of the UIMA Common Analysis System. *IBM Systems Journal*, 43(3):476 –489.

Nancy Ide and Keith Suderman. 2007. GrAF: A graph-based format for linguistic annotations. In *Proc. Linguistic Annotation Workshop*, pages 1–8, Prague, Czech Republic.

Todd Lingren, L. Deleger, K. Molnar, H. Zhai, J. Meinzen-Derr, M. Kaiser, L. Stoutenborough, Q. Li, and I. Solti. 2013. Evaluating the impact of pre-annotation on annotation speed and potential bias: natural language processing gold standard development for clinical named entity recognition in clinical trial announcements. In *Journal of the American Medical Informatics Association*, pages 951 – 991.

Thomas Morton and Jeremy LaCivita. 2003. WordFreak: an open tool for linguistic annotation. In *Proc. NAACL 2003*, demonstrations, pages 17–18, Edmonton, Canada.

Slav Petrov, Dipanjan Das, and Ryan McDonald. 2012. A universal part-of-speech tagset. In *Proc LREC 2012*, Istanbul, Turkey.

Guido Sautter, Klemens Böhm, Frank Padberg, and Walter Tichy. 2007. *Empirical Evaluation of Semi-automated XML Annotation of Text Documents with the GoldenGATE Editor*. Budapest, Hungary.

Pontus Stenetorp, Sampo Pyysalo, Goran Topić, Tomoko Ohta, Sophia Ananiadou, and Jun'ichi Tsujii. 2012. brat: a Web-based Tool for NLP-Assisted Text Annotation. In *Proc. EACL 2012 Demo Session*, Avignon, France.

Seid Muhie Yimam, Iryna Gurevych, Richard Eckart de Castilho, and Chris Biemann. 2013. WebAnno: A flexible,web-based and visually supported system for distributed annotations. In *Proc. ACL 2013 System Demonstrations*, pages 1–6, Sofia, Bulgaria.

Amir Zeldes, Julia Ritz, Anke Lüdeling, and Christian Chiarcos. 2009. ANNIS: A search tool for multi-layer annotated corpora. In *Proc. Corpus Linguistics 2009*, Liverpool, UK.

Web Information Mining and Decision Support Platform for the Modern Service Industry

Binyang Li[1,2], Lanjun Zhou[2,3], Zhongyu Wei[2,3], Kam-fai Wong[2,3,4], Ruifeng Xu[5], Yunqing Xia[6]

[1] Dept. of Information Science & Technology, University of International Relations, China
[2]Dept. of Systems Engineering & Engineering Management, The Chinese University of Hong Kong, Shatin, N.T., Hong Kong
[3]MoE Key Laboratory of High Confidence Software Technologies, China
[4] Shenzhen Research Institute, The Chinese University of Hong Kong
[5]Harbin Institute of Technology Shenzhen Graduate School, Shenzhen, China
[6]Department of Computer Science & Technology, TNList, Tsinghua University, China
{byli,ljzhou,zywei,kfwong}@se.cuhk.edu.hk

Abstract

This demonstration presents an intelligent information platform MODEST. MODEST will provide enterprises with the services of retrieving news from websites, extracting commercial information, exploring customers' opinions, and analyzing collaborative/competitive social networks. In this way, enterprises can improve the competitive abilities and facilitate potential collaboration activities. At the meanwhile, MODEST can also help governments to acquire information about one single company or the entire board timely, and make prompt strategies for better support. Currently, MODEST is applied to the pillar industries of Hong Kong, including innovative finance, modem logistics, information technology, etc.

1 Introduction

With the rapid development of Web 2.0, the amount of information is exploding. There are millions of events towards companies and billions of opinions on products generated every day (Liu, 2012). Such enormous information cannot only facilitate companies to improve their competitive abilities, but also help government to make prompt decisions for better support or timely monitor, e.g. effective risk management. For this reason, there is a growing demand of Web information mining and intelligent decision support services for the industries. Such services are collectively referred as modern service, which includes the following requirements:

(1) To efficiently retrieve relevant information from the websites;
(2) To accurately determine the latest business news and trends of the company;
(3) To identify and analyze customers' opinions towards the company;
(4) To explore the collaborative and competitive relationship with other companies;
(5) To leverage the knowledge mined from the business news and company social network for decision support.

In this demonstration, we will present a Web information mining and decision support platform, MODEST[1]. The objective of MODEST is to provide modern services for both enterprises and government, including collecting Web information, making deep analysis, and providing supporting decision. The innovation of MODEST is focusing on deep analysis which incorporates the following functions:

- Topic detection and tracking function is to cluster the hot events and capture the relationship between the relevant events based on the collected data from websites (*event* also referred as *topic* in this paper). In order to realize this function, Web mining techniques are adopted, e.g. topic clustering, heuristics algorithms, etc.
- The second function is to identify and analyze customers' opinions about the company. Opinion mining technology (Zhou et al., 2010) is adopted to determine the polarity of those news, which can help the company timely and appropriately adjust the policy to strengthen the dominant position or avoid risks.

[1] This work is supported by the Innovation and Technology Fund of Hong Kong SAR.

Proceedings of 52nd Annual Meeting of the Association for Computational Linguistics: System Demonstrations, pages 97–102, Baltimore, Maryland USA, June 23-24, 2014.

- The third function is to explore and analyze social network based on the company centric. We utilize social network analysis (SNA) technology (Xia et al., 2010) to discover the relationships, and we further analyze the content in fine-grained granularity to identify its potential partners or competitors.

With the help of MODEST, the companies can acquire modern service-related information, and timely adjust corporate policies and marketing plan ahead. Hence, the ability of information acquisition and the competitiveness of the enterprises can be improved accordingly.

In this paper, we will use a practical example to illustrate our platform and evaluate the performance of main functions.

The rest of this paper is organized as follows. Section 2 will introduce the system description as well as the main functions implementation. The practical case study will be illustrated in Section 3. The performance of MODEST will be evaluated in Section 4.Finally, this paper will be concluded in Section 5.

2 System Description

In this section, we first outline the system architecture of MODEST, and then describe the implementation of the main functionality in detail.

2.1 Architecture and Workflow

The MODEST system consists of three modules: data acquisition, data analysis, and result display. The system architecture is shown in Figure 1.

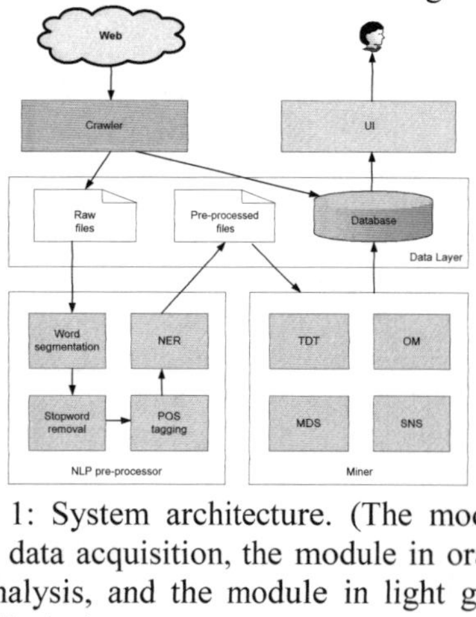

Figure 1: System architecture. (The module in blue is data acquisition, the module in orange is data analysis, and the module in light green is result display)

(1) The core technique in the data acquisition module is the crawler, which is developed to collect raw data from websites, e.g. news portals, blogosphere. Then the system parse the raw web pages and extract information to store in the local database for further processing.

(2) The data analysis module can be divided into two parts:

- NLP pre-processor: utilizes NLP (natural language processing) techniques and some toolkits to perform the pre-processing on the raw data in (1), including word segmentation, part-of-speech (POS) tagging[1], stopword removal, and named entity recognition (NER)[2]. We then create knowledgebase for individual industry, such as domain-specific sentiment word lexicon, name entity collection, and so on.
- Miner: makes use of data mining techniques to realize four functions, topic detection and tracking (TDT), multi-document summarization[3] (MDS), social network analysis (SNA), and opinion mining (OM). The results of data analysis are also stored in the database.

(3) The result display module read out the analysis results from the database and display them to users in the form of plain text, charts, figures, as well as video.

2.2 Function Implementation

Since the innovation of MODEST is focusing on the module of data analysis, we will describe its main functions in detail, including topic detection and tracking, opinion mining, and social networks analysis.

2.2.1 Topic Detection and Tracking

The TDT function targets on detecting and tracking the hot topics for each individual company. Given a period of data collected from websites, there are various discussions about the company. In order to extract these topics, clustering methods (Viermetz et al., 2007 and Yoon et al., 2009) are implemented to explore the topics. Note that during the period of data collection, different topics with respect to the same company may have relations. We, therefore, utilize hierarchical clustering methods[4]to capture the potential relations.

Due to the large amount of data, it is impossible to view all the topics at a snapshot. MODEST utilizes topic tracking technique (Wang et al., 2008) to identify related stories with a stream of

[1] www.ictclas.org
[2]http://ir.hit.edu.cn/demo/ltp
[3]http://libots.sourceforge.net/
[4]http://dragon.ischool.drexel.edu/

media. It is convenient for the users to see the latest information about the company.

In summary, TDT function provides the services of detecting and tracking the latest and emergent topics, analyzing the relationships of topics on the dynamics of the company. It meets the aforementioned demand, "to accurately grasp the latest business news and trends of the company".

2.2.2 Opinion Mining

The objective of OM function is to discover opinions towards a company and classify the opinions into positive, negative, or neutral.

The opinion mining function is redesigned based on our own opinion mining engine (Zhou et al., 2010). It separates opinion identification and polarity classification into two stages.

Given a set of documents that are relevant to the company, we first split the documents into sentences, and then identify whether the sentence is opinionated or not. We extract the features shown in Table 1 for opinion identification. (Zhou et al., 2010)

Table 1: Features adopted in the opinionated sentence classifier

Punctuation level features
The presence of direct quote punctuation "“" and "”"
The presence of other punctuations: "?" and "!"
Word-Level and entity-level features
The presence of known opinion operators
The percentage of known opinion word in sentence
Presence of a named entity
Presence of pronoun
Presence of known opinion indicators
Presence of known degree adverbs
Presence of known conjunctions
Bi-gram features
Named entities + opinion operators
Pronouns + opinion operators
Nouns or named entities + opinion words
Pronouns + opinion words
Opinion words (adjective) + opinion words(noun)
Degree adverbs + opinion words
Degree adverbs + opinion operators

These features are then combined using a radial basis function (RBF) kernel and a support vector machine (SVM) classifier (Drucker et al., 1997) is trained based on the NTCIR 8training data for opinion identification (Kando, 2010).

For those opinionated sentences, we then classify them into positive, negative, or neutral. In addition to the features shown in Table 1, we incorporate features of s-VSM (Sentiment Vector Space Model) (Xia et al., 2008) to enhance the performance. The principles of the s-VSM are listed as follows: (1) Only sentiment-related words are used to produce sentiment features for the s-VSM. (2) The sentiment words are appropriately disambiguated with the neighboring negations and modifiers. (3) Negations and modifiers are included in the s-VSM to reflect the functions of inversing, strengthening and weakening. Sentiment unit is the appropriate element complying with the above principles. (Zhou et al., 2010)

In addition to polarity classification, opinion holder and target are also recognized in OM function for further identifying the relationship that two companies have, e.g. collaborative or competitive. Both of the dependency parser and the semantic role labeling[1] (SRL) tool are incorporated to identify the semantic roles of each chunk based on verbs in the sentence.

The OM function provides the company with services of analyzing the social sentimental feedback on the dynamics of the company. It meets the aforementioned demand, "to identify and analyze customers' opinions towards the company".

2.2.3 Social Network Analysis

SNA function aims at producing the commercial network of companies that are hidden within the articles.

To achieve this goal, we maintain two lexicons, the commercial named entity lexicon and commercial relation lexicon. Commercial named entity are firstly located within the text and then recorded in the commercial entity lexicon in the pre-processor NER. Commercial relation lexicon record the articles/documents that involve the commercial relations. Note that the commercial relation lexicon (Table 2) is manually compiled. In this work, we consider only two general commercial relations, namely cooperation and competition.

Table 2: Statistics on relation lexicon.

Type	Amount	Examples
Competition	20	挑战(challenge), 竞争(compete), 对手(opponent)
Collaboration	18	协作(collaborate),协同(coordinate), 合作(cooperate)

SNA function produces the social network of a centric company, which can provide the compa-

[1]http://ir.hit.edu.cn/demo/ltp

ny with the impact analysis and decision-making chain tracking. It meets the aforementioned demand, "to explore the collaborative and competitive relationship between companies".

3 Practical Example

In this section, we use a case study to illustrate our system and further evaluate the performance of the main functions with respect to those companies. Due to the limited space, we just illustrate the main functions of topic detection, opinion mining and social network analysis.

3.1 Topic Detection and Opinion Mining

Figure 2(a) showed the results of topic detection and opinion mining functions for a Hong Kong local financial company *Sun Hung Kai Properties* (新鴻基地產). On top of the figure are the results of topic detection and tracking function. Multi-document summary of the latest news is provided for the company and more news with the similar topics can be found by pressing the button "更多" (*more*). Since there are a lot of duplicates of a piece of news on the websites, the summary is a direct way to acquire the recent news, which can improve the effectiveness of the company.

The results of opinion mining function are shown at the bottom of Figure 2(a), where the green line indicates negative while the red line indicates positive. In order to give a dynamic insight of public opinions, we provide the amount changes of positive and negative articles with time variant. This is very helpful for the company to capture the feedback of their marketing policies. As shown in Figure 2(a), there were 14 negative articles (負面信息) on Oct. 29, 2012, which achieved negative peak within the 6 months. The users would probably read those 14 articles and adjust the company strategy accordingly.

3.2 Social Network Analysis

Figure 2(b) shows the social network based on the centric company in yellow, *Sun Hung Kai Properties* (新鴻基地產). We only list the half of the connected companies with collaborative relationship from *Sun Hung Kai Properties*, and remove the competitive ones due to limited space. The thickness of the line indicates the strength of the collaboration between the two companies. The social network can explore the potential partners/competitors of a company. Furthermore, users are allowed to adjust the depth and set the nodes count of the network. The above analysis can provide a richer insight in to a company.

In the following section, we will make experiments to investigate the performance of the above functions.

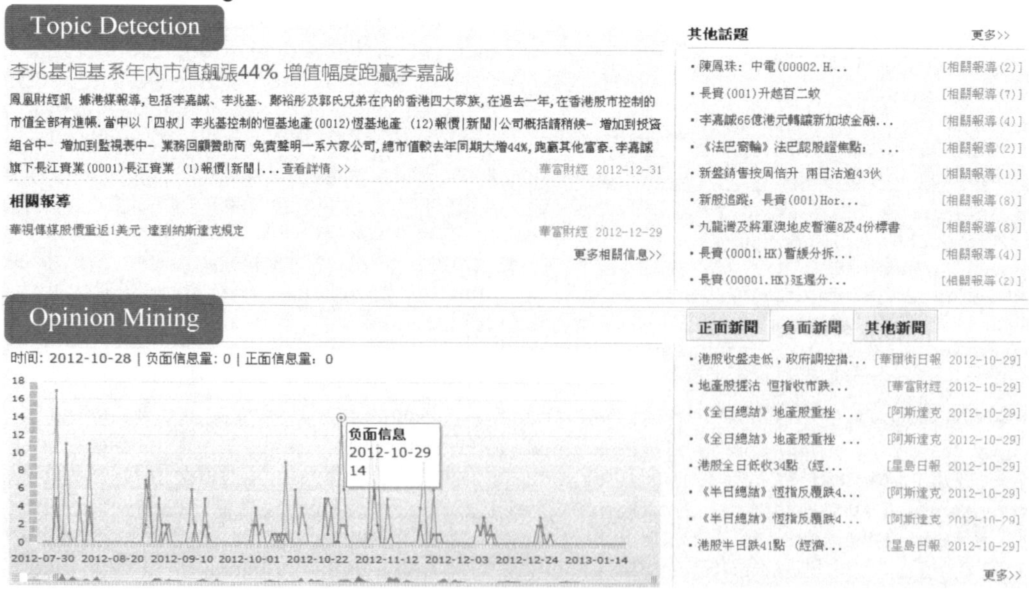

(a) Topic detection and opinion mining of *Sun Hung Kai Properties* (新鴻基地產). (For convenience, we translate the texts on the button in English)

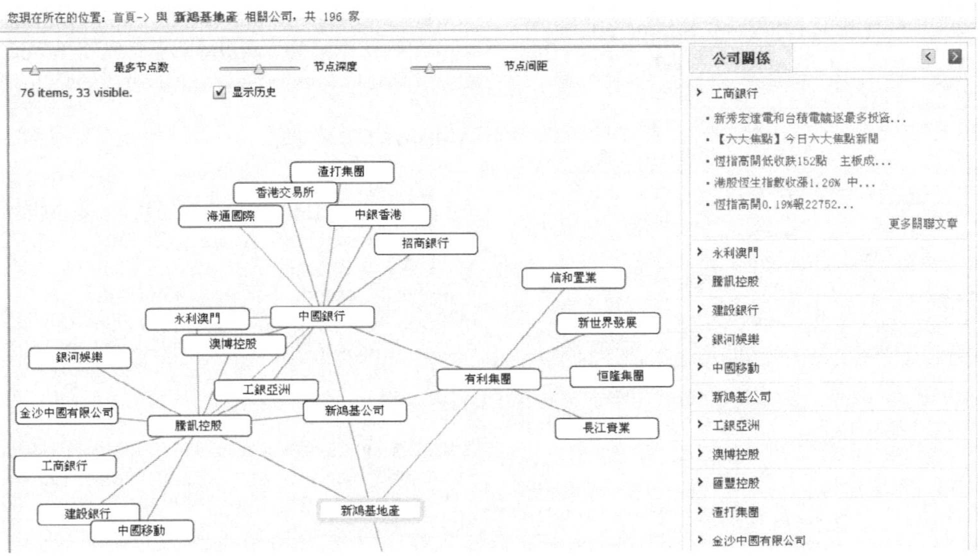

(b)Social network of *Sun Hung Kai Properties* (新鴻基地產). (The rectangle in yellow is the centric)

Figure 2: Screenshot of the MODEST system.

4 Experiment and Result

In our evaluation, the experiments were made based on 17692 articles collected from 52 Hong Kong websites during 6 months (1/7/2012~ 31/12/2012). We investigate the performance of MODEST based on the standard metrics proposed by NIST[1], including precision, recall, and F-score.

Precision (P) is the fraction of detected articles (U) that are relevantto the topic (N).

$$P = \frac{N}{U} \times 100\%$$

Recall (R) is the fraction of the articles (T) that are relevant to the topic that are successfully detected (N).

$$R = \frac{N}{T} \times 100\%$$

Usually, there is an inverse relationship between precision and recall, where it is possible to increase one at the cost of reducing the other. Therefore, precision and recall scores are not discussed in isolation. Instead, F-Score (F) is proposed to combine precision and recall, which is the harmonic meanof precision and recall.

$$F = \frac{2}{\frac{1}{P} + \frac{1}{R}} \times 100\% = \frac{2 \times P \times R}{P + R} \times 100\%$$

4.1 Topic Detection and Tracking

We first assess the performance of the topic detection function. The data is divided into 6 parts according to the time. For different companies, the amount of articles vary a lot. Therefore, we calculate the metrics for each individual dataset, and then compute the weighted mean value. The experimental results are shown in Table 3.

Table 3: Experimental results on topic detection.

Dataset	Recall	Precision	F-Score
1/7/12-31/7/12	85.71%	89.52%	85.38%
1/8/12-31/8/12	93.10%	93.68%	92.49%
1/9/12-30/9/12	76.50%	83.13%	76.56%
1/10/12-31/10/12	83.32%	88.53%	85.84%
1/11/12-30/11/12	86.11%	89.94%	87.98%
1/12/12-31/12/12	84.26%	87.65%	85.92%
Average	85.13%	88.78%	85.69%

From the experimental results, we can find that the average F-Score is about 85.69%.The dataset in the second row achieves the best performance while the dataset in the third only get 76.56% in F-Score. It is because that the amount of articles is smaller than the others and the recall value is very low. As far as we know, the best run of topic detection in (Allan et al., 2007) achieved 84%. The performance of topic detection in MODEST is comparable.

4.2 Opinion Mining

We then evaluate the performance of opinion mining function. We manually annotated 1568 articles, which is further divided into 8 datasets randomly. Precision, recall, and F-score are also used as the metrics for the evaluation. The experimental results are shown in Table 4.

[1]http://trec.nist.gov/

Table 4: Experimental results on opinion mining.

Dataset	Size	Precision	Recall	F-Score
dataset-1	200	76.57%	78.26%	76.57%
dataset-2	200	83.55%	89.64%	86.07%
dataset-3	200	69.12%	69.80%	69.44%
dataset-4	200	77.13%	75.40%	75.67%
dataset-5	200	76.21%	77.65%	76.74%
dataset-6	200	63.76%	66.22%	64.49%
dataset-7	200	78.56%	78.41%	78.43%
dataset-8	168	65.72%	65.15%	65.32%
Average	196	73.83%	75.07%	74.09%

From Table 4, we can find that the average F-Score can reach 74.09%. Note that the opinion mining engine of MODEST is the implementation of (Zhou et al., 2010), which achieved the best run in NTCIR. However, the engine is trained on NTCIR corpus, which consists of articles of general domain, while the test set focuses on the financial domain. We further train our engine on the data from the financial domain and the average F-Score improves to over 80%.

5 Conclusions

This demonstration presents an intelligent information platform designed to mine Web information and provide decisions for modern service, MODEST. MODEST can provide the services of retrieving news from websites, extracting commercial information, exploring customers' opinions about a given company, and analyzing its collaborative/competitive social networks. Both enterprises and government are the target customers. For enterprise, MODEST can improve the competitive abilities and facilitate potential collaboration. For government, MODEST can collect information about the entire industry, and make prompt strategies for better support.

In this paper, we first introduce the system architecture design and the main functions implementation, including topic detection and tracking, opinion mining, and social network analysis. Then a case study is given to illustrate the functions of MODEST. In order to evaluate the performance of MODEST, we also conduct the experiments based on the data from 52 Hong Kong websites, and the results show the effectiveness of the above functions.

In the future, MODEST will be improved in two directions:

- Extend to other languages, e.g. English, Simplified Chinese, etc.
- Enhance the compatibility to implement on mobile device.

The demo of MODEST and the related toolkits can be found on the homepage: http://sepc111.se.cuhk.edu.hk:8080/adcom_hk/

Acknowledgements

This research is partially supported by General Research Fund of Hong Kong (417112), Shenzhen Fundamental Research Program (JCYJ20130401172046450, JCYJ20120613152557576), KTO(TBF1ENG007), National Natural Science Foundation of China (61203378, 61370165), and Shenzhen International Cooperation Funding (GJHZ20120613110641217).

References:

James Allan, Jaime Carbonell, George Doddington, Jonathan Yamron, and Yiming Yang. 1998. Topic Detection and Tracking Pilot Study: Final Report. Proceedings of the DARPA Broadcast News Transcription and Understanding Workshop.

Harris Drucker, Chris J.C. Burges, Linda Kaufman, Alex Smola, and Vladimir Vpnik. 1997. Support Vector Regression Machines. Proceedings of Advances in Neural Information Processing Systems, pp. 155-161.

Noriko Kando.2010. Overview of the Eighth NTCIR Workshop. Proceedings of NTCIR-8 Workshop.

Bing Liu. 2012. Sentiment Analysis and Opinion Mining. Proceedings of Synthesis Lectures on Human Language Technologies, pp. 1-167.

Maximilian Viermetz, and Michal Skubacz. 2007. Using Topic Discovery to Segment Large Communication Graphs for Social Network Analysis. Proceedings of the IEEE/WIC/ACM International Conference on Web Intelligence, pp. 95-99.

Canhui Wang, Min Zhang, Liyun Ru, and Shaoping Ma. 2008. Automatic Online News Topic Ranking Using Media Focus and User Attention based on Aging Theory. Proceedings of the Conference on Information and Knowledge Management.

Yunqing Xia, Nianxing Ji, Weifeng Su, and Yi Liu. 2010. Mining Commercial Networks from Online Financial News. Proceedings of the IEEE International Conference on E-Business Engineering, pp. 17-23.

Ruifeng Xu, Kam-fai Wong, and Yunqing Xia. 2008. Coarse-Fine Opinion Mining-WIA in NTCIR-7 MOAT Task. In NTCIR-7 Workshop, pp. 307-313.

Seok-Ho Yoon, Jung-Hwan Shin, Sang-Wook Kim, and Sunju Park. 2009. Extraction of a Latent Blog Community based on Subject. Proceeding of the 18th ACM Conference on Information and Knowledge Management, pp. 1529-1532.

Lanjun Zhou, Yunqing Xia, Binyang Li, and Kam-fai Wong. 2010. WIA-Opinmine System in NTCIR-8 MOAT Evaluation. Proceedings of NTCIR-8 Workshop Meeting, pp. 286-292.

FAdR: A System for Recognizing False Online Advertisements

Yi-jie Tang and Hsin-Hsi Chen
Department of Computer Science and Information Engineering
National Taiwan University, Taipei, Taiwan
tangyj@nlg.csie.ntu.edu.tw;hhchen@ntu.edu.tw

Abstract

More and more product information, including advertisements and user reviews, are presented to Internet users nowadays. Some of the information is false, misleading or overstated, which can cause seriousness and needs to be identified. Authorities, advertisers, website owners and consumers all have the needs to detect such statements. In this paper, we propose a False **Ad**vertisements **R**ecognition system called **FAdR** by using one-class and binary classification models. Illegal advertising lists made public by a government and product descriptions from a shopping website are obtained for training and testing. The results show that the binary SVM models can achieve the highest performance when unigrams with the weighting of log relative frequency ratios are used as features. Comparatively, the benefit of the one-class classification models is the adjustable rejection rate parameter, which can be changed to suit different applications. Verb phrases more likely to introduce overstated information are obtained by mining the datasets. These phrases help find problematic wordings in the advertising texts.

1 Introduction

As online commerce and advertising keep growing, more and more consumers depend on information on the Internet to make purchasing decisions. This kind of information includes online advertisements posted by businesses, and discussions or reviews generated by users. However, false statements can also be presented to consumers. For example, some companies hire people to post fake product reviews in an attempt to promote their own products or reduce competitors' reputations (Ott et al., 2011). It is referred to as deceptive opinion spamming and explored in recent researches (Ott et al., 2011; Mukherjee et al., 2012; Mukherjee et al., 2013; Fei et al., 2013).

False statements and exaggerated content can also be seen in online advertisements. These statements can also be regarded as opinion spams, while the authors, that is, the advertisers, can be more easily identified. Yeh (2014) reported the top two types of illegal advertisements on the web, TV and broadcast are food (62.61%) and cosmetic (24.26%). Of the dissemination media, the web is the major source of false advertisements. Most inappropriate food-related advertisements contain overstated health claims. The medical effects and cure claims may also appear in cosmetic advertising. As a result, advertising regulations are enforced in many countries to protect consumers from fraudulent and misleading information. False, overstated or misleading information and mentions of curative effects can be prohibited by the authorities (FTC, 2000; DOH, 2009; CFIA, 2010).

To regulate online advertising, the authorities need to review a large number of advertisements and determine their legality, which is cost- and time-consuming. Advertisers also need to know the legality of their advertisements to avoid violating advertising laws. This becomes especially important when every Internet user can be an advertiser if s/he posts messages related to any product announcement, promotion, or sales. Website owners that accept advertisements have to present appropriate advertisement contents to users and avoid legal issues. Even Internet users should also identify false advertisements in order not to be misled. Thus, the recognition of false, misleading or overstated information is an emerging task.

This paper presents a False **Ad**vertisements **R**ecognition system called **FAdR**, and take two

Proceedings of 52nd Annual Meeting of the Association for Computational Linguistics: System Demonstrations, pages 103–108,
Baltimore, Maryland USA, June 23-24, 2014.

major sources of illegal advertisements on the web, i.e., food and cosmetic advertising, as examples. Section 2 surveys the related work. Section 3 introduces the datasets used in the experiments. Section 4 presents classification models and shows their performance. Section 5 mines the overstated phrases. Section 6 demonstrates the uses of **FAdR** system with screenshot. Both sentence and document levels are considered.

2 Related Work

Gokhman et al. (2012) collected data from the Internet and explored methods to construct a gold standard corpus for "deception" studies. Ott et al. (2011) studied methods to detect "disruptive opinion spams." Unlike conventional advertising spams, these fake opinions look authentic and are used to mislead users. Mukherjee et al. (2013) used reviewer's behavioral footprints to detect spammer. As they pointed out, one of the largest problems to solve this issue is that there is no appropriate datasets for fake and non-fake reviews.

Previous online advertising research mostly focuses on bidding, matching or recommendation of advertisements on websites. Ghosh et al. (2009) studied bidding strategies for advertisement allocations. Huang et al. (2008) proposed an advertisement recommendation method by classifying instant messages into the Yahoo categories. Scaiano and Inkpen (2011) used Wikipedia for negative keyphrase generation to hide advertisements that users are not interested in. This paper, in contrast, focuses on identifying false statements in online advertisements with classification models.

3 Datasets

We use the illegal advertising lists and statements made public by the Taipei City Government[1] as the illegal advertising datasets. The contents of the government data are split into sentences by colon, period, question mark and exclamation mark. Two types of datasets are built for illegal food and cosmetic advertising, named FOOD_ILLEGAL and COS_ILLEGAL, respectively. Some illegal sentences in the illegal food advertising dataset are shown below:

(1) 減少代謝廢物的堆積。
Reduces waste produced by metabolism process.

(2) 減少失眠及疼痛。
Stops insomnia and pain.

(3) 治療高血壓。
Cures hypertension.

In the government website, the authority does not regularly announce legal advertising data. We adopt one-class classifiers with only illegal data for this scenario, as shown in Section 4.1. To experiment on binary classifiers, we collect product descriptions from a shopping website[2] and verify their legality manually to construct the legal advertising datasets. The legal food and cosmetic adverting datasets are named FOOD_LEGAL and COS_LEGAL, respectively. The numbers of the sentences in FOOD_LEGAL, FOOD_ILLEGAL, COS_LEGAL, and COS_ILLEGAL are 5,059, 7,033, 10,520, and 11,381, respectively.

4 Classification Models

One-class Naïve Bayes and Bagging classifiers, and binary classifiers based on Naïve Bayes and SVM models are implemented.

4.1 One-Class Classifiers

We adopt the OneClassClassifier module (Hempstalk et al., 2008) in the WEKA machine learning tool to train one-class classifiers with illegal statements only. The OneClassClassifier module provides a rejection rate parameter for adjusting the threshold between target and non-target instances. The target class, which corresponds to the illegal class in this study, is the single class used to train the classifier. Higher rejection rate means that more legal statements will be preferred, but illegal statements may be still incorrectly classified into legal ones. Naïve Bayes and Bagging classifiers are chosen because they achieve best performance among the algorithms we have explored in this experiment.

Each instance in the dataset, i.e., a sentence, is represented by a word vector (w_1, w_2, …, w_{1000}), where w_i is a binary value indicating whether a word occurs in the sentence or not. The vocabulary is selected from the illegal advertising datasets. To properly filter out common words, we count top 1,000 frequent words in the Sinica Balanced Corpus of Modern Chinese[3] and remove them from the vocabulary. The remaining top 1,000 words are used for vector representation.

Total 532 illegal statements provided by the Department of Health form the training set. An

[1] http://www.health.gov.tw/Default.aspx?tabid=295

[2] http://www.7net.com.tw

[3] http://app.sinica.edu.tw/kiwi/mkiwi/

illegal and a legal advertising dataset make up the test set. The former consists of 317 illegal sentences from Taipei City Government's lists, and the latter contains 203 legal statement examples from the Department of Health.

Table 1 shows the accuracies of Naïve Bayes and Bagging classifiers in the food dataset. The rejection rates from 0.7 to 0.8 are preferable for most applications, because they result in higher accuracy for legal statement classification while not significantly reducing the performance of illegal statement detection. Using the 0.7 rejection rate produces high performance for the illegal class while 0.8 rejection rate does better for the legal class. The actual choice of rejection rate depends on the demands of users. For an advertiser, it is important to avoid all possible problematic statements. Thus, a lower rejection rate will be more suitable. If the system is used by the authorities, a rejection rate higher than 0.7 may be preferable because they don't misjudge too many legal advertisements.

Rejection rate		0.4	0.5	0.6	0.7	0.8	0.9
Naïve Bayes	Illegal	85.33%	82.39%	79.01%	74.49%	68.17%	59.14%
	Legal	31.07%	39.81%	53.40%	63.11%	72.82%	86.41%
Bagging	Illegal	92.78%	88.49%	84.65%	74.94%	69.07%	0.23%
	Legal	3.88%	17.48%	27.18%	65.72%	82.52%	99.77%

Table 1: Accuracies of Classifiers in Different Rejection Rates.

4.2 Binary Classifiers

We use FOOD_LEGAL and FOOD_ILLEGAL datasets, and COS_LEGAL and COS_ILLEGAL datasets to build binary classifiers for food and cosmetic advertising classification, respectively. Naïve Bayes classifiers and SVM classifiers implemented with libSVM (Chang & Lin, 2011) are adopted. Ten-fold cross validation is used for the training and testing tasks. Total 1,000 highly frequent words are selected in the same way as in Section 4.1 to form a word-based unigram feature set.

Two weighting schemes are considered. In the binary weighting, each sentence is represented by a word vector (w_1, w_2, ..., w_{1000}), where w_i is a binary value indicating whether a word occurs in the sentence or not. In the weighting of log relative frequency ratio, we follow the idea of collocation mining (Damerau, 1993). Relative frequency ratio between two datasets has been shown to be useful to discover collocations that are characteristic of a dataset when compared to the other dataset. It has been successfully applied to mine sentiment words from microblog and to model reader/writer emotion transition (Tang and Chen, 2011, 2012).

The log relative frequency ratio (*logRF*) is defined formally as follows. Given two datasets *A* and *B*, the log relative frequency ratio for each $w^i \in A \cup B$ is computed with the following formula.

$$logRF_{AB}(w^i) = \log \frac{\frac{f_A(w^i)}{|A|}}{\frac{f_B(w^i)}{|B|}}$$

$logRF_{AB}(w^i)$ is a log ratio of relative frequencies of word w^i in *A* and *B*, $f_A(w^i)$ and $f_B(w^i)$ are frequencies of w^i in *A* and in *B*, respectively, and $|A|$ and $|B|$ are total words in *A* and in *B*, respectively. *logRF* values are used to estimate the distribution of the words in datasets *A* and *B*. If w^i has higher relative frequency in *A* than in *B*, then $logRF_{AB}(w^i)>0$, and vice versa. In our experiments, *logRF* is used to present each unigram's distribution in the legal and illegal datasets, replacing the binary value for a unigram feature.

Tables 2 and 3 show the results of the classification models with different combinations of feature sets. When *logRF* is combined with Unigram, the accuracy is significantly improved in both the food and cosmetic datasets. We can also see that the performance of all FOOD models are higher than equivalent COS models. Possible reasons may be that the effects of cosmetics are related to body appearance, and inappropriate cure claims are also related to body improvement and appearance changes. There can be some overlaps between the words used in legal and illegal cosmetic advertising.

Classification Models →	Naïve Bayes		SVM	
Illegal vs. Legal → Features ↓	Illegal	Legal	Illegal	Legal
Unigram	92.59%	85.06%	89.46%	88.00%
Unigram + logRF	**94.32%**	**86.37%**	**94.70%**	**91.68%**

Table 2: Classification Accuracies for FOOD Datasets.

Classification Models →	Naïve Bayes		SVM	
Illegal vs. Legal → Features ↓	Illegal	Legal	Illegal	Legal
Unigram	86.48%	77.63%	82.47%	82.36%
Unigram + logRF	**88.20%**	**83.06%**	**88.46%**	**83.41%**

Table 3: Classification Accuracies for COS Datasets.

5 Overstated Phrase Mining

Since the authority focuses on health claims in advertising, almost all illegal statements announced by the government include an action related to health improvement and a name that refers to diseases or body conditions. Thus, we can observe that most of the illegal statements recognized and forbidden by the authority contain a health-related verb phrase consisting of a transitive verb and an object. These illegal advertising verb phrases can be mined from the datasets for the government's and advertisers' reference. We can also use these verb phrases to help the users of our system understand possible reasons why the sentences in advertisements are labeled as illegal.

We propose a mining method based on log relative frequency ratio, which is described in Section 4.2. We compute $logRF_{AB}(w^i)$ to obtain the words that are most likely to be used in illegal advertising. We identify transitive verbs and nouns in the word list based on POS tagging results generated by the CKIP parser[4], and then use them to examine if a verb phrase is presented in a sentence. Total 979 verb phrases are mined from the FOOD datasets, and 2,302 from the COS dataset. Table 4 shows some examples.

Dataset	Illegal advertising verb phrases	
	Transitive verb	Object noun
FOOD	增強 (improve)	體質 (physical condition)
	抑制 (inactivate)	細菌 (bacteria)
	分解 (decompose)	膽固醇 (cholesterol)
COS	淨化 (purify)	體質 (body)
	舒緩 (ease)	疼痛 (pain)
	治療 (cure)	面皰 (acne vulgaris)

Table 4: Example illegal verb phrases mined from the FOOD and COS datasets.

6 System Architecture

The **FAdR** system is composed of preprocessing (Pre-Processor), recognition (Recognizer), and explanation (Explainer) modules. Figure 1 shows the overall system architecture.

6.1 Pre-processing Module

Our classification models are sentence-based, so the main purpose of the Pre-processor in the system is detecting sentence boundaries. Four types of punctuations, including period, colon, exclamation, and question mark, are used to segment a document into sentences. Line breaks are also regarded as a sentence boundary marker because many advertisements in Chinese put sentences in separate lines and do not include any punctuation. Sentences with less than three characters or more than 80 characters are ignored.

Word segmentation is performed by using the CKIP segmenter, which is an online service and can be accessed through the TCP socket. Segmented data will be represented by the corresponding feature sets based on classification model and converted to a format that the Recognizer can read as input.

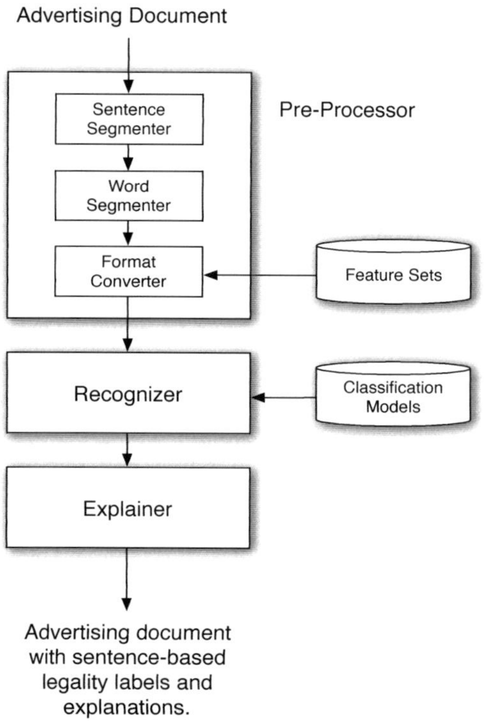

Figure 1. System architecture of **FAdR**

6.2 Recognition Module

All processed sentences are sent from the Pre-Processor to the Recognizer for legality identification.

Since our training tasks are done in WEKA, we can use the model files generated by WEKA for implementing the Recognizer. The Recognizer loads the pre-trained SVM models for food and cosmetic advertising classification, and then uses them for labeling the incoming sentences.

For the One-Class models, the model files are pre-generated by training with different rejection rates from 0.4 to 0.9. When the user adjusts the threshold, the Recognizer chooses the corresponding model to perform illegal sentences identification.

[4] http://ckipsvr.iis.sinica.edu.tw

6.3 Explanation Module

To give users more information on the possible reasons why the advertising contents are considered illegal, the Explainer uses the illegal verb phrase list, which is discussed in Section 5, to extract the problematic words from the input sentences. If the verb and the object noun in a verb phrase from the list both occur in an illegal sentence, then the verb phrase will be shown besides the recognition results in the user interface.

6.4 User Interface

Users can copy and paste the advertising contents to be recognized to the text field, or upload a document to the system. It usually takes less than 10 seconds on our server to process a document with 200 characters, so the system is suitable to quickly process a large amount of data.

If the users choose to use the one-class models, they can adjust the threshold value to fit different needs and receive useful results. Lowering the value can find as many problematic sentences as possible, but more legal sentences can also be misjudged. Increasing the value can avoid wrongly labeling legal sentences as illegal, but more illegal sentences can be missed.

Figure 2 shows a system screenshot. The recognition results of a food advertisement with 11 sentences are demonstrated. Sentences labelled as illegal are highlighted in red. Verb phrases possibly causing illegality are listed in grey colour for illegal sentences. The number of all sentences, the number of illegal sentences, and the final score are shown at the bottom. The correct score of an advertisement is defined as the number of correct sentences divided by total sentences in this advertisement. The sample advertisement used in Figure 2 and its English translation are shown as follows.

<A food advertisement>

日本茶第一品牌，全台首支融合三大天然色素的茶飲，可提升免疫力，消除壓力，增強體內抵抗力，增加體內抗體的形成。溫和不刺激，適合天天飲用。可降低自由基對細胞的過氧化傷害，強化人體免疫功能，健康好喝零負擔！

(The leading brand for Japanese tea. The first tea product combining three kinds of natural colourings in Taiwan. Can improve immunity. Can relieve stress. Can strengthen resistance to disease. Can increase antibodies in your body. It is mild and not irritative. Good for daily use. Can prevent body cells from being harmed by free radicals. Can strengthen immunity. It is healthy and tasty, and brings no body burden.)

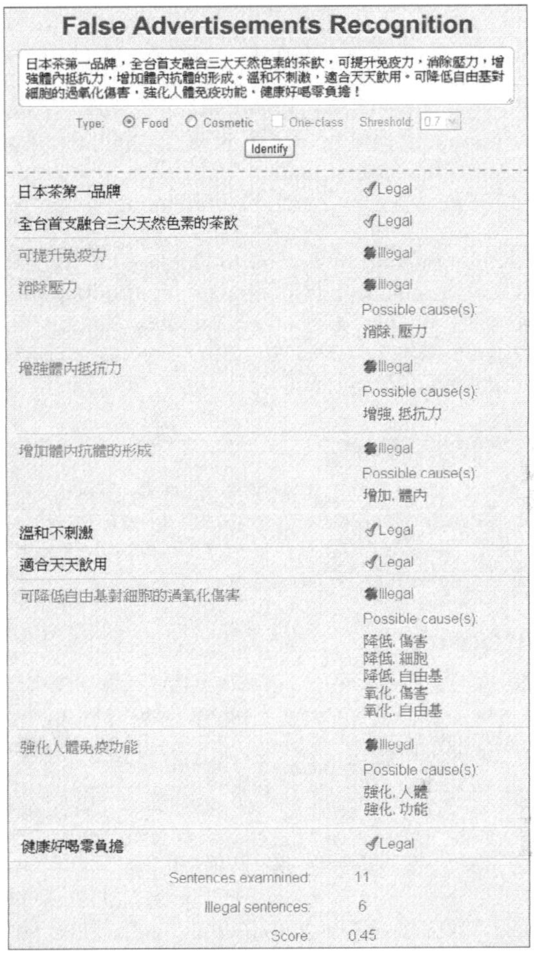

Figure 2: Screenshot for Illegal Sentence Recognition

7 Conclusion

Detecting false information on the Internet has become an important issue for users and organizations. In this paper, we present two types of classification methods to identify overstated sentences in online advertisements and build a false online advertisements recognition system **FAdR**. The recognition on both document and sentence levels is addressed in the demonstration.

In the binary models, using combinations of unigrams and the log relative frequency ratio as features can achieve highest performance. On the other hand, the one-class models can be used to build a system that is adjustable by users for different application domains.

The authorities or website owners can use a rejection rate of 0.7 or 0.8 to highlight most serious illegal advertisements. An advertisement with a score lower than 0.5 means it may critically violate the regulations, and need to be regarded as illegal advertising. Since not all advertisement posters are professional advertisers, they may need detailed information on the legality of every sentence. The illegal verb phrases found in a sentence provide clues to the advertiser. The system is also useful for consumers, as they can check if the advertisement contents can be trusted before making a purchase decision.

As future work, we will extend the methodology presented in this study to handle other types of advertisements and the materials in other languages. We will also investigate what linguistic patterns can be used to mine the overstated phrases in different languages.

Acknowledgments

This research was partially supported by National Taiwan University and Ministry of Science and Technology, Taiwan under 103R890858 and 102-2221-E-002-103-MY3.

References

Chih-Chung Chang and Chih-Jen Lin. 2001. LIBSVM: a Library for Support Vector Machines. Available at http://www.csie.ntu.edu.tw/~cjlin/libsvm.

CFIA. 2010. Advertising Requirements. Canadian Food Inspection Agency. Available at http://www.inspection.gc.ca/english/fssa/labeti/advpube.shtml.

Fred J. Damerau. 1993. Generating and Evaluating Domain-Oriented Multi-Word Terms from Text. *Information Processing and Management*, 29:433-477.

DOH. 2009. Legal and Illegal Advertising Statements for Cosmetic Regulations. Department of Health of Taiwan. Available at http://www.doh.gov.tw/ufile/doc/0980305527.pdf.

Geli Fei, Arjun Mukherjee, Bing Liu, Meichun Hsu, Malu Castellanos, and Riddhiman Ghosh. 2013. Exploiting Burstiness in Reviews for Review Spammer Detection. In *Proceedings of the International AAAI Conference on Weblogs and Social Media (ICWSM-2013)*, 175-184.

FTC. 2000. Advertising and Marketing on the Internet: Rules of the Road, Bureau of Consumer Protection. Federal Trade Commission, September 2000. Available at http://business.ftc.gov/sites/default/files/pdf/bus28-advertising-and-marketing-internet-rules-road.pdf.

Stephanie Gokhman, Jeff Hancock, Poornima Prabhu, Myle Ott, and Claire Cardie. 2012. In Search of a Gold Standard in Studies of Deception. In *Proceedings of the EACL 2012 Workshop on Computational Approaches to Deception Detection*, 23–30.

Arpita Ghosh, Preston McAfee, Kishore Papineni, and Sergei Vassilvitskii. 2009. Bidding for Representative Allocations for Display Advertising. CoRR, abs/0910-0880, 2009.

Hung-Chi Huang, Ming-Shun Lin and Hsin-Hsi Chen. 2008. Analysis of Intention in Dialogues Using Category Trees and Its Application to Advertisement Recommendation. In *Proceedings of the Third International Joint Conference on Natural Language Processing (IJCNLP 2008)*, 625-630.

Kathryn Hempstalk, Eibe Frank, and Ian H. Witten. 2008. One-Class Classification by Combining Density and Class Probability Estimation. In *Proceedings of the 12th European Conference on Principles and Practice of Knowledge Discovery in Databases and 19th European Conference on Machine Learning*, 505-519.

Arjun Mukherjee, Bing Liu, and Natalie Glance. 2012. Spotting Fake Reviewer Groups in Consumer Reviews. In *Proceedings of the International World Wide Web Conference (WWW 2012)*, 191-200.

Arjun Mukherjee, Abhinav Kumar, Bing Liu, Junhui Wang, Meichun Hsu, Malu Castellanos, and Riddhiman Ghosh. 2013. Spotting Opinion Spammers using Behavioral Footprints. In *Proceedings of SIGKDD International Conference on Knowledge Discovery and Data Mining (KDD 2013)*, 632-640.

Myle Ott, Yejin Choi, Claire Cardie, and Jeffrey T. Hancock. 2011. Finding Deceptive Opinion Spam by Any Stretch of the Imagination. In *Proceedings of the 49th Annual Meeting of the Association for Computational Linguistics*, 309–319.

M. Scaiano and D. Inkpen. 2011. Finding Negative Key Phrases for Internet Advertising Campaigns Using Wikipedia. In *Recent Advances in Natural Language Processing (RANLP 2011)*, 648–653.

Yi-jie Tang and Hsin-Hsi Chen. 2011. Emotion Modeling from Writer/Reader Perspectives Using a Microblog Dataset. In *Proceedings of IJCNLP Workshop on Sentiment Analysis where AI Meets Psychology*, 11-19.

Yi-jie Tang and Hsin-Hsi Chen. 2012. Mining Sentiment Words from Microblogs for Predicting Writer-Reader Emotion Transition. In *Proceedings of the 8th International Conference on Language Resources and Evaluation (LREC 2012)*, 1226-1229.

Ming-kung Yeh. 2014. *Weekly Food and Drug Safety*. No. 440, February, Food and Drug Administration, Taiwan. Available at http://www.fda.gov.tw/TC/PublishOther.aspx.

lex4all: A language-independent tool for building and evaluating pronunciation lexicons for small-vocabulary speech recognition

Anjana Vakil, Max Paulus, Alexis Palmer, and Michaela Regneri
Department of Computational Linguistics, Saarland University
{anjanav,mpaulus,apalmer,regneri}@coli.uni-saarland.de

Abstract

This paper describes *lex4all*, an open-source PC application for the generation and evaluation of pronunciation lexicons in any language. With just a few minutes of recorded audio and no expert knowledge of linguistics or speech technology, individuals or organizations seeking to create speech-driven applications in low-resource languages can build lexicons enabling the recognition of small vocabularies (up to 100 terms, roughly) in the target language using an existing recognition engine designed for a high-resource source language (e.g. English). To build such lexicons, we employ an existing method for cross-language phoneme-mapping. The application also offers a built-in audio recorder that facilitates data collection, a significantly faster implementation of the phoneme-mapping technique, and an evaluation module that expedites research on small-vocabulary speech recognition for low-resource languages.

1 Introduction

In recent years it has been demonstrated that speech recognition interfaces can be extremely beneficial for applications in the developing world (Sherwani and Rosenfeld, 2008; Sherwani, 2009; Bali et al., 2013). Typically, such applications target low-resource languages (LRLs) for which large collections of speech data are unavailable, preventing the training or adaptation of recognition engines for these languages. However, an existing recognizer for a completely unrelated high-resource language (HRL), such as English, can be used to perform small-vocabulary recognition tasks in the LRL, given a pronunciation lexicon mapping each term in the target vocabulary to a sequence of phonemes in the HRL, i.e. phonemes which the recognizer can model.

This is the motivation behind *lex4all*,[1] an open-source application that allows users to automatically create a mapped pronunciation lexicon for terms in any language, using a small number of speech recordings and an out-of-the-box recognition engine for a HRL. The resulting lexicon can then be used with the HRL recognizer to add small-vocabulary speech recognition functionality to applications in the LRL, without the need for the large amounts of data and expertise in speech technologies required to train a new recognizer. This paper describes the *lex4all* application and its utility for the rapid creation and evaluation of pronunciation lexicons enabling small-vocabulary speech recognition in any language.

2 Background and related work

Several commercial speech recognition systems offer high-level Application Programming Interfaces (APIs) that make it extremely simple to add voice interfaces to an application, requiring very little general technical expertise and virtually no knowledge of the inner workings of the recognition engine. If the target language is supported by the system – the Microsoft Speech Platform,[2] for example, supports over 20 languages – this makes it very easy to create speech-driven applications.

If, however, the target language is one of the many thousands of LRLs for which high-quality recognition engines have not yet been developed, alternative strategies for developing speech-recognition interfaces must be employed. Though tools for quickly training recognizers for new languages exist (e.g. CMUSphinx[3]), they typically require many hours of training audio to produce effective models, data which is by definition not

[1] http://lex4all.github.io/lex4all/
[2] http://msdn.microsoft.com/en-us/library/hh361572
[3] http://www.cmusphinx.org

Proceedings of 52nd Annual Meeting of the Association for Computational Linguistics: System Demonstrations, pages 109–114,
Baltimore, Maryland USA, June 23-24, 2014.

available for LRLs. In efforts to overcome this data scarcity problem, recent years have seen the development of techniques for rapidly adapting multilingual or language-independent acoustic and language models to new languages from relatively small amounts of data (Schultz and Waibel, 2001; Kim and Khudanpur, 2003), methods for building resources such as pronunciation dictionaries from web-crawled data (Schlippe et al., 2014), and even a web-based interface, the Rapid Language Adaptation Toolkit[4] (RLAT), which allows non-expert users to exploit these techniques to create speech recognition and synthesis tools for new languages (Vu et al., 2010). While they greatly reduce the amount of data needed to build new recognizers, these approaches still require non-trivial amounts of speech and text in the target language, which may be an obstacle for very low- or zero-resource languages. Furthermore, even high-level tools such as RLAT still demand some understanding of linguistics/language technology, and thus may not be accessible to all users.

However, many useful applications (e.g. for accessing information or conducting basic transactions by telephone) only require small-vocabulary recognition, i.e. discrimination between a few dozen terms (words or short phrases). For example, VideoKheti (Bali et al., 2013), a text-free smartphone application that delivers agricultural information to low-literate farmers in India, recognizes 79 Hindi terms. For such small-vocabulary applications, an engine designed to recognize speech in a HRL can be used as-is to perform recognition of the LRL terms, given a grammar describing the allowable combinations and sequences of terms to be recognized, and a pronunciation lexicon mapping each target term to at least one pronunciation (sequence of phonemes) in the HRL (see Fig. 1 for an example).

This is the thinking behind Speech-based Automated Learning of Accent and Articulation Mapping, or "Salaam" (Sherwani, 2009; Qiao et al., 2010; Chan and Rosenfeld, 2012), a method of cross-language phoneme-mapping that discovers accurate source-language pronunciations for terms in the target language. The basic idea is to discover the best pronunciation (phoneme sequence) for a target term by using the source-language recognition engine to perform phone decoding on one or more utterances of the term. As commercial

[4]http://i19pc5.ira.uka.de/rlat-dev

```
<lexicon version="1.0" xmlns="http://www
    .w3.org/2005/01/pronunciation-
    lexicon" xml:lang="en-US"  alphabet
    ="x-microsoft-ups">

  <lexeme>
    <grapheme>beeni</grapheme>
    <phoneme>B E NG I</phoneme>
    <phoneme>B EI N I I</phoneme>
  </lexeme>

</lexicon>
```

Figure 1: Sample XML lexicon mapping the Yoruba word *beeni* ("yes") to two possible sequences of American English phonemes.

recognizers such as Microsoft's are designed for word-decoding, and their APIs do not usually allow users access to the phone-decoding mode, the Salaam approach uses a specially designed "super-wildcard" recognition grammar to mimic phone decoding and guide pronunciation discovery (Qiao et al., 2010; Chan and Rosenfeld, 2012). This allows the recognizer to identify the phoneme sequence best matching a given term, without any prior indication of how many phonemes that sequence should contain.

Given this grammar and one or more audio recordings of the term, Qiao et al. (2010) use an iterative training algorithm to discover the best pronunciation(s) for that term, one phoneme at a time. Compared to pronunciations hand-written by a linguist, pronunciations generated automatically by this algorithm yield substantially higher recognition accuracy: Qiao et al. (2010) report word recognition accuracy rates in the range of 75-95% for vocabularies of 50 terms. Chan and Rosenfeld (2012) improve accuracy on larger vocabularies (up to approximately 88% for 100 terms) by applying an iterative discriminative training algorithm, identifying and removing pronunciations that cause confusion between word types.

The Salaam method is fully automatic, demanding expertise neither in speech technology nor in linguistics, and requires only a few recorded utterances of each word. At least two projects have successfully used the Salaam method to add voice interfaces to real applications: an Urdu telephone-based health information system (Sherwani, 2009), and the VideoKheti application mentioned above (Bali et al., 2013). What has not existed before now is an interface that makes this approach accessible to any user.

Given the established success of the Salaam method, our contribution is to create a more time-efficient implementation of the pronunciation-discovery algorithm and integrate it into an easy-to-use graphical application. In the following sections, we describe this application and our slightly modified implementation of the Salaam method.

3 System overview

We have developed *lex4all* as a desktop application for Microsoft Windows,[5] since it relies on the Microsoft Speech Platform (MSP) as explained in Section 4.1. The application and its source code are freely available via GitHub.[6]

The application's core feature is its lexicon-building tool, the architecture of which is illustrated in Figure 2. A simple graphical user interface (GUI) allows users to type in the written form of each term in the target vocabulary, and select one or more audio recordings (`.wav` files) of that term. Given this input, the program uses the Salaam method to find the best pronunciation(s) for each term. This requires a pre-trained recognition engine for a HRL as well as a series of dynamically-created recognition grammars; the engine and grammars are constructed and managed using the MSP. We note here that our implementation of Salaam deviates slightly from that of Qiao et al. (2010), improving the time-efficiency and thus usability of the system (see Sec. 4).

Once pronunciations for all terms in the vocabulary have been generated, the application outputs a pronunciation lexicon for the given terms as an XML file conforming to the Pronunciation Lexicon Specification.[7] This lexicon can then be directly included in a speech recognition application built using the MSP API or a similar toolkit.

4 Pronunciation mapping

4.1 Recognition engine

For the HRL recognizer we use the US English recognition engine of the MSP. The engine is used as-is, with no modifications to its underlying models. We choose the MSP for its robustness and ease of use, as well as to maintain comparability with the work of Qiao et al. (2010) and Chan and Rosenfeld (2012). Following these authors, we use an engine designed for server-side recognition

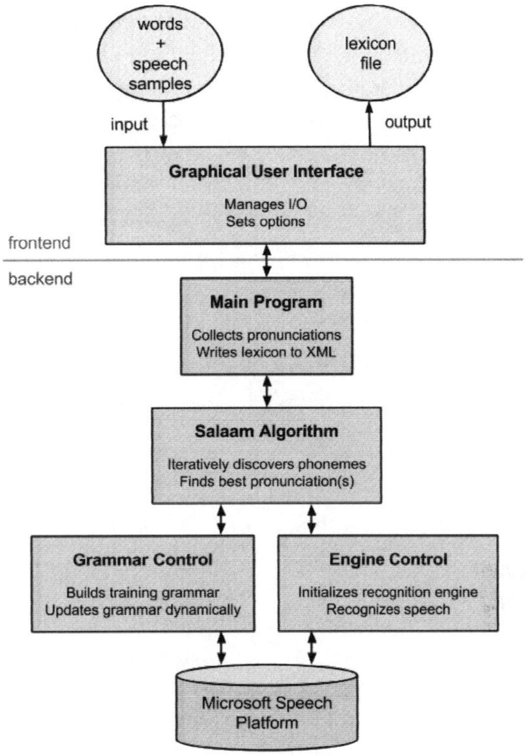

Figure 2: Overview of the core components of the *lex4all* lexicon-building application.

of low-quality audio, since we aim to enable the creation of useful applications for LRLs, including those spoken in developing-world communities, and such applications should be able to cope with telephone-quality audio or similar (Sherwani and Rosenfeld, 2008).

4.2 Implementation of the Salaam method

Pronunciations (sequences of source-language phonemes) for each term in the target vocabulary are generated from the audio sample(s) of that term using the iterative Salaam algorithm (Sec. 2), which employs the source-language recognizer and a special recognition grammar. In the first pass, the algorithm finds the best candidate(s) for the first phoneme of the sample(s), then the first two phonemes in the second pass, and so on until a stopping criterion is met. In our implementation, we stop iterations if the top-scoring sequence for a term has not changed for three consecutive iterations (Chan and Rosenfeld, 2012), or if the best sequence from a given pass has a lower confidence score than the best sequence from the

[5] Windows 7 or 8 (64-bit).

[6] http://github.com/lex4all/lex4all

[7] http://www.w3.org/TR/pronunciation-lexicon/

previous pass (Qiao et al., 2010). In both cases, at least three passes are required.

After the iterative training has completed, the n-best pronunciation sequences (with n specified by users – see Sec. 5.2) for each term are written to the lexicon, each in a `<phoneme>` element corresponding to the `<grapheme>` element containing the term's orthographic form (see Fig. 1).

4.3 Running time

A major challenge we faced in engineering a user-friendly application based on the Salaam algorithm was its long running time. The algorithm depends on a "super-wildcard" grammar that allows the recognizer to match each sample of a given term to a "phrase" of 0-10 "words", each word comprising any possible sequence of 1, 2, or 3 source-language phonemes (Qiao et al., 2010). Given the 40 phonemes of US English, this gives over 65,000 possibilities for each word, resulting in a huge training grammar and thus a long processing time. For a 25-term vocabulary with 5 training samples per term, the process takes approximately 1-2 hours on a standard modern laptop. For development and research, this long training time is a serious disadvantage.

To speed up training, we limit the length of each "word" in the grammar to only one phoneme, instead of up to 3, giving e.g. 40 possibilities instead of tens of thousands. The algorithm can still discover pronunciation sequences of an arbitrary length, since, in each iteration, the phonemes discovered so far are prepended to the super-wildcard grammar, such that the phoneme sequence of the first "word" in the phrase grows longer with each pass (Qiao et al., 2010). However, the new implementation is an order of magnitude faster: constructing the same 25-term lexicon on the same hardware takes approximately 2-5 *minutes*, i.e. less than 10% of the previous training time.

To ensure that the new implementation's vastly improved running time does not come at the cost of reduced recognition accuracy, we evaluate and compare word recognition accuracy rates using lexicons built with the old and new implementations. The data we use for this evaluation is a subset of the Yoruba data collected by Qiao et al. (2010), comprising 25 Yoruba terms (words) uttered by 2 speakers (1 male, 1 female), with 5 samples of each term per speaker. To determine same-speaker accuracy for each of the two speakers, we perform a leave-one-out evaluation on the five samples recorded per term per speaker. Cross-speaker accuracy is evaluated by training the system on all five samples of each term recorded by one speaker, and testing on all five samples from the other speaker. We perform paired two-tailed t-tests on the results to assess the significance of the differences in mean accuracy.

		Old	New	p
Same-speaker	Female average	72.8	**73.6**	0.75
	Male average	**90.4**	**90.4**	1.00
	Overall average	81.6	**82**	0.81
Cross-speaker	Trained on male	**70.4**	66.4	–
	Trained on female	76.8	**77.6**	–
	Average	**73.6**	72	0.63

Table 1: Word recognition accuracy for Yoruba using old (slower) and new (faster) implementations, with p-values from t-tests for significance of difference in means. Bold indicates highest accuracy.

The results of our evaluation, given in Table 1, indicate no statistically significant difference in accuracy between the two implementations (all p-values are above 0.5 and thus clearly insignificant). As our new, modified implementation of the Salaam algorithm is much faster than the original, yet equally accurate, *lex4all* uses the new implementation by default, although for research purposes we leave users the option of using the original (slower) implementation (see Section 5.2).

4.4 Discriminative training

Chan and Rosenfeld (2012) achieve increased accuracy (gains of up to 5 percentage points) by applying an iterative discriminative training algorithm. This algorithm takes as input the set of mapped pronunciations generated using the Salaam algorithm; in each iteration, it simulates recognition of the training audio samples using these pronunciations, and outputs a ranked list of the pronunciations in the lexicon that best match each sample. Pronunciations that cause "confusion" between words in the vocabulary, i.e. pronunciations that the recognizer matches to samples of the wrong word type, are thus identified and removed from the lexicon, and the process is repeated in the next iteration.

We implement this accuracy-boosting algorithm in *lex4all*, and apply it by default. To enable fine-tuning and experimentation, we leave users the option to change the number of passes (4 by default) or to disable discriminative training entirely, as mentioned in Section 5.2.

5 User interface

As mentioned above, we aim to make the creation and evaluation of lexicons simple, fast, and above all accessible to users with no expertise in speech or language technologies. Therefore, the application makes use of a simple GUI that allows users to quickly and easily specify input and output file paths, and to control the parameters of the lexicon-building algorithms.

Figure 3 shows the main interface of the *lex4all* lexicon builder. This window displays the terms that have been specified and the number of audio samples that have been selected for each word. Another form, accessed via the "Add word" or "Edit" buttons, allows users to add to or edit the vocabulary by simply typing in the desired orthographic form of the word and selecting the audio sample(s) to be used for pronunciation discovery (see Sec. 5.1 for more details on audio input).

Once the target vocabulary and training audio have been specified, and the additional options have been set if desired, users click the "Build Lexicon" button and specify the desired name and target directory of the lexicon file to be saved, and pronunciation discovery begins. When all pronunciations have been generated, a success message displaying the elapsed training time is displayed, and users may either proceed to the evaluation module to assess the newly created lexicon (see Sec. 6), or return to the main interface to build another lexicon.

5.1 Audio input and recording

The GUI allows users to easily browse their file system for pre-recorded audio samples (`.wav` files) to be used for lexicon training. To simplify data collection and enable the development of lexicons even for zero-resource languages, *lex4all* also offers a simple built-in audio recorder to record new speech samples.

The recorder, built using the open-source library NAudio,[8] takes the default audio input device as its source and records one channel with a sampling rate of 8 kHz, as the recognition engine we employ is designed for low-quality audio (see Section 4.1).

[8]http://naudio.codeplex.com/

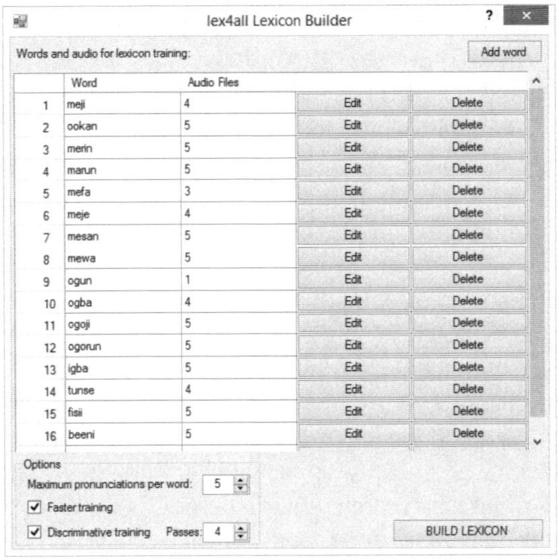

Figure 3: Screenshot of the lexicon builder.

5.2 Additional options

As seen in Figure 3, *lex4all* includes optional controls for quick and easy fine-tuning of the lexicon-building process (the default settings are pictured).

First of all, users can specify the maximum number of pronunciations (`<phoneme>` elements) per word that the lexicon may contain; allowing more pronunciations per word may improve recognition accuracy (Qiao et al., 2010; Chan and Rosenfeld, 2012). Secondly, users may train the lexicon using our modified, faster implementation of the Salaam algorithm or the original implementation. Finally, users may choose whether or not discriminative training is applied, and if so, how many passes are run (see Sec. 4.4).

6 Evaluation module for research

In addition to its primary utility as a lexicon-building tool, *lex4all* is also a valuable research aide thanks to an evaluation module that allows users to quickly and easily evaluate the lexicons they have created. The evaluation tool allows users to browse their file system for an XML lexicon file that they wish to evaluate; this may be a lexicon created using *lex4all*, or any other lexicon in the same format. As in the main interface, users then select one or more audio samples (`.wav` files) for each term they wish to evaluate. The system then attempts to recognize each sample using the given lexicon, and reports the counts and percentages of correct, incorrect, and failed recognitions.

Users may optionally save this report, along with a confusion matrix of word types, as a comma-separated values (`.csv`) file.

The evaluation module thus allows users to quickly and easily assess different configurations of the lexicon-building tool, by simply changing the settings using the GUI and evaluating the resulting lexicons. Furthermore, as the application's source code is freely available and modifiable, researchers may even replace entire modules of the system (e.g. use a different pronunciation-discovery algorithm), and use the evaluation module to quickly assess the results. Therefore, *lex4all* facilitates not only application development but also further research into small-vocabulary speech recognition using mapped pronunciation lexicons.

7 Conclusion and future work

We have presented *lex4all*, an open-source application that enables the rapid automatic creation of pronunciation lexicons in any (low-resource) language, using an out-of-the-box commercial recognizer for a high-resource language and the Salaam method for cross-language pronunciation mapping (Qiao et al., 2010; Chan and Rosenfeld, 2012). The application thus makes small-vocabulary speech recognition interfaces feasible in any language, since only minutes of training audio are required; given the built-in audio recorder, lexicons can be constructed even for zero-resource languages. Furthermore, *lex4all*'s flexible and open design and easy-to-use evaluation module make it a valuable tool for research in language-independent small-vocabulary recognition.

In future work, we plan to expand the selection of source-language recognizers; at the moment, *lex4all* only uses US English as the source language, but any of the 20+ other HRLs supported by the MSP could be added. This would enable investigation of the target-language recognition accuracy obtained using different source languages, though our initial exploration of this issue suggests that phonetic similarity between the source and target languages might not significantly affect accuracy (Vakil and Palmer, 2014). Another future goal is to improve and extend the functionality of the audio-recording tool to make it more flexible and user-friendly. Finally, as a complement to the application, it would be beneficial to create a central online data repository where users can upload the lexicons they have built and the speech samples they have recorded. Over time, this could become a valuable collection of LRL data, enabling developers and researchers to share and re-use data among languages or language families.

Acknowledgements

The first author was partially supported by a Deutschlandstipendium scholarship sponsored by IMC AG. We thank Roni Rosenfeld, Hao Yee Chan, and Mark Qiao for generously sharing their speech data and valuable advice, and Dietrich Klakow, Florian Metze, and the three anonymous reviewers for their feedback.

References

Kalika Bali, Sunayana Sitaram, Sebastien Cuendet, and Indrani Medhi. 2013. A Hindi speech recognizer for an agricultural video search application. In *ACM DEV '13*.

Hao Yee Chan and Roni Rosenfeld. 2012. Discriminative pronunciation learning for speech recognition for resource scarce languages. In *ACM DEV '12*.

Woosung Kim and Sanjeev Khudanpur. 2003. Language model adaptation using cross-lingual information. In *Eurospeech*.

Fang Qiao, Jahanzeb Sherwani, and Roni Rosenfeld. 2010. Small-vocabulary speech recognition for resource-scarce languages. In *ACM DEV '10*.

Tim Schlippe, Sebastian Ochs, and Tanja Schultz. 2014. Web-based tools and methods for rapid pronunciation dictionary creation. *Speech Communication*, 56:101–118.

Tanja Schultz and Alex Waibel. 2001. Language-independent and language-adaptive acoustic modeling for speech recognition. *Speech Communication*, 35(1-2):31 – 51.

Jahanzeb Sherwani and Roni Rosenfeld. 2008. The case for speech technology for developing regions. In *HCI for Community and International Development Workshop, Florence, Italy*.

Jahanzeb Sherwani. 2009. *Speech interfaces for information access by low literate users*. Ph.D. thesis, Carnegie Mellon University.

Anjana Vakil and Alexis Palmer. 2014. Cross-language mapping for small-vocabulary ASR in under-resourced languages: Investigating the impact of source language choice. In *SLTU '14*.

Ngoc Thang Vu, Tim Schlippe, Franziska Kraus, and Tanja Schultz. 2010. Rapid bootstrapping of five Eastern European languages using the Rapid Language Adaptation Toolkit. In *Interspeech*.

Enhanced Search with Wildcards and Morphological Inflections in the Google Books Ngram Viewer

Jason Mann[♣*] **David Zhang**[◇*] **Lu Yang**[♡*] **Dipanjan Das**[♠] **Slav Petrov**[♠]
[♣]Columbia University [◇]USC [♡]Cornell University [♠]Google Inc.
Contact: `dipanjand@google.com`, `slav@google.com`

Abstract

We present a new version of the Google Books Ngram Viewer, which plots the frequency of words and phrases over the last five centuries; its data encompasses 6% of the world's published books. The new Viewer adds three features for more powerful search: wildcards, morphological inflections, and capitalization. These additions allow the discovery of patterns that were previously difficult to find and further facilitate the study of linguistic trends in printed text.

1 Introduction

The Google Books Ngram project facilitates the analysis of cultural, social and linguistic trends through five centuries of written text in eight languages. The Ngram Corpus (Michel et al., 2011; Lin et al., 2012) consists of words and phrases (i.e., ngrams) and their usage frequency over time.[1] The interactive Ngram Viewer[2] allows users to retrieve and plot the frequency of multiple ngrams on a simple webpage. The Viewer is widely popular and can be used to efficiently explore and visualize patterns in the underlying ngram data. For example, the ngram data has been used to detect emotion trends in 20th century books (Acerbi et al., 2013), to analyze text focusing on market capitalism throughout the past century (Schulz and Robinson, 2013), detect social and cultural impact of historical personalities (Skiena and Ward, 2013), or to analyze the correlation of economic crises with a literary 'misery index' reflected in printed text during crises periods (Bentley et al., 2014).

Query: *"President Kennedy, President Reagan, President Nixon"*

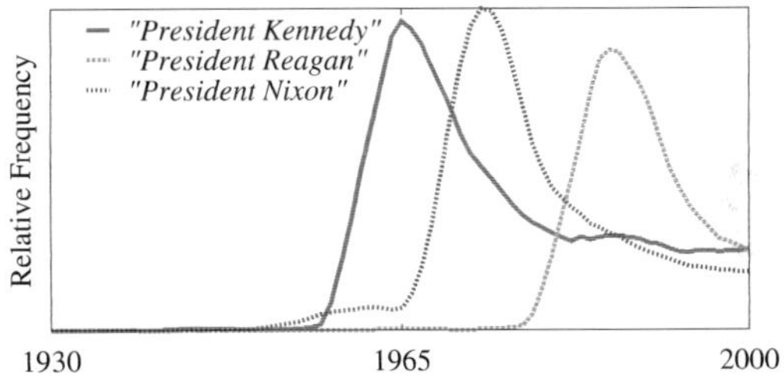

Figure 1: Mention frequencies for three different American presidents queried one-by-one.

A limitation of the Viewer, however, is that all the reasoning has to be done by the user, and only individual, user-specified ngrams can be retrieved and plotted. For example, to compare the popularity of different presidents, one needs to come up with a list of presidents and then search for them one-by-one. The result of the query '`President Kennedy, President Nixon, President Reagan`' is shown in Figure 1. To determine the most popular president, one would need to search for all presidents, which is cumbersome and should ideally be automated.

In this paper, we therefore present an updated version of the Viewer that enhances its search functionality. We introduce three new features that automatically expand a given query and retrieve a collection of ngrams, to facilitate the discovery of patterns in the underlying data. First, users can replace one query term with a placeholder symbol '$\star$' (wildcard, henceforth), which will return the ten most frequent expansions of the wildcard in the corpus for the specified year range. Second, by adding a specific marker to any word in a query ('`_INF`'), ngrams with all

* The majority of this work was carried out during an internship at Google.

[1] The Ngram Corpus is freely available for download at `http://books.google.com/ngrams/datasets`.

[2] See `http://books.google.com/ngrams`.

Proceedings of 52nd Annual Meeting of the Association for Computational Linguistics: System Demonstrations, pages 115–120,
Baltimore, Maryland USA, June 23-24, 2014.

morphological inflections of that word will be retrieved. Finally, the new Viewer supports capitalization searches, which return all capitalization variants of the query ngram. Figure 2 provides examples for these three new types of queries.

While it is fairly obvious how the above search features can be implemented via brute-force computation, supporting an interactive application with low latency necessitates some precomputation. In particular, the wildcard search feature poses some challenges because the most frequent expansions depend on the selected year range (consider the frequency with which presidents are mentioned during different decades, for example). To this end, we provide details of our system architecture in §2 and discuss how the new search features are implemented in §3. In addition, we present an overhaul of the Ngram Viewer's user interface with interactive features that allow for easier management of the increase in data points returned.

Detailed analysis and interpretation of trends uncovered with the new search interface is beyond the scope of this paper. We highlight some interesting use cases in §4; many of the presented queries were difficult (or impossible) to execute in the previous versions of the system. We emphasize that this demonstration updates only the Viewer, providing tools for easier analysis of the underlying corpora. The ngram corpora themselves are not updated.

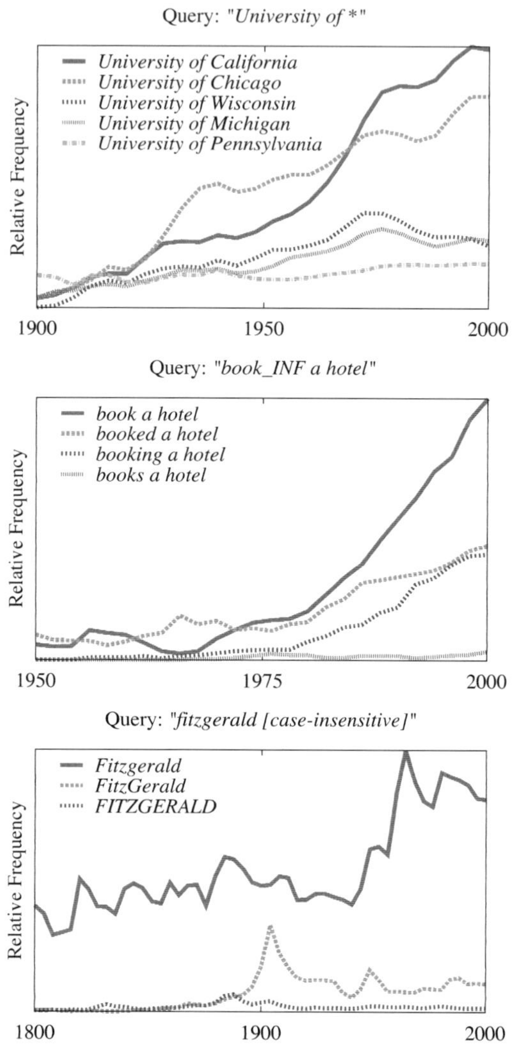

Figure 2: In the new enhanced search features of the Ngram Viewer, a single query is automatically expanded to retrieve multiple related ngrams. From top to bottom, we show examples of the wildcard operator ('*'), the '_INF' marker that results in morphological inflections, and the case insensitive search functionality. Due to space considerations we show only a subset of the results returned by the Ngram Viewer.

2 System Overview

We first briefly review the two editions of the Ngram Corpus (Michel et al., 2011; Lin et al., 2012) and then describe the extensions to the architecture of the Viewer that are needed to support the new search features.

2.1 The Ngram Corpus

The Google Books Ngram Corpus provides ngram counts for eight different languages over more than 500 years; additionally, the English corpus is split further into British vs. American English and Fiction to aid domain-specific analysis. This corpus is a subset of all books digitized at Google and represents more than 6% of all publicized texts (Lin et al., 2012). Two editions of the corpus are available: the first edition dates from 2009 and is described in Michel et al. (2011); the second edition is from 2012 and is described in Lin et al. (2012). The new search features presented here are available for both editions.

Michel et al. (2011) extract ngrams for each page in isolation. More specifically, they use whitespace tokenization and extract all ngrams up to length five. These ngrams include ones that potentially span sentence boundaries, but do not include ngrams that span across page breaks (even when they are part of the same sentence). Lin et al. (2012) on the other hand perform tokenization, text normalization and segmentation into sentences. They then add synthetic _START_ and _END_ tokens to the beginning and end of the sentences to enable the distinction of sentence medial ngrams from those near sentence boundaries. They also ensure that sentences that span across page boundaries are included. Due to these differences, as well as the availability of additional book data, improvements to the optical character recognition algorithms and metadata extraction for dating the books, the ngrams counts from the two editions are not the same.

The edition from Lin et al. (2012) additionally includes syntactic ngrams. The corpus is tagged using the universal part-of-speech (POS) tag set of Petrov et al. (2012): NOUN (nouns), VERB (verbs), ADJ (adjectives), ADV (adverbs), PRON (pronouns), DET (determiners and articles), ADP (prepositions and postpositions), CONJ (conjunctions). Words can be disambiguated by their POS tag by simply appending the tag to the word with an underscore (e.g. book_NOUN) and can also be replaced by POS tags in the ngrams, see Lin et al. (2012) for details. The corpus is parsed with a dependency parser and head-modifier syntactic relations between words in the same sentence are extracted. Dependency relations are represented as '=>' in the corpus. Our new enhanced search features for automatic expansions can also be applied to these syntactic ngrams. In fact, some of the most interesting queries use expansions to automatically uncover related ngrams, while using syntax to focus on particular patterns.

The Viewer supports the composition of ngram frequencies via arithmetic operators. Addition (+), subtraction (−) and division (/) of ngrams are carried out on a per year basis, while multiplication (∗) is performed by a scalar that is applied to all counts in the time series. Where ambiguous, the wildcard operator takes precedence over the multiplication operator. Parentheses can be used to disambiguate and to force the interpretation of a mathematical operation.

2.2 Architecture

The Ngram Viewer provides a lightweight interface to the underlying ngram corpora. In its basic form, user requests are directed through the server to a simple lookup table containing the raw ngrams and their frequencies. This data flow is displayed in the top part of Figure 3 and is maintained for queries that do not involve the new expansion features introduced in this work.

The expansion queries could in principle be

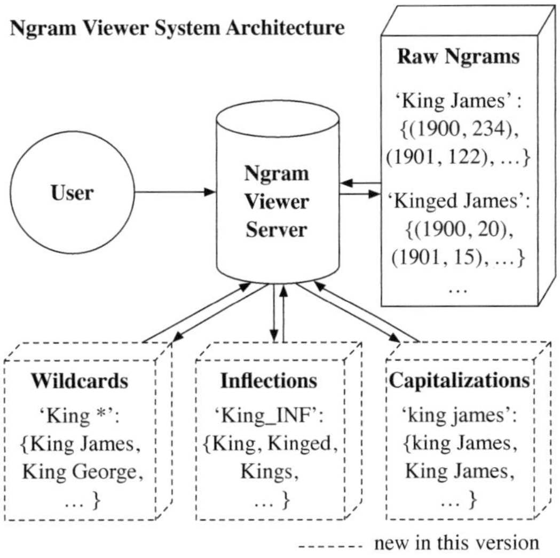

Figure 3: Overview of the Ngram Viewer architecture.

implemented by scanning the raw ngrams on the fly and returning the matching subset: to answer the query 'President *', one would need to obtain all bigrams starting with the word President (there are 23,693) and extract the most frequent ten. Given the large number of ngrams (especially for larger n), such an approach turns out to be too slow for an interactive application. We therefore pre-compute intermediate results that can be used to more efficiently retrieve the results for expansion queries. The intermediate results are stored in additional lookup tables (shown at the bottom in Figure 3). When the user executes an expansion search, the query is first routed to the appropriate lookup table which stores all possible expansions (including expansions that might not appear in the corpus). These expanded ngrams are then retrieved from the raw ngram table, sorted by frequency and returned to he user. We describe the intermediate results tables and how they are generated in the next section.

Note that we only support one expansion operation per query ngram. This is needed in order to avoid the combinatorial explosion that would result from mixing multiple expansion operators in the same query.

3 New Features

The three new search features are implemented via the same two-step approach. As shown in Figure 3, we add three new lookup tables that store intermediate results needed for efficiently support-

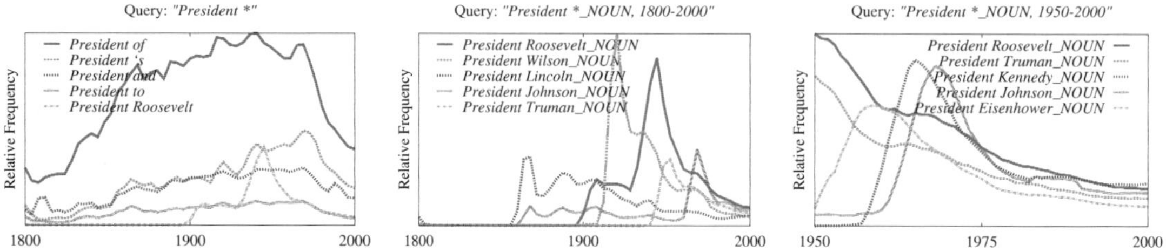

Figure 4: Different wildcard queries for bigrams starting with `President`. Specification of a POS tag along with the wildcard operator results in more specific results, and the results vary depending on the selected yaer range.

ing the new search types. In all cases the lookup tables provide a set of possible expansions that are then retrieved in the original raw ngram table. Below we describe how these intermediate results are generated and how they are used to retrieve the final results.

3.1 Wildcards

Wildcards provide a convenient way to automatically retrieve and explore related ngrams. Because of the large number of possibilities that can fill a wildcard slot, returning anything but the top few expansions is likely to be overwhelming. We therefore return only the ten most frequent expansions. Determining the most frequent expansions is unfortunately computationally very expensive because of the large number of ngrams; the query '`the *`' for example has 2,353,960 expansions.

To avoid expensive on-the-fly computations, we precompute the most frequent expansions for all possible queries. The problem that arises is that the ten most frequent expansions depend on the selected year range. Consider the query '`President *`'; we would like to be able get the correct result for any year range. Since our data spans more than 500 years, precomputing the results for all year ranges is not a possibility. Instead, we compute the possible wildcard expansions for each year. The top expansions for the entire range are then taken from the union of top expansions for each year. This set is at most of size $10n$ (where n is the year range) and in practice typically a lot smaller. Theoretically it is possible for this approximation to miss an expansion that is never among the top ten for a particular year, but is cumulatively in the top ten for the entire range. This would happen if there were many spikes in the data, which is not the case.

To make the wildcard expansions more relevant, we filter expansions that consist entirely of punctuation symbols. To further narrow down the expansions and focus on particular patterns, we allow wildcards to be qualified via POS tags. Figure 4 shows some example wildcard queries involving bigrams that start with the word '`President`.' See also Table 1 for some additional examples. Note that it is possible to replace POS tags with wildcards (e.g., `cook_*`) which will find all POS tags that the query word can take.

3.2 Morphological Inflections

When comparing ngram frequencies (especially across languages, but also for the same language), it can be useful to examine and potentially aggregate the frequencies of all inflected forms. This can be accomplished by manually deriving all inflected forms and then using arithmetic operations to aggregate their counts. Our new inflected form search accomplishes this automatically. By appending the keyword `_INF` to a word, a set of ngrams with all inflected forms of the word will be retrieved. To generate the inflected forms we make use of Wiktionary[3] and supplement it with automatically generated inflection tables based on the approach of Durrett and DeNero (2013).

Because there are at most a few dozen inflected forms for any given word, we can afford to substitute and retrieve all inflections of the marked word, even the ones that are not grammatical in a given ngram context. This has the advantage that we only need to store inflected forms for individual words rather than entire ngrams. If a generated ngram has no support in the corpus, we simply omit it from the final set of results. We do not perform any additional filtering; as a result, an inflection search can produce many results, especially for morphologically rich languages like Russian. We have therefore updated the user interface to better deal with many data lines (§4).

[3] See `http://www.wiktionary.org/`. Because Wiktionary is an evolving resource, results for a particular query may change over time.

Query	Possible Replacements
* 's Theorem	Lagrange 's Theorem, Gauss 's Theorem, Euler 's Theorem, Pascal 's Theorem
War=>*_NOUN	War=>World_NOUN, War=>Civil_NOUN, War=>Second_NOUN, War=>Cold_NOUN
любовь_INF	любил, люблу, любит, любить, любила, любимый, любишь
book_INF	book, books, booked, booking
book_INF_NOUN	book, books
cook_*	cook_NOUN, cook_VERB
the cook (case insensitive)	THE COOK, the cook, The Cook, the Cook, The cook

Table 1: Examples expansions for wildcard, inflection, and capitalization queries.

3.3 Capitalization

By aggregating different capitalizations of the same word, one can normalize between sentence-initial and sentence-medial occurrences of a given word. A simple way to accomplish this is by searching for a lowercased, capitalized and all caps spelling of the query. This however can miss CamelCase spelling and other capitalization variants (consider FitzGerald for example). It is of course not feasible to try all case variants of every letter in the query. Instead, we perform an offline precomputation step in which we collect all ngrams that map to the same lowercased string. Due to scanning errors and spelling mistakes there can be many extremely rare capitalization variants for a given query. We therefore filter out all variants that have a cumulative count of less than 1% of the most frequent variant for a given year range. Capitalization searches are enabled by selecting a case-insensitive check box on the new interface.

4 Use Cases

The three features introduced in this paper represent a major extension of the capabilities of the Ngram Viewer. While the second edition of the Ngram Corpus (Lin et al., 2012) introduced syntactic ngrams, the functionality of the Viewer had remained largely unchanged since its first launch five years ago. Together, the updated Corpus and Viewer enable a much more detailed analysis of the underlying data. Below we provide some uses cases highlighting the ways in which sophisticated queries can be crafted. While the results produce some intriguing patterns, we leave their analysis to the experts.

Since we have made no modifications to the underlying raw ngrams, all of the plots in this paper could have also been generated with the previous version of the Viewer. They would, however, have required the user to manually generate and issue all query terms. For example, Figure 1 shows manually created queries searching for specific presidents; contrarily, Figure 4 shows single wildcard queries that automatically retrieve the ten most frequently mentioned presidents and uncover additional trends that would have required extra work on behalf of the user.

The wildcard feature used on its own can be a powerful tool for the analysis of top expansions for a certain context. Although already useful on its own, it becomes really powerful when combined with POS tags. The user can attach an underscore and POS tag to either a wildcard-based or inflection-based query to specify that the expansions returned should be of a specific part of speech. Compare the utility of the generic wildcard and a search with a noun part-of-speech specification in a query examining president names, 'President *' vs. 'President *_NOUN' shown in Figure 4. The former gives a mixture of prepositions, particles, and verbs along with names of presidents, and because the latter specifies the noun tag, the top expansions turn out to be names and more in line with the intention of the search. Also, note in Figure 4 the difference in expansions that searching over two different time ranges provides. In Table 2, we compare the combination of the wildcard feature with the existing dependency link feature to highlight a comparison of context across several languages.

It is worth noting that the newly introduced features could result in many lines in the resulting chart. Hence, we have updated the Viewer's user interface to better handle charts involving many ngrams. The new interactive functionality allows the user to highlight a line by hovering over it, keep that focus by left clicking, and clear all focused lines by double clicking. A right click on any of the expansions returned by an issued query combines them into the year-wise sum total of all the expansions. We added another feature to the

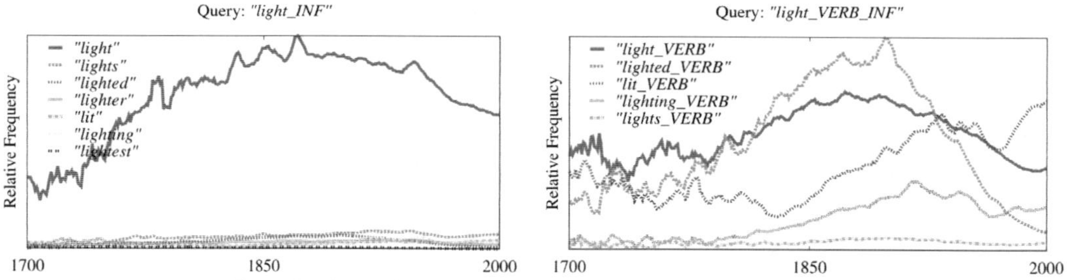

Figure 5: Comparison of specification of POS tag in wildcard search.

English (All)	American English	British English	German	French	Russian	Italian	Chinese (Simplified)	Spanish	Hebrew
drinks	drinks	drinks	trinkt	boit	пьёт	beve	喝	bebe	שתה
water	water	water	Bier (beer)	vin (wine)	он (he)	vino (wine)	酒 (wine)	agua (water)	יין (wine)
wine	wine	wine	Kaffee (coffee)	sang (blood)	чай (tea)	acqua (water)	茶 (tea)	vino (wine)	מים (water)
milk	coffee	tea	Wein (wine)	eau (water)	воду (water)	sangue (blood)	水 (water)	sangre (blood)	ה (the)
coffee	beer	blood	Wasser (water)	cafe (coffee)	Он (He)	birra (beer)	咖啡 (coffee)	vaso (glass)	כוס (cup)
beer	milk	beer	Tee (tea)	verre (glass)	вино (wine)	caffé (coffee)	人 (person)	cerveza (beer)	תה (tea)

Table 2: Comparison of the top modifiers of the verb drinks, or its equivalent in translation, in all corpora, retrieved via the query drinks_VERB=>*_NOUN and equivalents in the other languages. The modifiers can appear both in subject and in object position because we have access only to unlabeled dependencies.

interface that creates static URLs maintaining all the raw ngrams retrieved from any query. This prevents statically linked charts from changing over time, and allowing for backwards compatibility.

One of the primary benefits of the capitalization feature is the combination of multiple searches in one, which allows the user to compare case-insensitive usages of two different phrases. An alternative use is in Figure 2(c), where capitalization search allows the immediate identification of changing orthographic usage of a word or phrase; in this case the figure shows the arrival of F. Scott Fitzgerald in the early to mid 20th century, as well as the rise in popularity of the CamelCase variety of his surname at the turn of the 19th century.

Searches using inflections can be useful for the same reasons as the capitalization feature, and also be used to compare changes in spelling; it is particularly useful for the analysis of irregular verbs, where the query can return both the regular and irregular forms of a verb.

5 Conclusions

We have presented an update to the Ngram Viewer that introduces new search features. Users can now perform more powerful searches that automatically uncover trends which were previously difficult or impossible to extract. We look forward to seeing what users of the Viewer will discover.

6 Acknowledgements

We would like to thank John DeNero, Jon Orwant, Karl Moritz Hermann for many useful discussions.

References

A. Acerbi, V. Lampos, and R. A. Bentley. 2013. Robustness of emotion extraction from 20th century english books. In *Proceedings of the IEEE International Conference on Big Data*.

A. R. Bentley, A. Acerbi, P. Ormerod, and V. Lampos. 2014. Books average previous decade of economic misery. *PLOS One*, 9(1).

G. Durrett and J. DeNero. 2013. Supervised learning of complete morphological paradigms. In *Proceedings of NAACL-HLT*.

Y. Lin, J.-B. Michel, E. L. Aiden, J. Orwant, W. Brockman, and S. Petrov. 2012. Syntactic annotations for the Google Books Ngram Corpus. In *Proceedings of the ACL*.

J.-B. Michel, Y. K. Shen, A. P. Aiden, A. Veres, M. K. Gray, The Google Books Team, J. P. Pickett, D. Hoiberg, D. Clancy, P. Norvig, J. Orwant, S. Pinker, M. A. Nowak, and E. Lieberman Aiden. 2011. Quantitative analysis of culture using millions of digitized books. *Science*.

S. Petrov, D. Das, and R. McDonald. 2012. A universal part-of-speech tagset. In *Proc. of LREC*.

J. Schulz and L. Robinson. 2013. Shifting grounds and evolving battlegrounds. *American Journal of Cultural Sociology*, 1(3):373–402.

S. Skiena and C. Ward. 2013. *Who's Bigger?: Where Historical Figures Really Rank*. Cambridge University Press.

Simplified Dependency Annotations with GFL-Web

Michael T. Mordowanec **Nathan Schneider** **Chris Dyer** **Noah A. Smith**
School of Computer Science
Carnegie Mellon University
Pittsburgh, PA 15213, USA
michael.mordowanec@gmail.com, {nschneid,cdyer,nasmith}@cs.cmu.edu

Abstract

We present GFL-Web, a web-based interface for syntactic dependency annotation with the lightweight FUDG/GFL formalism. Syntactic attachments are specified in GFL notation and visualized as a graph. A one-day pilot of this workflow with 26 annotators established that even novices were, with a bit of training, able to rapidly annotate the syntax of English Twitter messages. The open-source tool is easily installed and configured; it is available at: https://github.com/Mordeaux/gfl_web

1 Introduction

High-quality syntactic annotation of natural language is expensive to produce. Well-known large-scale syntactic annotation projects, such as the Penn Treebank (Marcus et al., 1993), the English Web Treebank (Bies et al., 2012), the Penn Arabic Treebank (Maamouri et al., 2004), and the Prague dependency treebanks (Hajič, 1998; Čmejrek et al., 2005), have relied on expert linguists to produce carefully-controlled annotated data. Because this process is costly, such annotation projects have been undertaken for only a handful of important languages. Therefore, developing syntactic resources for less-studied, lower-resource, or politically less important languages and genres will require alternative methods. To address this, simplified annotation schemes that trade cost for detail have been proposed (Habash and Roth, 2009).[1]

The Fragmentary Unlabeled Dependency Grammar (FUDG) formalism (Schneider et al., 2013) was proposed as a simplified framework for annotating dependency syntax. Annotation effort is reduced by relaxing a number of constraints placed on traditional annotators: partial fragments can be specified where the annotator is uncertain of part of the structure or wishes to focus only on certain phenomena (such as verbal argument structure). FUDG also offers mechanisms for excluding extraneous tokens from the annotation, for marking multiword units, and for describing coordinate structures. FUDG is written in an ASCII-based notation for annotations called Graph Fragment Language (GFL), and text-based tools for verifying, converting, and rendering GFL annotations are provided.

Although GFL offers a number of conveniences to annotators, the text-based UI is limiting: the existing tools require constant switching between a text editor and executing commands, and there are no tools for managing a large-scale annotation effort. Additionally, user interface research has found marked preferences for and better performance with graphical tools relative to text-based interfaces—particularly for less computer-savvy users (Staggers and Kobus, 2000). In this paper, we present the **GFL-Web** tool, a web-based interface for FUDG/GFL annotation. The simple interface provides instantaneous feedback on the well-formedness of a GFL annotation, and by wrapping Schneider et al.'s notation parsing and rendering software, gives a user-friendly visualization of the annotated sentence. The tool itself is lightweight, multi-user, and easily deployed with few software dependencies. Sentences are assigned to annotators via an administrative interface, which also records progress and provides for a text dump of

[1] These can be especially effective when some details of the syntax can be predicted automatically with high accuracy (Alkuhlani et al., 2013).

Proceedings of 52nd Annual Meeting of the Association for Computational Linguistics: System Demonstrations, pages 121–126, Baltimore, Maryland USA, June 23-24, 2014.

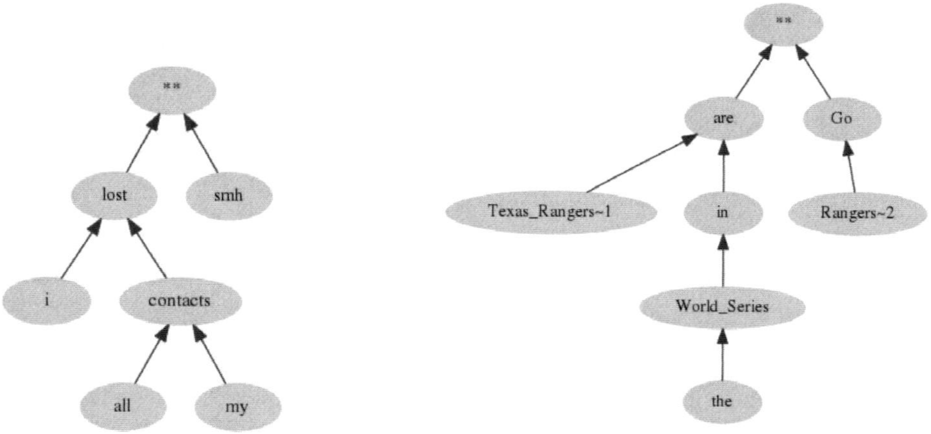

(a) @Bryan_wright11 i lost all my contacts , smh .

(b) Texas Rangers are in the World Series ! Go Rangers !!!!!!!!! http://fb.me/D2LsXBJx

Figure 1: FUDG annotation graphs for two tweets.

all annotations. The interface for annotators is designed to be as simple as possible.

We provide an overview of the FUDG/GFL framework (§2), detail how the tool is set up and utilized (§3), and discuss a pilot exercise in which 26 users provided nearly 1,000 annotations of English Twitter messages (§4). Finally, we note some of the technical aspects of the tool (§5) and related syntactic annotation software (§6).

2 Background

GFL-Web is designed to simplify the creation of dependency treebanks from noisy or under-resourced data; to that end, it exploits the lightweight FUDG/GFL framework of Schneider et al. (2013). Here we outline how FUDG differs from traditional Dependency Grammar (§2.1) and detail major aspects of GFL (§2.2).

2.1 FUDG

Figure 1 displays two FUDG graphs of annotations of Twitter messages ("tweets", shown below in tokenized form). Arrows point upwards from dependents to their heads. These tweets illustrate several characteristics of the formalism, including:

- The input may contain multiple independent syntactic units, or "utterances"; the annotation indicates these by attaching their heads to a special root node called **.
- Some input tokens are omitted if deemed extrinsic to the syntax; by convention, these include most punctuation, hashtags, usernames, and URLs.
- Multiword units may be joined to form composite lexical nodes (e.g., `World_Series` in figure 1b). These nodes are not annotated with any internal syntactic structure.
- Tokens that are used in the FUDG parse must be unambiguous. If a word appears multiple times in the input, it is disambiguated with ~ and an index (e.g., `Rangers~2` in figure 1b).

(Some of the other mechanisms in FUDG, such as coordinate structures and underspecification, are not shown here; they are not important for purposes of this paper.)

2.2 GFL

The Graph Fragment Language is a simple ASCII-based language for FUDG annotations. Its norms are designed to be familiar to users with basic programming language proficiency, and they are intuitive and easy to learn even for those without. The annotation in figure 1a may be expressed in GFL as:[2]

```
i > lost** < ({all my} > contacts)
smh**
```

In GFL, angle brackets point from a dependent (child) to its head (parent). Parentheses group nodes together; the head of this group is then attached to another node. The double asterisk (**) marks a root node in an annotations containing multiple utterances. Curly braces group nodes that modify the same head.

GFL corresponding to Figure 1b is:

[2]The abbreviation smh stands for *shaking my head*.

Sentence: Texas Rangers are in the World Series ! Go Rangers !!!!!!!!! http://fb.me/D2LsXBJx

Input format:

```
---
% ID data_set_name:417
% TEXT
Texas Rangers~1 are in the World Series ! Go Rangers~2 !!!!!!!!!
http://fb.me/D2LsXBJx
% ANNO
Texas Rangers~1 are in the World Series  Go Rangers~2
http://fb.me/D2LsXBJx
```

Figure 2: Illustration of the GFL-Web input format for a tweet. The ANNO section will be shown to the user as the default annotation; punctuation has been stripped out automatically to save time.

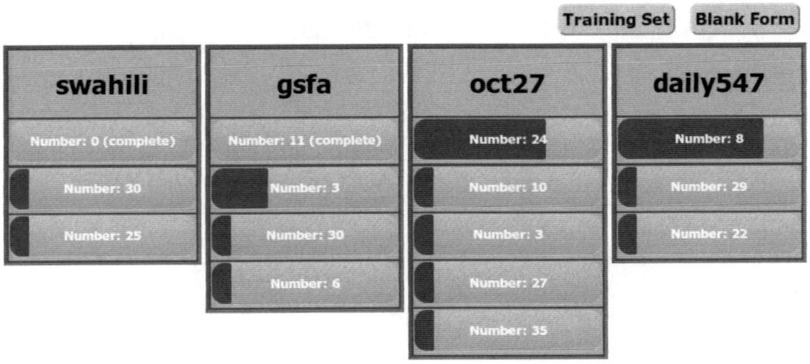

Figure 3: User home screen showing assigned batches for annotation, with links to the training set and blank annotation form.

```
[Texas Rangers~1] > are** < in
in < (the > [World Series])
Go** < Rangers~2
```

This uses square brackets for multiword expressions. Similar to a programming language, there are often many equivalent GFL annotation options for a given sentence. The annotation can be split across multiple lines so that annotators can approach smaller units first and then link them together.

3 Using GFL-Web

The GFL-Web tool uses the Python programming language's Flask microframework for server-side scripting. This allows it to be deployed on a web server, locally or via the Internet. This also enables the interface to rely on scripts previously created for analyzing GFL. Once installed, the researcher need only configure a few settings and begin entering data to be annotated.

3.1 Setup

There are a few simple configuration options. The most useful of these options specify how many sentences should be in each batch that is assigned to an annotator, and how many sentences in each batch should be doubly annotated, for the purpose of assessing inter-annotator agreement. By default, the batch size is 10, and the first 2 sentences of each batch overlap with the previous batch, so 4/10 of the sentences in the batch will be annotated by someone else (assuming no two consecutive batches are assigned to the same user). The program requires tokenized input, with indices added to distinguish between words that appear twice (easily automated). The input format, figure 2, allows for easy editing with a text editor if so desired.

Once the input files have been placed in a designated directory, an **admin interface** can be used to assign batches of data to specific users (annotators).

3.2 Annotation

Annotators log in with their username and see a **home screen**, figure 3. The home screen always offers links to a **training set** to get them up to speed, as well as a **blank** annotation form into which they can enter and annotate any sentence. Beneath these is a table of batches of sentences which have been assigned to the user. Clicking

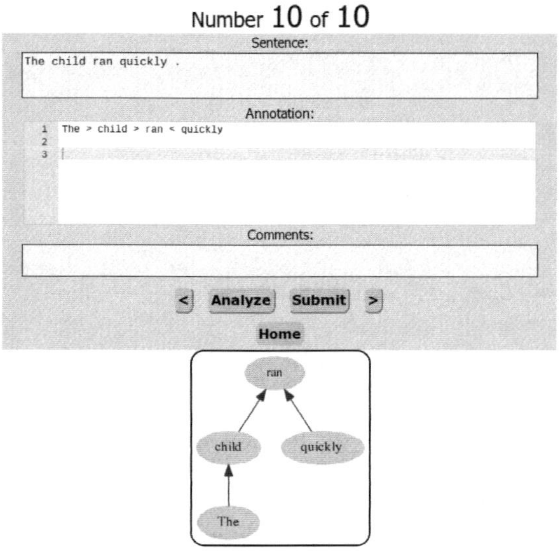

Figure 4: A well-formed GFL annotation is indicated by a green background and visualization of the analysis graph.

any of these will take the annotator to an annotation page, which displays the text to be annotated, an input field, and a comments box.

The annotation interface is simple and intuitive and provides instant feedback, preventing the annotator from submitting ill-formed annotations. Annotators press the Analyze button and receive feedback before submitting annotations (figure 4). Common GFL errors such as unbalanced parentheses are caught by the program and brought to the attention of the annotator with an informative error message (figure 5). The annotator can then fix the error, and will be able to submit once all errors are resolved.

The training set consists of 15 sentences selected from Rossman and Mills (1922), shown in the same annotation interface. Examples become increasingly more complicated in order to familiarize the user with different syntactic phenomena and the entry-analyze-review workflow. A button displays the FUDG graph from an expert annotation so the novice can compare it to her own and consult the guidelines (or ask for help) where the two graphs deviate.

4 Pilot User Study

We conducted a pilot annotation project in which 26 annotators were trained on GFL-Web and asked to annotate English Twitter messages from the *daily547* and *oct27* Twitter datasets of Gimpel et al. (2011). The overwhelming majority were all trained on the same day, having no prior knowledge of GFL. Most, but not all, were native speakers of English. Those who had no prior knowledge of dependency grammar in general received a short tutorial on the fundamentals before being introduced to the annotation workflow. All participants who were new to FUDG/GFL worked through the training set before moving on to the Twitter data. Annotators were furnished with the English annotation guidelines of Schneider et al. (2013).[3]

4.1 Results

In the one-day event, 906 annotations were generated. Inter-annotator agreement was high—.9 according to the *softComPrec* measure (Schneider et al., 2013)—and an expert's examination of a sample of the annotations found that 75% of contained no major error.

Annotators used the analysis feature of the interface—which displays either a visual representation of the tree or an error message—an average of 3.06 times per annotation. The interface requires they analyze each annotation at least once. Annotators have the ability to resubmit annotations if they later realize they made an error, and each annotation was submitted an average of 1.16 times. Disregarding instances that took over 1,000 seconds (under the assumption that these represent annotators taking breaks), the median time between the first analysis and the first submission of an annotation was 30 seconds. We take this as evidence that annotators found the instant feedback features useful in refining their annotations.

4.2 Post-Pilot Improvements

Annotator feedback prompted some changes to the interface. The annotation input box was changed to incorporate bracket-matching. The graph visualization for a correct annotation was added for each example in the training set so new annotators could compare their tree to an example. Presumably these changes would further reduce annotators' training time and improve their efficiency. Progress bars were added to the user home screen to show per-batch completion information.

4.3 Other Languages

In addition to English, guidelines for Swahili, Zulu, and Mandarin are currently in development.

[3] https://github.com/brendano/gfl_syntax/blob/master/guidelines/guidelines.md

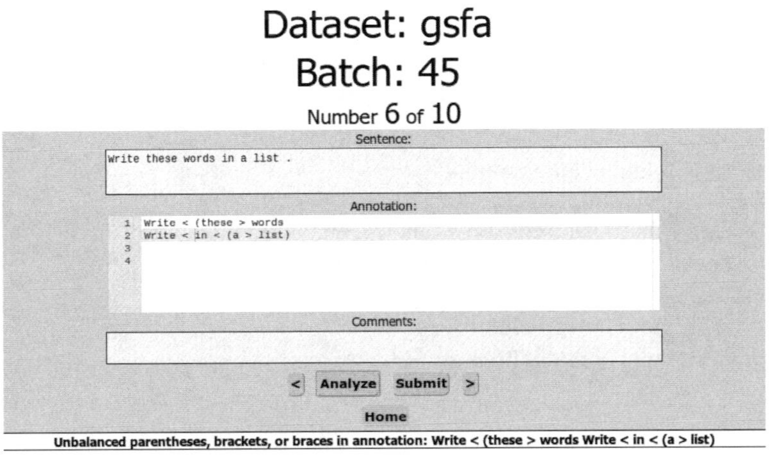

Figure 5: An example error notification. The red background indicates an error, and the cause of the error is displayed at the bottom of the screen.

5 Technical Architecture

GFL-Web and its software dependencies for analyzing and visualizing GFL are largely written in Python. The tool is built with Flask, a Python framework for web applications. Data is stored and transmitted to and from the browser in the Javascript Object Notation (JSON) format, which is supported by libraries in most programming languages. The browser interface uses AJAX techniques to interact dynamically with the server.

GFL-Web is written for Python version 2.7. It wraps scripts previously written for the analysis and visualization of GFL (Schneider et al., 2013). These in turn require Graphviz (Ellson et al., 2002), which is freely available.

Flask provides a built-in server, but can also be deployed in Apache, via WSGI or CGI, etc.

6 Other Tools

In treebanking, a good user interface is essential for annotator productivity and accuracy. Several existing tools support dependency annotation; GFL-Web is the first designed specifically for the FUDG/GFL framework. Some, including WebAnno (Yimam et al., 2013) and brat (Stenetorp et al., 2012), are browser-based, while WordFreak (Morton and LaCivita, 2003), Abar-Hitz (Ilarraza et al., 2004), and TrEd (Pajas and Fabian, 2000–2011) are client-side applications. All offer tree visualizations; to the best of our knowledge, ours is the only dependency annotation interface that has text as the exclusive mode of entry. Some, such as WebAnno and brat, aim to be fairly general-purpose, supporting a wide range of annotation schemes; by contrast, GFL-Web supports a single annotation scheme, which keeps the configuration (and codebase) simple. In the future, GFL-Web might incorporate elements of monitoring progress, such as display of evaluation measures computed with existing FUDG/GFL scripts.

Certain elements of the FUDG/GFL framework can be found in other annotation systems, such as the PASSAGE syntactic representation (Vilnat et al., 2010), which allows for grouping of words into units, but still requires dependency relations to be labeled.

Finally, we note that new approaches to corpus annotation of *semantic* dependencies also come with rich browser-based annotation interfaces (Banarescu et al., 2013; Abend and Rappoport, 2013).

7 Conclusion

While the creation of high-quality, highly specified, syntactically annotated corpora is a goal that is out of reach for most languages and genres, GFL-Web facilitates a rapid annotation workflow within a simple framework for dependency syntax. More information on FUDG/GFL is available at `http://www.ark.cs.cmu.edu/FUDG/`, and the source code for GFL-Web is available at `https://github.com/Mordeaux/gfl_web`.

Acknowledgments

The authors thank Archna Bhatia, Lori Levin, Jason Baldridge, Dan Garrette, Jason Mielens, Liang Sun, Shay Cohen, Spencer Onuffer, Nora Kazour, Manaal Faruqui, Wang Ling, Waleed Ammar, David Bamman, Dallas Card, Jeff Flanigan, Lingpeng Kong, Bill McDowell, Brendan O'Connor, Tobi Owoputi, Yanchuan Sim, Swabha Swayamdipta, and Dani Yogatama for annotating data, and anonymous reviewers for helpful feedback. This research was supported by NSF grant IIS-1352440.

References

Omri Abend and Ari Rappoport. 2013. Universal Conceptual Cognitive Annotation (UCCA). In *Proc. of ACL*, pages 228–238. Sofia, Bulgaria.

Sarah Alkuhlani, Nizar Habash, and Ryan Roth. 2013. Automatic morphological enrichment of a morphologically underspecified treebank. In *Proc. of NAACL-HLT*, pages 460–470. Atlanta, Georgia.

Laura Banarescu, Claire Bonial, Shu Cai, Madalina Georgescu, Kira Griffitt, Ulf Hermjakob, Kevin Knight, Philipp Koehn, Martha Palmer, and Nathan Schneider. 2013. Abstract Meaning Representation for sembanking. In *Proc. of the 7th Linguistic Annotation Workshop and Interoperability with Discourse*, pages 178–186. Sofia, Bulgaria.

Ann Bies, Justin Mott, Colin Warner, and Seth Kulick. 2012. English Web Treebank. Technical Report LDC2012T13, Linguistic Data Consortium, Philadelphia, PA.

Martin Čmejrek, Jan Cuřín, Jan Hajič, and Jiří Havelka. 2005. Prague Czech-English Dependency Treebank: resource for structure-based MT. In *Proc. of EAMT*, pages 73–78. Budapest, Hungary.

John Ellson, Emden Gansner, Lefteris Koutsofios, Stephen C. North, and Gordon Woodhull. 2002. Graphviz—open source graph drawing tools. In Petra Mutzel, Michael Jünger, and Sebastian Leipert, editors, *Graph Drawing*, pages 483–484. Springer, Berlin.

Kevin Gimpel, Nathan Schneider, Brendan O'Connor, Dipanjan Das, Daniel Mills, Jacob Eisenstein, Michael Heilman, Dani Yogatama, Jeffrey Flanigan, and Noah A. Smith. 2011. Part-of-speech tagging for Twitter: annotation, features, and experiments. In *Proc. of ACL-HLT*, pages 42–47. Portland, Oregon.

Nizar Habash and Ryan Roth. 2009. CATiB: The Columbia Arabic Treebank. In *Proc. of ACL-IJCNLP*, pages 221–224. Suntec, Singapore.

Jan Hajič. 1998. Building a syntactically annotated corpus: the Prague Dependency Treebank. In Eva Hajičová, editor, *Issues of Valency and Meaning. Studies in Honor of Jarmila Panevová*, pages 12–19. Prague Karolinum, Charles University Press, Prague.

Arantza Díaz De Ilarraza, Aitzpea Garmendia, and Maite Oronoz. 2004. Abar-Hitz: An annotation tool for the Basque dependency treebank. In *Proc. of LREC*, pages 251–254. Lisbon, Portugal.

Mohamed Maamouri, Ann Bies, Tim Buckwalter, and Wigdan Mekki. 2004. The Penn Arabic Treebank: building a large-scale annotated Arabic corpus. In *NEMLAR Conference on Arabic Language Resources and Tools*, pages 102–109. Cairo.

Mitchell P. Marcus, Beatrice Santorini, and Mary Ann Marcinkiewicz. 1993. Building a large annotated corpus of English: the Penn Treebank. *Computational Linguistics*, 19(2):313–330.

Thomas Morton and Jeremy LaCivita. 2003. WordFreak: An open tool for linguistic annotation. In *Proc. of HLT-NAACL: Demonstrations*, pages 17–18. Edmonton, Canada.

Petr Pajas and Peter Fabian. 2000–2011. Tree Editor TrEd 2.0. `http://ufal.mff.cuni.cz/tred/`.

Mary Blanche Rossman and Mary Wilda Mills. 1922. *Graded Sentences for Analysis, Selected from the Best Literature and Systematically Graded for Class Use*. L. A. Noble.

Nathan Schneider, Brendan O'Connor, Naomi Saphra, David Bamman, Manaal Faruqui, Noah A. Smith, Chris Dyer, and Jason Baldridge. 2013. A framework for (under)specifying dependency syntax without overloading annotators. In *Proc. of the 7th Linguistic Annotation Workshop and Interoperability with Discourse*, pages 51–60. Sofia, Bulgaria.

Nancy Staggers and David Kobus. 2000. Comparing response time, errors, and satisfaction between text-based and graphical user interfaces during nursing order tasks. *Journal of the American Medical Informatics Association*, 7(2):164–176.

Pontus Stenetorp, Sampo Pyysalo, Goran Topić, Tomoko Ohta, Sophia Ananiadou, and Jun'ichi Tsujii. 2012. brat: a web-based tool for NLP-assisted text annotation. In *Proc. of EACL: Demonstrations*, pages 102–107. Avignon, France.

Anne Vilnat, Patrick Paroubek, Eric Villemonte de la Clergerie, Gil Francopoulo, and Marie-Laure Guénot. 2010. PASSAGE syntactic representation: a minimal common ground for evaluation. In *Proc. of LREC*, pages 2478–2485. Valletta, Malta.

Seid Muhie Yimam, Iryna Gurevych, Richard Eckart de Castilho, and Chris Biemann. 2013. WebAnno: A flexible, web-based and visually supported system for distributed annotations. In *Proc. of ACL: Demonstrations*, pages 1–6. Sofia, Bulgaria.

Author Index